THE PREHISTORY OF PRIVATE PROPERTY

THE PREHISTORY OF PRIVATE PROPERTY

Implications for Modern Political Theory

Karl Widerquist and Grant S. McCall

EDINBURGH
University Press

Edinburgh University Press is one of the leading university presses in the UK. We publish academic books and journals in our selected subject areas across the humanities and social sciences, combining cutting-edge scholarship with high editorial and production values to produce academic works of lasting importance. For more information visit our website: edinburghuniversitypress.com

Edinburgh University Press Ltd
The Tun – Holyrood Road, 12(2f) Jackson's Entry, Edinburgh EH8 8PJ

First published in hardback by Edinburgh University Press 2021

Typeset in 11/13 Adobe Sabon by
IDSUK (DataConnection) Ltd,
printed and bound by CPI Group (UK) Ltd
Croydon, CR0 4YY

A CIP record for this book is available from the British Library

ISBN 978 1 4744 4742 3 (hardback)
ISBN 978 1 4744 4743 0 (paperback)
ISBN 978 1 4744 4744 7 (webready PDF)
ISBN 978 1 4744 4745 4 (epub)

CONTENTS

PREFACE

Prehistory is often treated as the stuff of myth. Although archaeology, anthropology, and other fields provide good evidence about humans in the deep past, many people—even otherwise good academic researchers—feel free to make wild assertions about prehistory, the "state of nature," or any remote peoples without fear that anyone will ask them to back up their claims with evidence.

You might expect philosophers and political theorists to be immune from making such wild assertions. Even if philosophers' work isn't primarily empirical, their job is to be truth seekers: to expand human knowledge by looking for weaknesses in past theories, improving or replacing them with new theories supported by the strongest evidence and argument they can find, and to submit their theories to the scrutiny of their peers, who in turn will probe those theories for weaknesses. If this process works, human knowledge continually trends toward improvement as it seems to have done over most of history. It's a good method.

But it's an imperfect method. Normative theorists have nothing but the scrutiny of their peers to improve their theories. Although they do their best to improve theories when contradictory evidence is apparent, researchers, like all people, share the prejudices of their day. Modern social science and philosophy inherited a lot of shared prejudices from earlier eras, including ideas about "civilized man" and "the savage," about settled people and nomads, about the benefits of existing institutions, and so on. The evidence that contradicts shared prejudice is hard to find in a world where scientific knowledge is too large for any single person to grasp, and academic inquiry is divided into increasingly separate subfields. It's possible for researchers in one field to continue passing on claims that have long been refuted by researchers in other fields. Anthropologists are not trolling through philosophy journals looking for claims to debunk. Shared prejudices remain alive in one discipline until people within that discipline take the time to challenge them.

Contemporary theories contain so many shared prejudices about prehistory and about stateless peoples that a genre of literature debunking false claims about history and prehistory has developed in recent years. Such works include: *Privatization in the Ancient Near East and Classical World* by Michael Hudson and Baruch A. Levine (1996); *The Myth of the Noble Savage* by Tar Ellingson (2001); *The Art of Not Being Governed* and *Against the Grain* by James C. Scott (2009, 2017); *Debt: The First 5,000 Years* by David Graeber (2011); *Communal Property: A Libertarian Analysis* by Kevin Carson (2011); *Paleofantasy* by Marlene Zuk (2013); "Farewell to the 'childhood of man'" by David Wengrow and David Graeber (2015); *Sapiens* by Yuval Noah Harari (2015); "The Early Modern 'Creation' of Property and its Enduring influence" by Erik Olsen (2019); "The Anti-Nomadic Bias of Political Theory" by Erik Ringmar (2020); *Plunder of the Commons* by Guy Standing (2019); *Edges of the State* by John Protevi (2019); "Property, Legitimacy, Ideology: A Reality Check" by Enzo Rossi and Carlo Argenton (forthcoming); *Civilized to Death* by Christopher Ryan; and many more.

This book is the second (and hopefully last) book in our contribution to this debunking genre.

The first book, *Prehistoric Myths in Modern Political Philosophy* (Widerquist and McCall 2017), which is available for free download,[1] debunks false beliefs associated with what we call, "the Hobbesian hypothesis" or "the mutual advantage hypothesis": the empirical claim that everyone is better-off in society today than they were or would be in a society without either the state or the private property rights system. *Prehistoric Myths* shows how Thomas Hobbes and John Locke relied on versions of this false empirical claim in their respective justifications of state sovereignty and the property rights system. It shows how centuries of political philosophers have followed Hobbes and Locke using this hypothesis in arguments without presenting much if any evidence for it. It then uses the best evidence

---

[1] See http://oapen.org/search?identifier=625284

available from anthropology to show that this hypothesis and related claims are false. Although many, perhaps most, people are better-off today, a significant number of people have not only failed to share in the benefits of these institutions; they are worse-off than an otherwise similar individual could expect to be in a small-scale society with neither of these institutions. Until we start treating the least advantaged people better, we live in a parasitic society.

Our new book debunks three more claims, which we introduce in Chapter 1.

Karl Widerquist and Grant S. McCall, May 2020

ACKNOWLEDGMENTS

We started working on this project (which now involves two books, an online appendix, and several articles) over a dozen years ago—several years before we met each other. We can't possibly list all the people who helped in those years. We explicitly thank our wives and our families and anonymously thank and apologize to everyone else who has given us feedback and encouragement since the Bush Administration.

See the preface and acknowledgments of our first book for more-but-still-insufficient acknowledgments.

–Karl Widerquist and Grant S. McCall,
on our respective front porches during
the COVID-19 outbreak in
New Orleans, May 10, 2020

Chapter 1

INTRODUCTION

The true myths of our time are the beliefs we accept without thinking. They get far less scrutiny than the ones we self-consciously choose to accept. Many common beliefs about prehistory and about the origin and development of private property rights are speculative to the point of mythmaking. Nothing is wrong with speculation. But something is wrong with misidentifying speculation as fact. Something's very wrong with basing political power structures and onerous duties on dubious and often self-serving speculations or unnoticed myths. And that is exactly what we do. We are often unaware of the destructive myths embedded in common beliefs about our institutions. These "prehistoric myths" are so ingrained in our cultural thinking that they can be hard to recognize, much less debunk.

Pure normative theory has an important place in philosophical reasoning, but a priori reasoning is one thing and applied empirical reasoning is another. Any theory that includes even one empirical claim is an applied theory that can be definitively established only with empirical evidence. As both of our books show, philosophers have a bad habit of slipping unsupported empirical premise into an otherwise a priori, normative argument, calling little attention to it, and inviting readers to accept it without question. Obscurity and ambiguity have helped perpetuate belief in these claims for centuries and given then their "mythical" status.

A "myth" is not always a bad thing. Myths often communicate greater truths in ways people can more easily understand and remember. But some myths are destructive myths. These myths communicate greater falsehoods in ways that affect us sometimes beyond our conscious awareness. For example, the Garden of Eden story can be interpreted as telling the greater truth that all people begin as innocent

1

children who don't understand right and wrong, but when they eventually learn right from wrong, they inevitably choose to do wrong, making everyone's lives harder. Or it can be interpreted as telling the greater lie that it's all Eve's fault. That's an example of a destructive, self-serving, and dubious myth.

This book uses the word "prehistory" in a broad sense. Prehistory can refer to the time before written language first appeared on Earth, ending around 3000–2500 BCE. It can refer to the time before any particular society developed written records of its own, ending gradually around the world at different times after 3000 BCE and still continuing in a few remote places. But prehistory can also mean the history that precedes and leads up to some particular phenomenon. *The Prehistory of Private Property* is the history before the establishment of the private property system from the deep past to the enclosure and colonial movements that slowly made the private property system ubiquitous over last 100–500 or so years.

This book debunks three prehistoric myths that are often used in justifications of economic inequality. The use of these claims has been so unclear and ambiguous that instead of one historical chronology, this book presents six short ones. First, it presents the intellectual history of a claim, showing the role it plays in past and present theories. Then, the book presents the economic and political history that debunks the claim. The intellectual histories show that these claims are *empirical*, that they are used as necessary *premises* in many contemporary political theories philosophy that have significant *effects* on what policies people believe are justified—showing the need for an empirical examination of the truth of these claims.

We define these claims as:

1. *The inequality hypothesis* (Part One): Inequality (meaning significant hierarchy or stratification) is natural and inevitable. That is, equality is incompatible with negative freedom or impossible altogether.
2. *The market freedom hypothesis* (Part Two): Negative freedom is better preserved under capitalism than under any other economic system.
3. *The individual appropriation hypothesis* (Part Three): There is something natural about individualistic, unequal private property rights. Or, the application of the normative principles of

appropriation and voluntary transfer to real-world history supports a strong private property system with significant ethical limits on any collective power to tax, regulate, or redistribute property.

The appropriation hypothesis is obviously about prehistory, involving the origin and development of property rights. The others are less obviously so: for example, the claim that equality is impossible raises the question whether it is everywhere and always impossible, including among peoples living in conditions very unfamiliar to contemporary Westerners; the claim that capitalism promotes freedom better than all other systems raises the question whether it does so better than all other societies throughout history and prehistory. All three claims can be falsified with historic and prehistoric anthropological evidence.

1. PREVIEW

The three main sections of this book are each dedicated to one central empirical claim, first showing how it is used and the second addressing the evidence for and against it.

Part One. Chapter 2 discusses the history of the belief that inequality is natural and inevitable showing the many contradictory ways it has been used to justify many different hierarchical structures. Chapter 3 shows how versions of this hypothesis remain influential in the form of a claimed trade-off between negative freedom and equality. Chapter 4 shows that many indigenous communities known to anthropology have successfully maintained freedom and significant political, social, and economic equality, for perhaps tens or hundreds of thousands of years. It concludes that inequality is not natural, inevitable, or the necessary by-product of negative freedom.

Part Two. Chapter 5 discusses the history of the market freedom hypothesis and how it is used in contemporary political theory. Chapter 6 argues that some small-scale stateless societies are more consistent with negative freedom than any other form of socio-political organization known to anthropology, including the market economy. If freedom is an overriding value, either freedom must be to restored people in industrial societies or everyone must become a nomadic hunter-gatherer. This finding implies both that the justification of any other system relies at least partially on some other value such as opportunity and that aid to the disadvantaged is not necessarily freedom-reducing. Redistribution can counteract the loss of freedom experienced by propertyless people under the private property system, thereby increasing negative freedom overall. Importantly, the small-scale societies that are the most equal also tend to be the freest. The strategies that tend to promote both freedom and equality involve conceding real power to all individuals, even the least advantaged, by giving them direct and unconditional access to common resources.

Part three. Chapters 7 shows how the appropriation hypothesis is used in contemporary theory. Chapter 8 discusses the origin and history of the appropriation hypothesis, showing how the appropriation story gradually obtained its mythic status. Chapter 9 considers attempts to build a rights-based justification in pure theory without relying on empirical premises. Chapter 10 discusses the evidence people who use the appropriation hypothesis have offered in support, showing that it is cursory and inconclusive at best.

Chapter 11 shows that nomadic hunter-gatherers, who have an excellent claim to be the original appropriators of the vast majority of the earth's land, treated land—and to some extent food and tools—as a common resource. Chapter 12 shows that stateless farmers, who also have a good claim to be original appropriators, tended to establish complex, overlapping, flexible, nonspatial, at least partially collective land-tenure institutions with significant common access rights for all members of the community. Chapter 13 discusses early and medieval state societies, showing that most of them had small or nonexistent privatized sectors; traditional agricultural villages continued to have complex land-tenure systems in many places in the world; and privatization began not from the bottom up through individual appropriation but from the top down with government officials exercising their power to name themselves titleholders. Chapter 14 shows how two aggressive and violent processes—the enclosure movement and colonial movement—privatized most of the earth's land and created the now-ubiquitous private property system between about 1500 and 2000 CE.

Chapter 15 discusses the findings and implications of Part Three, showing that the normative principles usually associated with the natural rights justification of private property (e.g. appropriation and voluntary transfer) applied to real human history actually support common or collective claims to property rather than an unequal privatized system. Unequal private property systems tend to develop only via state aggression against people who have betters claim to a connection with original appropriation and who have chosen to reject those institutions.

Chapter 16 concludes with some of the lessons this book has for contemporary political philosophy and the efforts to expand freedom and equality. Greater equality and freedom are possible. They require ceding much more power to disadvantaged and disaffected people than any society does today.

The organization of this book into six histories creates the opportunity to read selectively without losing continuity. If you're convinced that any of these empirical claims are used in contemporary theory, you can skip the intellectual history and focus on the economic and political histories. Or, if you're convinced a claim is false but doubt it is actually used as an empirical claim in relevant theories, focus on the intellectual histories. The intellectual histories are further divided into sections explaining who argued what when and additional sections analyzing the meaning of those arguments, allowing more selective reading.

2. PRELIMINARY ISSUES

We try to explain what readers need to know as we go, but we have to discuss a few preliminary issues at the outset. This book is cross-disciplinary. It uses anthropological and historical evidence to address issues in normative political philosophy.

A. *Political Theory Issues*

Normative political philosophy (also called normative political theory) addresses questions such as what principles of justice should guide political policy and what do those principles imply about it. The normative issues this book addresses mostly involve issues of unequal power and wealth. The central issue of this book is property rights in "external assets." That is, assets external to the human body including land, the natural resources land contains, and the things people make out of land and natural resources. "Property" in this book refers to external assets under the presumption that people own themselves.

Political theorists usually conceive of a property right not as *one* right but as *a bundle of rights and duties* (or incidents) that people can hold over a thing. In Tony Honoré's (1987: 161–175) analysis, "Full liberal ownership" (sometimes called "sole proprietorship," "fee-simple ownership," and various other names) includes eleven incidents: the right to possess, the right to use, the right to manage, the right to income, the right to capital, the right to security, transmissibility, absence of term, the duty to prevent harm, the liability to execution, and residuary character.

Property can be owned collectively by the people or publicly by the government. If the government is of, by, and for the people, there is no distinction between collective and public property. Property, especially land, can be treated as "a commons" for the use of every individual but the property of no individual. For example, the streets, the atmosphere, and the oceans are part of the commons. A commons can be thought of as unowned or as collectively owned. The incidents of ownership can be owned by different parties, making each party's ownership weaker than full liberal ownership.

Two moral views of property are common in contemporary political theory. In one view, property is an arbitrary creation of the state, a tool that can be used for good or bad, and should be used if and when it benefits the people as a whole.

In the other view (which is the primary focus of this book), property is naturally private, taking the form of full liberal ownership unless the owner decides to divide the incidents. If so, ownership tends to become unequal, and government powers of taxation, regulation, and redistribution infringe on many privately owned incidents, including possession, use, income, capital, security, and transmissibility.

The belief that at least some property rights are natural is extremely common in Western society today, but the most thorough arguments for that belief come from a school of thought whose members tend to call themselves "libertarians." They are sometimes called or have some overlap with right-libertarians, propertarians, classical liberals, neoliberals, anarcho-capitalists, and so on. We use the term "propertarianism" for all theories involving a natural rights justification of unequal private property: the belief that natural rights, including the right to be free from interference (negative freedom), imply the necessity of a private property rights system with strong (perhaps overriding) ethical limits on any collective powers of taxation, regulation, or redistribution.

Propertarians tend to be extreme in their advocacy of private property, but the ideas that this book addresses are mainstream: that economic inequality is inevitable, that the market economy promotes freedom better than other systems, and that unequal property rights are natural rights even if some infringements on these rights are acceptable. Propertarians should be congratulated for articulating the most thorough arguments for these widely held beliefs even if they take their implications further than most people do.

John Locke (1960 [1689]) and Robert Nozick (1974) are our main sources of historical and contemporary propertarianism (respectively), but because no one figure speaks for all propertarians, we also address many more.

B. Anthropology Issues

This book's empirical evidence comes largely from sociocultural anthropology and archaeology. Sociocultural anthropologists' main method is ethnography, which usually involves participant observation (often on a long-term basis), as well as other approaches involving interviewing ethnographic informants (McCall and Simmons 1969). Archaeologists attempt to make inferences about the past based on arrangements of material objects that survive to the present. Archaeologists use deductive reasoning to build scientific frameworks to make inferences about the nature of human cultural lifeways in the past (Binford and Binford 1968; Hegmon 2003; Schiffer 2016).

Anthropologists use ethnography and archaeology together to create a framework for understanding lifeways of the deep past among peoples with similar practices—such as organizational scale or subsistence strategy. Doing so is inherently difficult and easily overdone. "[S]tateless societies do not represent an evolutionary stage, innocent of higher organization" (Wengrow and Graeber 2015: 12), as early anthropologists unfortunately believed. Small-scale societies have undergone the same dynamics of historical interaction and adaptation to shifting environmental and demographic contexts as any other modern group and, therefore, cannot be taken as somehow more closely related to the past (Binford 2001; Wilmsen 1989).

But it would also be a mistake to refuse to use any ethnographic information to help theorize about the past. Efforts to do so are controversial (Headland and Reid 1989; Lee 1992; Schrire 1984; Wilmsen

1989), yet there are clear logical reasons why our knowledge of the past must be partially based on observations of modern peoples. It would be absurd to deny that there are common organizing principles governing the lifeways of both modern people and those of the past, including even our deep evolutionary past. Let us be crystal clear: no modern society is an analog for our ancestors, though the behavior of modern peoples reflects basic aspects of economic, social, and political life that were shared by past human societies. The ways in which modern peoples cope with the various dimensions of their lives as human beings can help us make sense of the past in building robust social scientific theory, which is capable of working even in situations outside of our modern experiences. If particular solutions to problems tend to work well under similar conditions, past and modern peoples confronted by similar environmental, economic, and social situations are likely to respond in similar ways. It is therefore useful for anthropologists to consult with and observe modern peoples, who are themselves familiar with the economic problems, practices, and technologies employed by peoples in the past, and also with the forms of material patterning these solutions might leave behind (Binford 2001; Kelly 1995; O'Connell 1995). But it is also important for ethnoarchaeology to understand the diversity or variability of modern societies as a method for contextualizing the activities of peoples in the past (Kirch and Green 2001: 42).

Unfortunately, our knowledge of prehistory is based on a tiny sample of the material patterning left behind by past peoples. There are many things about our past that we may never know; or, as Jean-Philippe Rigaud and Jan F. Simek (1987) complain in allusion to Johnson (1927), many prehistorians believe that our archaeological arms are "too short to box with God." Though we are not necessarily convinced by this genre of pessimism, the problem that it poses is actually much greater for the authors we criticize than it is for us. These philosophers make factual claims and use them in arguments to justify onerous duties: because it has been everywhere and always like this, or because things began like that (etc.), they claim certain obligations are justified. Any such argument requires those empirical claims to be facts, not speculations. If our arms are long enough to box with God, then philosophers must concretely succeed in finding evidence to support their claims about how things happened in the past. If not, then they simply cannot make those kinds of claims. Although we believe that we can falsify all or most of the claims in question, the inherent ambiguity in our understanding of the past is in itself enough to raise fundamental doubts about their claims.

Before proceeding, we have to define a few of the anthropological terms we use—sometimes reluctantly. Anthropological taxonomies tend to be controversial because they involve using limited data to make generalizations about diverse peoples, and they often link us with the colonialist and racist baggage of the nineteenth-century origins of the field.

The distinction between hunter-gatherers and farmers is straightforward. Hunter-gatherer societies obtain all their subsistence from forms of foraging: hunting, gathering, fishing, and scavenging, and keep no domesticated animals other than dogs. Societies that plant crops or keep livestock are considered agricultural even if most of their consumption still comes from foraging. The earliest anthropologists presumed there was a single, uniform, "primitive," hunter-gatherer lifeway and a uniform evolutionary path toward larger-and-larger-scale farming. Both ethnographic and archaeological evidence has disproved this belief. Hunter-gatherers and non-state farmers are as diverse as state societies.

Anthropologists also classify peoples by socio-political organization— such as states and stateless societies. There are infinite possible forms of socio-political organization. No two are exactly alike. They can be understood as existing on a multidimensional spectrum, but many anthropologists have found it useful to divide them into four classifications—though not without controversy. A "hunter-gatherer band" (also called an "immediate-return society" or a "family-level society") is a nomadic group of usually 15–60 people who get all of their consumption from foraging and do not store food. Membership is fluid. Many bands break up into nuclear families for part of the year (Bird-David 1994; Boehm 2001: 72–73, 86–87; Ingold 1986: 235; Johnson and Earle 2000: 32–33, 54–65, 120; Leacock 1998: 142–143; Lee and Daly 1999: 3–4; Lee and DeVore 1968b: 9; Silberbauer 1982: 24; Turnbull 1968: 135–137; Woodburn 1968b: 103).

An autonomous village is a slightly larger-scale group of usually 100–600 people who do not have specialist rulers. Leaders usually exist, but their power is limited, and they produce their own food like everyone else. Autonomous villages might be farmers or foragers. Autonomous village still exist today and have been observed by ethnographers (Bandy 2004; Boehm 2001: 3–4, 93; Carneiro 1970:

734–738; Johnson and Earle 2000: 179–180, 191–192; Lee 1990: 236; McCall 2009: 161; Renfrew 2007: 142; Roscoe 2002; Wilson 1988: 3).

Chiefdoms are slightly larger-scale groups usually with populations from the "low thousands to tens of thousands" with specialist leaders who hold power at a regional scale and do not need to produce their own food. Chiefs tend to have greater power the larger and more densely populated their territory is. The economic specialization of chiefs and elites often goes along with permanent socio-economic stratification. Chiefdoms tend to be based on farming, though there are also striking examples of forager chiefdoms. A significant number of chiefdoms survived into the nineteenth and twentieth centuries and have been studied by ethnographers. Many remain in existence today as semi-autonomous political units with separate legal systems within nation-states today, especially in places like sub-Saharan Africa, Southeast Asia, and the South Pacific (Bellwood 1987: 31–33; Drennan and Peterson 2006; Earle 1997: 15–16; 2000; 2002; Renfrew 2007: 152, 164, 173–176; Thomas 1999: 229; Yoffee 2004: 5–6, 23–41).

These terms are controversial for three reasons. First, most of them were used originally by people holding the now-discredited belief that they represented "stages" in a uniform evolutionary progression. Second, they represent ranges on a spectrum, which could be divided in many other plausible ways, and all of the forms bleed into one another with many in-between examples. Third, giving any name to a range on a spectrum can obscure the diversity within the named range. Bands are diverse, as are autonomous villages and chiefdoms. The existence of the spectrum and the diversity within the named ranges are important to keep in mind.

We use these terms not because we are thrilled with them or because we are true believers in either their absolute empirical reality or theoretical justification. For example, as Lewis Binford (2006) points out, the term "band" refers to a scale of social organization that had already disappeared by the time that the first modern ethnographies were being carried out among the classic so-called "band" societies in the middle of the twentieth century. Other more political complaints about these typologies also have merit (e.g. Johnson and Earle 2000). However, especially in a project of this nature, we need a heuristic framework for organizing our discussion and for making systematic comparisons between classes of phenomena; in other words, between societies of different political scales. Even just from the perspective of terminology and semantics, we need convenient "handles" for referring to scale differences between political systems so that we don't have to repeat cumbersome lists of characteristics every time we want to make a point. Thus, we use these terms trepidatiously but unapologetically.

Definitions of the state are less controversial but more complex. Anthropologists and political theorists define the state differently. The definition in political theory makes sovereignty the state's essential feature: "a human community that (successfully) claims the monopoly of the legitimate use of physical force within a given territory." (Weber 2004: 33). The most famous anthropological definition of the state makes its central defining characteristic the presence of a city, as well as a discrete list of about nine other features, including surplus agriculture, labor specialization, public infrastructure and monuments, writing systems, long-distance foreign trade, and so on (Childe 1950, 1957). This definition is controversial because it is not necessarily useful for early states in all regions and because it emphasized the achievements of early states seen as ancestral to Western civilization at the expense of others especially in places like the New World and sub-Saharan Africa (Connah 2001).

The difference between anthropology's and political theory's definitions is not a major problem because the strength and scale of political authority are highly correlated. Virtually all observed societies large enough to support cities also have a sovereign government, and most societies that can't be described as having anything more than a village do not. Some in-between-scale societies might meet the political theorists' definition without meeting the anthropologists' definition of statehood.

Our two books are not directly about indigenous peoples. They are about a few selected erroneous beliefs embedded in Western political thought. However, the pigeonholing of indigenous peoples to fit preconceived imperialist notions is a concern of the indigenous rights movement, and therefore this book might be of some interest to people in that movement. One of the common examples of pigeonholing is the mistaken belief that all indigenous peoples have some close connection to stateless societies. The majority of indigenous peoples lived in state societies long before Western colonization, and as the colonial movement was going on outside Europe, a parallel movement of "enclosure" created similar changes inside Europe. These books are as much about European history as any other. Primarily, our books offer indigenous readers the same thing they offer everyone else: a better understanding of how erroneous beliefs about stateless societies grew out of the colonial and enclosure movements but remain influential in contemporary political theory, which effects economic and social policy throughout the world.

Finally, anyone who writes anything positive about indigenous or stateless peoples has to face the allegation that they are "romanticizing" the "noble savage." See our earlier book for a response to that common but nonsubstantive criticism (Widerquist and McCall 2017: 21–22).

Part One

The inequality hypothesis

Chapter 2

HIERARCHY'S APOLOGISTS, PART ONE: 5,000 YEARS OF CLEVER AND CONTRADICTORY ARGUMENTS THAT INEQUALITY IS NATURAL AND INEVITABLE

All things bright and beautiful, all creatures great and small,
All things wise and wonderful: the Lord God made them all. . . .
The rich man in his castle, the poor man at his gate,
He made them, high or lowly, and ordered their estate.

Anglican hymn by Cecil F. Alexander (2013)[1]

When Captain Cook happened upon the Hawaiian Islands in 1778, he found the largest-scale political units that existed in Polynesia at that time. The Hawaiian Islands were made up of either large-scale chiefdoms or small-scale states, depending on where you're willing to draw the line. The island chain's polities were led by paramount chiefs who owned the land and appointed local chiefs and land managers called konohiki who in turn allocated land to peasants in exchange for corvée labor. Paramount chiefs held life-and-death power over their subjects and lived off their subject's labor. The paramount chief held a position at the top of a single hierarchy of political and economic power as well as religious and social position (Earle 1997: 7, 79–82). The paramount chief was the highest born, most direct descendant of the mythical, semi-divine founder of the Hawaiian people, and only the chiefs were endowed with the founder's divine essence. Those with successively lower places in the hierarchy were

---

[1] The publisher notes that most hymnals now omit this verse.

successively lower-ranking, less-direct descendants, who were, there-fore, less worthy of wealth, power, and social position than the higher descendants. They were better suited to taking orders, working more, and receiving less (Earle 1997: 44–45; Flannery and Marcus 2012: 55, 59–60, 65).

All of this might have seemed like a silly superstition or a terrible injustice to Captain Cook and his men, who saw their own society as civilized, reasonable, and enlightened. Of course, their society also had enormous economic, political, and social inequality—a king, a hereditary House of Lords, and a House of "Commons" that repre-sented only the small minority of male property owners. This structure held power over an enormous empire, in which only a tiny portion of the population had any significant share of political or economic power, and in which most people were unenfranchised subjects and many were slaves. The ideological beliefs justifying the British Empire seemed quite reasonable and natural to the British, but they must have seemed equally bizarre to Hawaiians.

The dominant ideologies in these two societies, as in all or most societies, justified the level and form of inequality that happened to exist there, portraying it as natural and inevitable. Also, like most such ideologies, it strikes outsiders as less than fully convincing—if not bizarre and implausible.

Both Britain and Hawaii enforced these "natural" hierarchies with strong legal and social sanctions. In that way—as this chapter shows—both societies reflect a pattern that has existed throughout the world from prehistoric chiefdoms to modern industrial states. Although every unequal or hierarchical society has strong human-created rules and human-enforced powers that ensure the existence of inequality, popular beliefs do not credit those rules as the source of inequality. Dominant ideologies almost always assert the rules enforcing hierar-chical relations merely reflect the natural and inevitable hierarchy, or in a variant that has become common in modern Western parlance, the inequality that is naturally consistent with freedom. Even reformist ideologies tend to assert—whether out of tactical or sincere motives—that the existing inequalities are corruptions of the true and natural inequality that necessarily exists.

This chapter reviews the history of the belief that inequality is natural or inevitable, showing that this belief played a role in very differently unequal societies from prehistory to modern times. The following chapter shows that ideas of natural and inevitable inequality remain popular in contemporary political thought. These two chapters are not a history of justifications of inequality per se but of the role played in such theories by the claims that inequality is natural, inevitable, or an inevitable consequence of freedom.

What we ultimately want to know—and what Chapter 4 examines—is whether this claim is true. In the discussion below, two central claims (along with several supporting claims) stand out as testable with research into the anthropology and archaeology of small-scale societies: (1) inequality is necessary, natural, or inevitable, and (2) equality and freedom are necessarily, naturally, or inevitably in conflict.

Claim 1 can be examined with the question: has anthropology observed societies with substantial equality of the relevant kind? Claim 2 can be examined with the question: if anthropology has observed egalitarian societies, has equality come at the expense of freedom (as defined by those making the claim of a trade-off)? The following section fills out these claims more explicitly. The discussion throughout these two chapters reveals other testable claims involved in explaining the supposed inevitability of inequality in different societies.

The history in these two chapters itself casts doubt on the hypothesis that inequality is natural and inevitable, because it reveals so many conflicting explanations of why inequality is supposed to be inevitable. This history suggests reasons people might want to believe inequality is natural, and it underscores the lack of evidence that has been given to support the idea—even in the contemporary academic discussion. But the doubt cast by this chapter's review of the history of these claims is no substitute for the empirical discussion in Chapter 4.

Almost every society with substantial inequality has some popular ideology claiming that the inequality of that society is not only justified but natural or inevitable and not ultimately attributable to the coercive legal structure that supports inequality. Therefore, this chapter is free to be selective and will focus mainly (but not entirely) on Western societies.

1. SOME THINGS TO LOOK FOR IN THE DISCUSSION BELOW

Before beginning this survey, we need to address two questions: what do we mean by inequality? And, what do we mean by necessary, natural, or inevitable inequality? Human beings are different and unequal in many ways: in height, weight, lactating ability, strength, intelligence, skill, effort, smell, and so on. If this is what one means by inequality, it is obvious—and uninteresting—that all humans and all societies are unequal in many ways. But differing in these ways does not imply that people necessarily differ in political power (call it "power"), economic power (call it "wealth"), and rank (call it "social position"). Economic, political, and social inequalities are outcomes of human interactions. They are affected by the way humans interact and the rules and conventions humans create.

We are primarily interested in inequality in the form of stratification, which we define as structured or systemic inequalities that have a notion of being permanent or long-lasting even if they are seldom unchangeable. Stratified societies are inevitably hierarchical even if hierarchy does not always have the same connotations of permanence. Kenneth M. Ames (2007: 490) defines three kinds of societies in terms of stratification:

> In egalitarian societies, there is equal access to positions of prestige and to basic resources; in rank societies there is differential access to positions of prestige but equal access to basic resources. In stratified societies, there is unequal access to both positions of prestige and basic resources, with people in high strata also having structural organizational power.

In these terms, the two claims are clearly testable. Claim 1 is that only stratified societies exist; there are no societies in which people have equal access to basic resources and equal influence over the group's structural organizational power. Differential access to these elements—rather than the physical differences between people—plays the central role in the debate over inequality. Claim 2 is that if any such societies do exist, they are unfree in the relevant sense—which we take to be negative freedom (see Chapter 5).

Consider two other ways to state the question. Are sustained inequalities in power, wealth, and/or social position necessary, natural, or inevitable? Do innate human differences or the dynamics of feasible types of social interaction necessarily lead to substantial, systemic inequalities of power, wealth, or social position?

The words natural and inevitable can be used interchangeably in some but not all contexts. Natural inequality can be used to refer to all inequality that is the necessary result of human social interaction even if individual humans do not have great innate differences between them. Under this meaning, natural and inevitable are interchangeable. But natural inequality can also refer to inequality that stems from innate differences in human beings. Under this meaning, we explain below, natural and inevitable inequality might not be interchangeable.

It is tempting to define "natural inequality" as the belief that inequality of power, wealth, and social position stem from innate differences between people and "inevitable inequality" as the belief that inequalities of power, wealth, and social position are the necessary result of human interaction whether or not they stem from natural differences among people.

But there are three reasons not to impose these definitions on a historical study. First, there is a great deal of overlap between them. Second, few people in the history surveyed below use these terms in these ways. Third, most people who believe inequality is natural also believe that it is inevitable and vice versa. As the history below shows, even those whose justification of inequality does not require claims of innate difference tend to make claims that inequalities in power, wealth, or social position do reflect innate differences. Conversely, one could believe that although inequality is the natural expression of human differences, it would be possible to stop those differences from creating inequalities of power, wealth, and/or social position.

We are more concerned with the claim that inequality is inevitable and less concerned with whether it is innate. But we will examine claims about the causes of inequality because they inform the question of whether it is inevitable. To be clear about this issue, we use the phrase "natural or inevitable" and distinguish between them where necessary.

These terms are further complicated because the term "inevitable" can be used universally or conditionally. By saying that inequality is inevitable one can mean that it exists in all circumstances or that it exists in all societies that have some characteristic—such as freedom or peacefulness.

Although the claim of natural or inevitable inequality is only a small part of the discussion of inequality, the history of the use of this claim is enormous. Claims about natural or inevitable inequality have been made since prehistory and have been used to justify enforced social hierarchies as different as monarchy, slavery, serfdom, chiefdom, the caste system, sexism, class-based capitalism, and so on (Trigger 2003: 142, 264).

Once one notices how pervasive the claims of natural and inevitable inequality are, it becomes apparent how much the explanations for inequality in different societies conflict with each other. One group's ideology says inequality on the basis of A is inevitable because of reason B while another asserts basis C for reason D, and often A and C or B and D are mutually exclusive. Differences in human characteristics are converted very differently into inequalities of power, wealth, and social position in different societies. Societies differ both in what characteristics they pick out for favor and in how much they reward favored characteristics. This is true even within Western industrial market economies. Some societies with similar economic, cultural, and political systems have very different levels of economic inequality and mobility. Societies with very different cultures differ even more in the type, form, degree, and justification of inequality.

Inequalities of wealth and power are not simply expressions of differences in ability, ambition, or any other characteristic. As this chapter shows, how human differences are converted into social, economic, and political inequalities depends heavily on socially contrived rules and customs that vary substantially over time and place. Knowledge that these contrived rules sound implausible to outsiders suggests caution to anyone who might think their society's hierarchy at all approximates a true natural inequality. The conflict between so many explanations for inevitable inequality probably raises doubts about all of them. These conflicting explanations cannot all be true. Perhaps none of them is true. If so, either inequality is not inevitable or inequality has some underlying cause that has a strong tendency to be misidentified.

Nevertheless, it sometimes seems like everyone everywhere thinks that their society has it just about right. Although imperfect, the inequalities in their society are very close to being the inevitable political, economic, and social expression of natural human differences.

If the stated explanations for the inevitability of inequality are all doubtful, why are they so widely accepted? A functionalist or determinist explanation would be that ideologies tend to become prevalent or even dominant because they justify and therefore help to preserve useful institutions or institutions favorable to the group in power (Jost and Hunyady 2005). For example, if technology requires an

agricultural economy based on large-scale centrally managed irrigation, an ideology favoring the centralization of power will tend to
become dominant. Functionalism doesn't itself explain the mechanism by which those ideologies become accepted.

Two explanations for such a mechanism are immediately apparent.
First, powerful people toward the top of the hierarchy are strongly
invested in it. To protect their position, they have reason to promote—
perhaps disingenuously—the belief that existing inequality is natural
and inevitable and to silence challenges to that belief.

Second, people have a tendency to believe things favorable to
themselves. People at the top of the hierarchy are, therefore, likely to
believe—genuinely—that the hierarchy is justified and perhaps inevitable (Shepperd et al. 2008). Of course, people lower in the hierarchy
apparently have as much reason to disbelieve natural inequality as
those at the top have to believe it. However, those at the top are likely
to be more powerful, more respected, better educated, more influential, and so on. Therefore, they are in much better position to make
their belief dominant.

Although these explanations are plausible, they don't explain why
these "system-justifying ideologies" are popular not only with the
elites but also with the masses who would seem to have a powerful
reason to disbelieve them (Jost and Hunyady 2005: 261). People at
the bottom of the scale might want more changes to the system than
others, but the revolutionary who rejects wholesale the dominant
ideology of her of his society—the Harriet Tubman or the Frederick
Douglas—is truly rare even in greatly unequal societies.

Melvin Lerner (1980: 24–25) proposes an answer, suggesting that
all people—not just those who most obviously benefit from current
social organization—have strong reasons to believe in a just world. In
order to function, people need to believe that their actions will produce something like the results they want. In order to go on with their
daily lives, people need to believe that the world, or their small corner
of it, "is essentially a just world, where, given the qualifiers, 'by and
large' and 'in the long run,' people can and do get what they deserve"
(p. 25). To quote *The Truman Show*, we all "accept the reality of the
world with which we are presented" (Manning 2013).

The history recounted below provides inductive evidence in favor
of the system-justifying and belief-in-a-just-world theories, especially
in light of the poor evidence that most people have accepted for the

belief in the naturalness and inevitability of their societies' idiosyncratic forms of stratification.

Hopefully, this chapter puts the modern philosophical discussion in historical context. If contemporary claims of natural inequality discussed in Chapter 3 turn out to be well-supported by evidence, contemporary theories of natural inequality are important exceptions to a very long-term trend. If the evidence is inconclusive, our modern philosophers and scientists might simply be part of a long line of thinkers who succumb to these biases and came up with clever and conflicting rationalizations to justify inequality by seeing cultural constructs of their society as the natural order of the universe.

2. THE OLDEST CLAIMS OF NATURAL INEQUALITY?

Prehistoric societies are, by definition, nonliterate, and so we have no record what societies in the deep past said about inequality. The best we can do is to look at common beliefs among historically observed societies with similar subsistence techniques as those in the past.

The tendency of Westerners to perceive all indigenous peoples as collective representatives of some state of nature has supported the misconception that inequality has everywhere and always existed. For example, the stratified Hawaiian chiefdoms discussed above were actually relatively large-scale societies of the sort that developed only very recently, at least by the standards of prehistoric archaeologists. The hierarchical nature of those societies is unknown to people in smaller-scale forms of social organization.

As Chapter 4 discusses in much greater detail, most hunter-gatherer societies (which predate the emergence of chiefdoms by hundreds of thousands of years) cultivate norms recognizing no one as having greater right to power, wealth, or social position than anyone else. To the extent that people in observed hunter-gatherer bands assert beliefs in natural inequality, those tend to be based on seniority, ethnocentrism, and gender.

Seniority doesn't seem to be a very significant form of inequality, at least as it pertains to power and wealth, and it is certainly very far from the forms of stratification people usually intend to justify with claims of natural or inevitable inequality. Although younger adults in band societies might defer to the influence of their elders, they are rarely if ever under their power; they do not noticeably differ from their elders in wealth or access to resources; and they fully expect to become elders in their turn.

Ethnocentric beliefs have been ubiquitous around the world and throughout history (including in observed small-scale, non-state societies), and they're often used to justify conflict and inequality, but they only work to justify inequality *within* a society if it has ethnic divisions. Band and autonomous village societies tend to have only one ethnic group in a given polity, partly because they quickly recognize new members as part of the group or even as fictive kin. Therefore, although ethnocentrism plays a part in inter-group conflicts between bands, it isn't often used as a justification for inequality within the group. Ethnocentrism plays a part in intra-group inequality only in much larger-scale societies, probably beginning with the appearance of chiefdoms, some of which held slaves captured from neighboring groups.

That leaves gender as the basis for the oldest belief in natural inequality within society. There is a great deal of variability in the manifestation of gender inequality within small-scale societies, usually stemming from differing economic roles in terms of sex-based division of labor (Hayden et al. 1986; Leacock 1978). Although men tend to do more of the hunting and women more of the gathering and childcare, in the smallest-scale societies, this common division of labor usually does not translate into significant differences in power. Women in most observed hunter-gatherer bands have substantial power, autonomy, and often general equality with men. Typically, the smaller the scale and the more closely the sexes work together, the less sexist their beliefs tend to be. Some bands have greater gender equality than most state societies have had until perhaps the twentieth century. For example, when the seventeenth-century Jesuit missionary, Paul Le Jeune, encountered the Montagnais-Naskapi of the St. Lawrence valley, he wrote with revulsion about the political power and relative equality of women (Leacock 1978). Many contemporary egalitarian forager societies, such as the Ju/'hoansi, exhibit general equality in terms of gender status (Lee 1979).

In contrast, small-scale societies with greater degrees of sedentism and differentiation in terms of sex-based division of labor often have high levels of gender inequality. The Baruya, for example, are an acephalous (leaderless), horticultural autonomous village society in Papua New Guinea who believe that sperm is a life force that not only produces children but also has many other benefits such as bringing on puberty in both genders and enabling women to produce milk for their offspring. Baruya men use this belief to justify male privilege and sexual domination. Because Baruya men produce this life force and women receive it, many Baruyas claim men are essentially givers and women are takers (Dubreuil 2010: 182). Although the factual claims in Baruya explanation of gender inequality probably seem laughably false and extreme to most Western societies today, contemporary state societies probably have gender inequalities that are absent in Baruya society and would seem implausible to them.

The Baruya might be extreme in their sexism compared to most stateless farmers, but to the extent that band and autonomous village societies believe in natural inequality, the belief in gender inequality is most common. With our usual qualifiers about the extent to which modern hunter-gatherer bands and autonomous villages are similar to prehistoric societies of similar scale, we can say that sexism is the oldest -ism.

3. PREHISTORIC JUSTIFICATIONS FOR STRATIFICATION

Historically known chiefdoms, all around the world (in North and South America, sub-Saharan Africa, Europe, the Middle East, Asia, and the Pacific Islands), often had ideologies similar to that of Hawaiian chiefdoms in which a chief or a group of chiefs claimed natural superiority based on descent from a mythical, often semi-divine founder (Earle 1991a, 1991b: 14–15, 2002). Hawaiians shared some version of this ideology with all other Polynesian groups, presenting an interesting case that provides some evidence for the antiquity of that ideology. Polynesians are the most geographically dispersed indigenous people who can be identified as a related group by both linguistic and DNA evidence. On first contact with the West, Polynesians occupied islands in a triangular area nearly 5,000 miles per side defined roughly by the three points of New Zealand, Hawaii, and Easter Island.

All or most Polynesian peoples had a similar ideology behind their chiefs or headmen. There are three reasons to surmise that they brought this ideology with them when they dispersed out of Melanesia (Kirch 1984). First, some version of this hereditary ranking system existed in virtually every Polynesian society no matter how large or small. It would be very unlikely for such diverse societies to invent the same institution separately over and over again.

Second, most Polynesian societies have very similar names for people of high-ranking birth (Feinberg 1982). Separated people, even if they initially speak the same or similar languages, often pick different words for new ideas. For example, consider how different the North American word "cell" (phone) is from the British word "mobile." If the differing Polynesian groups had separately invented the ideology supporting their separately invented chiefdoms after they separated from each other, it is very unlikely that they would have all chosen similar words to describe it.

Third, not all Polynesian societies were technically chiefdoms. Some had significantly smaller-scale and less integrated political systems with alternate bases for political control (Kirch 1984). The chosen form seems to have depended on functionality given the available resources and the population density of their islands. And for the most part Polynesian village-level societies chose institutions typical of observed small-scale societies throughout the world with one important exception: most or all Polynesian village-level societies recognized—at least nominally—some form of hereditary headman, even if the smaller-scale Polynesian societies granted him little or no power. And their word for headman was usually linguistically related to other Polynesian languages' words for chief.

Together, all this evidence strongly supports the conclusion that Polynesians descended from a group of people who lived in chiefdoms and that those chiefs claimed superiority of birth for reasons similar to those claimed by Polynesian chiefs at the time of contact with literate societies. If so, the ideology of hierarchy by reason of naturally high birth is thousands of years old. Exactly when Polynesians began to disperse out of Melanesia is a matter of contention among anthropologists. Genetic evidence suggests that dispersal began 3,000 or 4,000 years ago (1000 or 2000 BCE), if not earlier. Archaeological evidence seems to suggest that it might not have gotten into full swing until 1,000–1,500 years ago (Kirch 1984; Patrick 2010). It seems safe to say that the chiefdom political system began along the Pacific fringes of Southeast Asia during the early-to-middle Holocene; that is, by 5,000–6,000 years ago at the latest. If dispersal began by 1,500 years ago, as the archaeological evidence suggests, we have traced the ideology back at least one-fourth of the way to the first appearance of chiefdoms in

Southeast Asia. If dispersal began 4,000 years ago, as genetic evidence suggests, we have traced the ideology more than halfway back to that first appearance of chiefdoms in Southeast Asia, and a significant proportion of the way back to the first chiefdoms on Earth. The ideology evident among the Hawaiian paramount chiefdom at the time of European contact was durable and adaptable, manifesting variable ways over time and over a huge swath of the Pacific.

The evidence from very different Polynesian societies also attests to the power of this ideology. If it can survive when it is obviously not to the liking of those in low birth, and in societies with little or no inequality to justify, it must have some power in human minds—as much as it seems implausible to those who haven't grown up with it.

4. IDEOLOGIES OF ARCHAIC STATES

The preponderance of evidence suggests that extreme inequality and despotic rulers developed in most of the states in all seven of the areas where primary states developed, i.e. where states developed without outside influence: Central and South America, sub-Saharan Africa, Egypt, Mesopotamia, and South and East Asia. Early states also had remarkably similar justifying ideologies—despite an obvious lack of direct contact between some of them. Like the Polynesian chiefs, most rulers of archaic states claimed to be the highest-born descendants of divine or divinely favored founding ancestors. Some rulers (in times and places as far-flung as Egypt in 2000 BCE and South America in 1500 CE) actually claimed to be divine themselves (Bard 2008; Cobo 1979). This idea was a popular export. Roman Emperors started claiming divine status only a few decades after their nominally republican predecessors claimed the right to kill anyone who would declare himself a monarch.

As in Polynesian chiefdoms, dominant ideologies in archaic states tended to claim that it was natural for a single person to be at the top of what people in industrial capitalist societies tend to think of as very different hierarchies. The monarch might hold pre-eminent political and economic power as well as pre-eminent social and religious status—inheriting all of them in the way that modern Western people inherit economic power. The combination of powers was fused not only for the monarch but also throughout the socio-economic and political hierarchy. In the earliest states, no one seemed to think that economic and political inequality required separate justifications. The separation of economic and political power has been a gradual process over the course of thousands of years (Hudson 1996a), and it is only in the modern era that separate justifications for economic and political power became prominent.

5. CLASSICAL PHILOSOPHY

Virtually all classical philosophers—including Roman republicans and Greek democrats—considered enormous inequalities between people to be natural. Greek democracy was for a small group of people—excluding all women, most men, and especially all non-Greeks. Belief in the natural equality of male citizens was combined with the belief in their natural superiority to women, slaves, foreigners, and noncitizen residents called metics. The size of the citizen population in Athens was so small compared to noncitizens that by modern standards it is better described as an oligarchy.

The Athenian citizenry included thousands of people, some very rich and some very poor. Even the small sliver of equality afforded to this relatively small group was too much for many Athenian philosophers. Although Athenian philosophy was to some extent a product of the relative freedom of the city-state's democracy, philosophy was not a driving force behind Athenian democracy. In fact, philosophy and democracy—the two great ancient Greek contributions to modern political thought—grew up largely in opposition to each other, and that anti-democratic and anti-egalitarian tradition still influences modern philosophy (Roberts 1994: 1–20, especially 3).

Plato's dialogues are egalitarian in two important ways: they recognize some equality between the sexes (at least in their ability to become rulers or "Guardians"), and they call for a meritocracy rather than a strictly inherited aristocracy. These two nods to egalitarian ideas make the dialogues unusual for their time, but the apparent egalitarian sentiments of his work end there. Of course, being fictional dialogues they are not designed to clearly state exactly what Plato or Socrates believed. It is fairer to say that they present ideas to be considered, but no genuinely egalitarian ideas are among those considered. Slaves and metics are necessary for the polis's functioning, but their welfare is of little concern to the polis's government. Even the free citizens are assumed to be vastly unequal. The meritocratic system in Plato's (2013b) *Republic* is designed to bring out the natural inequality of people. It rejects democracy, political equality, and hereditary privilege in favor of a system of trials to sort people so that those who are naturally wiser and more virtuous can rule over other classes. Once tests determine individuals' places in the hierarchy, their social, economic, and political positions are permanently fixed. Plato is so distrusting of the lower orders (even among the free citizens) that the *Republic* suggests leaders tell a "noble lie" to disguise their true intentions from the less worthy members of the public. In "Crito," Plato (2013a) uses a runaway slave to exemplify a person worthy of extreme moral disapproval.

Although somewhat friendlier to democracy than Plato's dialogues, Aristotle's work argued for the natural subordination of women, slaves, and non-Greeks. The climate was too hot in the Middle East and too cold in most of Europe to produce men capable of full citizenship like the Greeks. Even the elite democracy practiced among Athenian men was to him inherently unstable and a threat to the natural hierarchy that exists between the male citizens (Roberts 1994). He discussed a cycle by which too much democracy would lead to demagoguery, unachievable promises of economic equality, and eventually to tyranny. Aristotle explicitly defended slavery. He would not have found it necessary to do so unless there were ancient Greeks who opposed slavery, but records of those opponents are sketchy. It is hard to find any rigorous attack on slavery in surviving philosophical literature of the period (Burns 2002, 2003).

Despite the outpouring of philosophy in the Hellenistic and Roman worlds, few prominent philosophers rejected natural hierarchy. Despite a Roman law tradition proclaiming the freedom and equality of all men, the elite class of the Roman Empire took their authority and the existence of slavery for granted and felt little need to make a serious defense of it (McLynn 2009). Other pre-Christian Greek and Roman philosophers from Xenophon in the fourth century BCE to Plotinus in the third century CE espoused ideas of natural inequality (Lovejoy 1960: 62–64; Roberts 1994: 6; Strauss 1953: 142–143).

6. CHRISTIANITY AND OTHER ABRAHAMIC RELIGIONS IN THE MEDIEVAL PERIOD

Religion has the potential to provide a counterpoint to secular assertions of natural hierarchy. In fact, some anthropologists speculate that one of the initial functions of religion in the Paleolithic era was to justify the egalitarianism observed in modern band societies (see Chapter 4). According to Kent Flannery and Joyce Marcus (2012: 59–60), the justification for equality in this life among many band and autonomous village societies is that the only true alphas or betas are in the heavens or in the afterlife: the living are all equally gammas. If so, egalitarian religions might have held sway throughout the period when most people lived in small-scale societies and conditions were favorable. But as societies increased in scale, these religious ideas proved sufficiently malleable to help inegalitarianism re-emerge. Early chiefs found it easy to claim that the ultimate alphas in heaven especially anointed the chiefs for leadership and privilege in this life—altering the religion just enough to justify hierarchy. People have made this use of religion ever since.

The Abrahamic faiths all stress the equality of humanity before God, the fraternity of believers, and the responsibility of the better-off to help people in need, but by the time they came to dominate Europe, North Africa, and the Middle East, they were all being used to justify extreme stratification. Most followers of the Abrahamic faiths believe God shapes Earth's history to fit a plan. Therefore, if hierarchy exists, God either made or let it happen. Perhaps, then, the unseen hand of God is the ultimate cause of inequality—rather than the willful decisions of the humans who make and enforce the rules that appear to be the proximate cause of inequality. If so, perhaps everyone should accept the inevitability and justice of existing inequalities. Perhaps God's divine providence gave everyone a station in life in accordance with his divine plan, and their worth as an individual is to accept that station and fulfill that role.

A closely related idea, called "the Great Chain of Being," offered another explanation of, and justification for, natural hierarchy. Although this theory was not stressed in the sacred literature of any of the Abrahamic faiths (having roots in Greco-Roman philosophy), it was strongly embraced in medieval and early modern Christian, Jewish, and Islamic theology and even by some modern philosophers and writers such as Baruch Spinoza, Gottfried Wilhelm Leibniz, and Alexander Pope (Béteille 2003; Lovejoy 1960; Pole 1978).

According to the theory, the universe must be perfect, and a perfect universe must be a plenitude. That is, it must be *full*, with every possible place occupied. And every place in that plenitude is defined hierarchically in order from the highest and closest to God to the lowest and farthest away. Every species of plant and animal, and every inanimate object occupied one of those places. At a smaller scale, every individual human held a particular place in this hierarchy as well, also ordered from high to low (Béteille 2003: 77–79; Lovejoy 1960: 58–64, 82; Pole 1978: 16–19).

Why a full universe should be thought more perfect than a selectively curated universe with the most beautiful mix of things (whether high, low, or equal) is a mystery, but the long chain of reasoning that ended at the Great Chain of Being seemed eminently reasonable to many if not most ancient, medieval, and early modern thinkers. The idea was so well-accepted that theologians and philosophers made little effort to verify it either by reference to sacred texts or by empirical investigation (Stark 1998: 1–13).

Theologians from all three Abrahamic faiths used ideas like divine providence and the Great Chain of Being to give doctrinal support to extreme stratification. Christian thinkers as early as St. Augustine, writing in the fifth century, argued that philosophy was addressed only to a small number of well-bred natural elites (Fortin 1987a: 202). The tenth-century Islamic philosopher, Al-Farabi, argued that people are naturally divided into classes, and that a supreme ruler must order the ranks of people into a hierarchy, educating them and assigning them duties appropriate for the virtues of which they are capable (Mahdi 1987: 210). The twelfth-century Jewish philosopher, Maimonides, declared that divine law endowed kings with life-and-death power over the people (Lerner 1987: 240). The thirteenth-century Christian philosopher, St. Thomas Aquinas, defended monarchy and slavery as institutions that might be necessary and are capable of being just. He embraced the Great Chain of Being and argued that differences in people's bodily natures ensured they were not equally disposed to knowledge, virtue, or wisdom (Fortin 1987b: 253–257, 264–268; Lovejoy 1960: 73–79; Strauss 1953: 142–143). Both Luther and Calvin—Christian reformers writing more than 1,100 years after St. Augustine—endorsed the belief that God gave people stations and vocations appropriate to that station (Forrester 1987).

This sort of thinking provided a surprisingly powerful and popular justification for inequality in Europe throughout the medieval period and well into the modern age, only being seriously challenged in Europe following the earthquake and tsunami that hit Lisbon in 1755 (Stark 1998: 1–13). The Great Chain of Being was taken to be scientific truth for at least 1,500 years (Béteille 2003: 75–76). The worth of individuals was in fulfilling the roles assigned to them by God's providence. Equality before God, even among the brotherhood of believers, was relegated to judgment day (Béteille 2003). The eighteenth-century philosopher, Andrew Michael Ramsay (1722: 32), often called "the Chevalier," asserted that men with "Superiority of their Mind, Wisdom, Virtue and Valour, are born fit to govern, whilst the vast Number of others . . . to obey," because "the Order of Providence" and "the Order of Nature contrived it thus." Following the lead of more than a millennium of philosophical and theological thought, he felt no need to provide evidence that the people in power actually have this superiority.

7. INEQUALITY ON THE EGALITARIAN PLATEAU

In the early modern period, arguments relying on a divinely ordered hierarchy increasingly became unpopular. More and more political philosophers came to feel obliged to begin on what is now called the "egalitarian plateau." That is, inequalities should be justified in terms of some notion of fundamental moral equality (Gosepath 2011). Few, however, felt obliged to *end* with the conclusion that their society needed a significant decrease in inequality—especially not in economic inequality and often not social and political inequality either.

The more prominent trend has been the system-justifying attempt to explain why respect for sometimes enormous inequality of outcome reflects respect for some deeper principle of moral equality on that egalitarian plateau. Many prominent philosophers of the seventeenth, eighteenth, and nineteenth centuries argue that outcome inequality is not only moral but natural and/or inevitable despite the moral equality of all people. Current inequalities might be somewhat corrupted, but with the necessary reforms, whether large or small, the more natural and more humane hierarchy that will inevitably emerge might not be so different from the current hierarchy, if perhaps a little less extreme or with more deserving people in each place.

The problem we intend to show in the modern philosophical treatment of natural inequality is that theorists have too readily used very poor evidence to justify severe departures from that plateau.

Hobbes's (1962 [1651]) social contract theory is not an argument for innate inequalities in natural abilities, but it is an early example of a "functionalist" argument for inevitably unequal political power.

A functionalist explanation for inequality is a justification based on some good that inequality does for everyone without arguing that the people at the top of the hierarchy are inherently better than anyone. No one *deserves* to be the leader in Hobbes's theory, but he argues that people cannot live together in peace without a sovereign political power to maintain order. He favors an absolute monarchy, although admits that sovereign power could conceivably be democratic. Therefore, he does not necessarily argue that inequality is an inevitable feature of human society, but his argument is often taken to mean that there must be at least some hierarchy: even under democracy some people have to have power over others to enforce the rules that keep the peace. Some contemporary philosophers make this claim of hierarchy explicit (see below).

If Hobbes's (1962 [1651]) argument is used as a functionalist argument for hierarchy, it is also an argument for *inevitable* inequality. Although it does not imply that inequality exists in *all possible* human conditions, it does say that inequality exists whenever humans live together in peace. Therefore, under this version of the functionalist argument, inequality inevitably exists in all human *societies*, because if humans cannot live together in peace, they cannot form a society (the basic reason behind Hobbes's depiction of the state of nature as solitary).

The title of Robert Filmer's (1949 [1680]) book, *Patriarcha*, is a religious-based justification of hierarchy, but it begins on—or at least closer to—the egalitarian plateau than do most earlier justifications of monarchy. It does not require everyone to have a place specifically designated by God, and only one divine action is essential. God gave the earth and the right to rule it to the first man, Adam, who passed it on to his sons, and after generations of division the worlds' kings have inherited Adam's power. One who accepts the historical premises of Filmer's argument could accept this part of his argument while rejecting divine providence, rejecting the Great Chain of Being, and accepting some notion of moral equality. A moral equal might happen to inherit the right to be king because the previous king just happened to bequeath the kingdom to them. Notice how similar Filmer's justification of monarchy is to the Polynesian justification of the power of chiefs. In Filmer's story, the leader's power is inherited from a mythical founder, Adam, who—although not technically semi-divine—has a supernatural birth, a supernatural lifespan, and divinely granted authority.

After Locke (1960 [1689]) refuted Filmer's argument—in part for its historical implausibility—he outlined a theory of appropriation (discussed in much greater detail elsewhere in this book), which includes his own version of the mythical founding ancestor. Locke does not seek to justify the political inequality of kings but the economic and social inequality of landowners. Although Locke, like many political theorists of his time and later, accepted the prevailing institution of limiting voting rights to property owners, the idea that justifications for political and economic inequality were one and the same thing (present to some extent in both Filmer and Hobbes) is absent in Locke, and political theories have increasingly treated them separately.

In Locke's (1960 [1689]) theory, landowners gain their authority by having a connection to a mythical "original appropriator." Locke's appropriator is the first person (presumed male) who, generations ago, took a piece of unclaimed land and improved it with his labor, thereby gaining the natural right to permanent, tradable, and heritable ownership of that land. Current property holders are to be taken as the heirs of the original appropriator of the particular plot of land they hold.

Had Locke known about the story popular in Hawaii at the time, he probably would have taken it to be "primitive," and he would have had at least three reasons to believe his argument was more sophisticated than theirs. First, Locke's original appropriator is neither semi-divine nor supernatural. All the appropriator can claim is the possession of the type of human virtues favored by God (such as hard work and foresight). And his original appropriator was modeled on settlers in British colonies at the time—if in an idealized way. Second, Locke does not require an implausible chain of father-to-son connections between current property holders and the original appropriators. The land might have been bought and sold or awarded in a legal settlement for wrongdoing many times between original appropriation and today. Third, Locke (1960 [1689]) and most present-day Lockeans deny the need to show *any* connection between the original appropriator and current property holders. The story is about what could have happened rather than what actually happened (see Chapters 7–9).

However, the pre-contact Polynesians had at least two potential claims to greater sophistication that Locke. First, they could say that they were aware that their myth is just a myth. Perhaps the chief tells the myth because he has to say something to justify his power, and perhaps the people repeat the myth because the chief does not allow freedom of speech. Second, Polynesian chiefs can claim that there is more truth in their myth than in Locke's myth. As discussed elsewhere in this book, colonizing expeditions were led by some person who owned the canoes and who (under a Lockean theory) would have appropriated any uninhabited lands they found. Polynesian colonization was relatively recent. It is possible that—in at least some of the hundreds of Polynesian chiefdoms scattered across the Pacific—the chief in power was the heir of the leader of the original settlement expedition to that region. No landowner in Britain can make that claim.

Locke (1960 [1689]) does not claim inequality exists in the state of nature (before the establishment of money, trade, and government), but once trade is established Locke argues that property holdings necessarily become unequal over time. He wants to change society very little. The current inequality between the Crown and landowners gives too much power to the Crown, but the general pattern of inequality between landowners and propertyless workers is not only ethical but inevitable in any society that respects the rights to life, liberty, and property. Society might need to tweak landownership a bit to ensure the right person owns each estate and perhaps to make sure every propertyless person has access to employment or charity as appropriate, but greater changes are unneeded and possibly unsustainable.

Although Hobbes and Locke didn't rely heavily on natural differences between people, many other thinkers of the period did. John Milton, for example, drew a distinction between those capable of great deeds and the ignorant masses, who, he believed, neither desired liberty nor were capable of using it (Berns 1987: 442–445). Spinoza favored a rather aristocratic form of democracy, because he believed people's natural differences necessitate a hierarchy that could not be eliminated without destroying social order (Rosen 1987: 460).

Jean-Jacques Rousseau, David Hartley, Étienne Bonnot de Condillac, William Godwin, Mary Wollstonecraft, and Thomas Paine were all relatively egalitarian, but they also accepted that skills and talents were rooted in nature in ways that ensured significant political, economic, and/or social inequality, although they disagreed about exactly what talents were most important. The Baron de Montesquieu argued that there weren't great natural differences between people, but he also argued that commerce would necessarily produce great inequalities. This argument, connected with Lockean property theory, later became connected to the claim that inequality is the necessary product of freedom, whether or not innate inequalities exist (Carson 2007: 20–22).

Adam Smith's (1976 [1776]) arguments were instrumental in making the connection between inequality and freedom, because he advocated private ownership and "free trade" that would lead to inequality. However, he was not as inegalitarian as most philosophers at the time. Smith did not believe that natural differences between people, whether in virtue, effort, or talent, were the primary motivation for trade. Instead, trade allows people to realize the productive benefits of specialization. Like Locke, Smith accepted that any trade-based economy results in some inequality of outcome and requires an ownership class to make investments. But Smith was also critical of many existing privileges, which he saw as the results of government-created market distortions. He was more concerned that these distortions caused inefficiency than inequality, but he was aware that most of them were put in place to maintain inequality, and he believed that the less-regulated economic system he advocated would become more equal than the economy of royal privileges he criticized. Therefore, although Smith may not be as egalitarian as Paine and the others mentioned with him, neither is he as inegalitarian as some of his contemporary followers.

Although the U.S. "Declaration of Independence" recognizes all men to be created equal, the idea of natural inequalities leading inevitably to hierarchy was popular with many of the framers of the United States, including the authors of the Declaration. For example, John Adams thought inequality was a fact of nature that could not be rationally denied. "Nature, which has established in the universe a chain of being, and universal order . . . has ordained that . . . no two men are perfectly equal in person, property, understanding, activity, and virtue, or ever can be made so by any power less than that which created them" (Kirk 1985: 97–98). Thomas Jefferson believed government action was needed to ensure that the higher positions in society were held by the natural aristocrats of virtue and talent rather than the artificial aristocrats of wealth and birth. Like many thinkers of his era he believed that equal opportunity would lead to a more just but similarly unequal hierarchy (Carson 2007: 11–13).

Perhaps the clearest statement of this sort of thinking comes not from a philosopher but from the novelist Owen Wister (1902). The narrator of his novel, *The Virginian*, says:

> It was through the Declaration of Independence that we Americans acknowledged the eternal inequality of man. For by it we abolished a cut-and-dried aristocracy . . . we decreed that every man should thenceforth have equal liberty to find his own level. By this very decree we acknowledged and gave freedom to true aristocracy . . . [because] true democracy and true aristocracy are one and the same thing.

All the other unequal societies had the wrong kind of stratification. But Wister's narrator just happens to be born in the one society that finally got natural inequality right. The book is a Western, taking place just as the government was violently forcing the Native Americans off the land to make this natural inequality happen.

Even Karl Marx was a believer in natural inequality. He is best-known for his revolutionary egalitarian sentiments, but that ideal was to be reached only in the far-off higher phase of communism. Before then, society would require the dictatorship of the proletariat as it progressed through the transitional phase of state socialism. Marx's idea of economic justice in this phase is surprisingly similar to liberal writers of the era:

> [An] equal right is an unequal right for unequal labor. It recognizes no class differences, because everyone is only a worker like everyone else; but it tacitly recognizes unequal individual endowment, and thus productive capacity, as a natural privilege. It is, therefore, a right of inequality, in its content, like every right. (Karl Marx n.d.)

Every specific hierarchical system had critics in the era, but the idea of natural hierarchy in general seems to have few critics.

8. CONSERVATISM

The conservative movement took shape in the late 1700s in defense of monarchy and aristocracy against some of the ideas discussed in the last section. Edmund Burke is now recognized as the founder of conservatism, largely because he introduced a theory that sounds like a secularized adaptation of divine providence.

In conservative theory, the world is too complex for any social reformer to understand. Prevailing social arrangements and even common prejudices reflect the accumulated wisdom of our ancestors through generations of trial and error. Accumulated wisdom, rather than (or along with) divine providence assure that current economic, social, and political inequality is better for everyone, even the people at the bottom of the hierarchy. The function of these rules is beyond our comprehension and better than any more-than-incremental improvements a reformer might devise. The differences in hierarchies across cultures is not taken as evidence against this theory but as evidence that different hierarchies are appropriate for different cultures and races (Kirk 1985: 34–38, 52–58).

Burke called social and political equality "that monstrous fiction, which, by inspiring false ideas and vain expectations into men destined to travel in the obscure walk of laborious life, serves only to aggravate and embitter that real inequality, which it never can remove." Burke applies this reasoning to political as well as socio-economic inequality, arguing that substantial equality of power is simply not possible; democratic leveling "perverts the natural order of things" (Mansfield 1987: 695–696).

Many conservatives continued to use theological explanations for natural inequality alongside their secular theory. Burke argued that each individual's "station" in life was assigned by the "divine tactic" of a just God. Joseph de Maistre (1996), writing in the late 1700s, declared, "simple good sense and the experience of centuries do not permit us to doubt [t]his privilege of aristocracy is really a natural law."

Many nineteenth-century British conservatives continued to believe in a divinely ordained, unalterable distribution of authority and mental capacity, which corresponded closely to the actual existing hierarchy in Britain from the landed aristocracy down (Shapin and Barnes 1976). Conservative arguments relying on natural inequality and divine providence exist in the works of John Adams, Samuel Taylor Coleridge, Thomas Babington Macaulay, James Fenimore Cooper, W. H. Mallock, Paul Elmer More, and others (Kirk 1985: 137, 191, 408, 437–438).

Some American conservatives credited God for ordaining inequality and even slavery. John C. Calhoun (1851) argued that liberty must not "be bestowed on a people [Black Americans] too ignorant, degraded and vicious, to be capable either of appreciating or of enjoying it," because "an all-wise Providence has reserved it." Any effort to get rid of the hierarchy, "must ever prove abortive, and end in disappointment." According to Calhoun, the belief that people are born free and equal, even in a "state of nature," is "contrary to all observation. . . . It never did, nor can exist; as it is inconsistent with the preservation and perpetuation of the race." Seemingly incongruously with his arguments against equal freedom, Calhoun (1851) also argued, "the necessary effect of leaving all free to exert themselves to better their condition, must be a corresponding inequality."

As late as the 1980s, the conservative author, Russell Kirk (1985: 34, 58, 65), praised divine providence as the primary reason for conservatism, unfortunately no longer holding the place it deserves in the political debate. In description of Burke's work, Kirk wrote, "In nature, obviously, men are unequal; unequal in mind, in body, in energies, in every material circumstance." This quote flows gracefully from innate personal differences to socially and legally constructed differences with no mention of the significance of that shift or even that it is a shift.

Many conservative statements provide testable claims. Herbert McCloskey (1958: 31), reporting on an extensive survey of conservative literature listed as one of the "essential elements of the conservative outlook" the belief that "Men are naturally unequal, and society requires 'orders and classes' for the good of all. All efforts at levelling are futile and lead to despair."

9. (PSEUDO-)SCIENTIFIC EXPLANATIONS FOR INEQUALITY

In the nineteenth and twentieth centuries, scientific-sounding—and often contradictory—explanations for natural inequality became popular. Some authors believe the natural superiors could come from any social station if the right education and opportunities were available; others believed that natural differences were highly heritable and that the natural aristocracy would probably correspond closely to existing imperfectly selected aristocracy.

This belief in natural aristocracy was so widespread that much of the education in Britain and the United States was predicated on the belief that the lower classes had a significantly different mode of thought than the higher classes. Steven Shapin and Barry Barnes (1976: 232–235) describe this belief as the "head and hand" analogy, by which every society supposedly resembles the human body. Some people are like the head. Their mentality is intellectual, complex, and active. Some people are like the hands. Their mentality is sensual, simple, and passive or automatic. The higher orders not only exceed their subordinates in mental capacity; they have an entirely different *way* of thinking. According to Shapin and Barnes (1976: 246), a wide consensus of people writing about education in mid-nineteenth-century Britain wrote confidently as if these differences in mentality were something that members of all cultures would recognize.

This belief in a fundamental intellectual divide between the upper and lower classes paved the way for the eugenics movement of the late nineteenth and early twentieth centuries. Francis Galton founded the movement, defining it as the scientific effort to improve the human gene pool by better breeding (Hasian 1996: 1).

Although eugenics shares the head-and-hand ideology's belief in the innate superiority of the upper class, eugenics is even less respectful toward the lower class. The head needs the hand. Although the head must take paternalistic authority over the hand, the head must respect what hand's contribution to a mutually beneficial team. The eugenic superior has no need for the eugenic inferior at all. The lower classes are nothing but a drag on the progress of their biological superiors. Although the fit person might have charitable concern that the unfit do not suffer if they manage to get born, the most important thing for the long-term improvement of the human race is to eliminate inferiors by selective breeding.

The movement collected a lot of data but never proved at all scientific. It had a very primitive understanding of how genetics worked. The recommendations of leading eugenicists turned out to be influenced by class and race prejudice much more than even a superficial analysis of the data they collected. The main eugenic strategies were little more than efforts to get the lower classes to breed less and the upper classes to breed more (Hasian 1996).

Eugenics made an enormous impact both on political thought and on practical legislation in the late nineteenth and early twentieth centuries, most infamously in Germany but also in many other Western countries including Britain and the United States. Many laws (some overtly racist or sexist) were justified on eugenic grounds, including government-sponsored contests to assess families on their fitness, bonuses for the fitter races to have more children, miscegenation laws, selective immigration laws, eugenic screening programs for military and other institutions, coercive sterilization, and prohibitions against marriage by the feeble-minded, drunkards, and other supposedly unfit individuals (Winter 2014).

At its extreme, the eugenicist's goal is to create the first human society with no need for inequality. In this sense, eugenics is not permanently committed to the inevitability of inequality. As long as the genetic make-up of the human race remains as it is, inequality is natural and inevitable, but as eugenic breeding does its work no one knows how equal a well-bred society might become.

Belief in eugenics was not confined to those who wanted to extend upper-class privileges. It was nearly ubiquitous across the political spectrum. The Catholic Church and some other Christian groups were exceptions, but many and perhaps most liberals, socialists, social democrats, reformers, and conservatives adopted eugenic thinking in the first half of the twentieth century. Supporters on the right tended to believe that fitness closely tracked current social position, while supporters on the left tended to believe that it did not. But both sides agreed that heredity caused enormous, unalterable inequality in nearly all physical and mental aspects of humanity—including the tendency to criminal behavior (Hasian 1996; Kevles 1985; Winter 2014).

Charles Darwin wasn't a eugenicist, but he gave his cousin, Francis Galton, credit for proving that genius tends to be inherited. Prominent supporters of eugenics in Britain and the United States included Major Leonard Darwin, Charles Davenport, George Eastman, Havelock Ellis, Charles W. Eliot, Irving Fisher, Henry Ford, Henry Goddard, Emma Goldman, David Starr Jordan, John Maynard Keynes, Harold Laski, Ottoline Morrell, Hermann J. Muller, Karl Pearson, Gifford Pinchot, John D. Rockefeller, Jr., Theodore Roosevelt, George Bernard Shaw, Charles R. Van Hise, and Beatrice and Sidney Webb (Kevles 1985: 10, 63, 64, 88). Even the Black American activist Booker T. Washington attended a eugenics conference to explain that "the negro" was *becoming* "more like you" (Winter 2014).

Thomas Henry Huxley (1998), though not necessarily a eugenicist, claimed that scientific observation supported the belief that inequality was ubiquitous. After admitting, "inequalities of condition must be less obvious among nomads than among settled people," he added, "[I]t is a profound mistake to imagine that, in the nomadic condition, any more than in any other which has yet been observed, men are either 'free' or 'equal.'"

Although eugenic thinking has not yet completely disappeared from Western thought, the eugenics movement was already becoming discredited before the Second World War exposed the connection between Nazi eugenics strategies and the holocaust. Several scientific factors were important to discrediting the movement. These included the realization that it would take hundreds or thousands of generations of consistent breeding to have any noticeable effect on the kinds of factors eugenicists hoped to change, and the realization that so many environmental factors affected human positions that it was nearly impossible to say that any person's position was attributable to genetic factors (Kevles 1985: especially 84, 85, 173).

The most pertinent aspect of the eugenics movement for our purposes is the readiness of so many prominent people across the political spectrum to accept it, demonstrating how many people were looking to science or resorting to pseudo-science to confirm rather than to challenge long-held cultural beliefs about the natural inequality of people.

The ubiquity of eugenic thinking at the time seems to be an excellent example of system-justifying ideologies (Jost and Hunyady 2005) and explanation of a belief in a just world (Lerner 1980). Because it is painful to believe that injustice is behind so much suffering or to believe that it could happen to anyone, most people—even those who sincerely wanted to relieve suffering—wished to believe that some aspect of the sufferer's nature is to blame rather than society's contrived rules.

10. CONCLUSION

The long history and the large number of contradictory explanations for natural inequality should give contemporary thinkers pause before accepting claims about natural inequality, especially in light of the poor evidence that supporters have provided for their theories. The possibilities of self-serving bias, system-justifying ideologies, and just-world theory all suggest that prevailing thought might be biased in favor of accepting inequalities. Yet, the following chapter shows that poorly supported, contradictory claims of natural and inevitable inequality remain popular in the contemporary philosophical and social science literature.

Chapter 3

HIERARCHY'S APOLOGISTS, PART TWO: NATURAL INEQUALITY IN CONTEMPORARY POLITICAL PHILOSOPHY AND SOCIAL SCIENCE

The belief in natural inequality survives in many guises in contemporary social science and political philosophy, most particularly in connection with justifying enormous inequality of property rights and the inequalities of power and social position that go along with it. Hobbesian and to a lesser extent Burkean ideas remain powerful in contemporary political thought. But propertarian and Lockean writers draw most of our attention because they pay the most attention to this issue.

1. PROPERTY RIGHTS AND FREEDOM

Probably the most popular assertion of natural inequality in recent literature is the claim—most commonly asserted by propertarians— that inequality is the natural and inevitable outcome of a free society. This idea has its roots in Smith, Hume, Montesquieu, Locke, and even Aristotle, although none of them clearly endorsed the now-prevalent version of it or made it the centerpiece of their argument as contemporary propertarians do. By the late twentieth century, belief in this conflict became popular both in philosophy and in practical politics as an important part of the rights-based or freedom-based argument for private property rights with little or no taxation, regulation, or redistribution.

Nozick's (1974: 160–163) argument that "liberty upsets patterns" is probably the most influential expression of the belief in the inevitable conflict between freedom and equality. He asks the reader to begin with whatever distribution of property they most prefer (calling it D1). This

42

distribution could be any level of equality or distribution according to talent, virtue, merit, or any other criteria. Beginning with the reader's favored D1, Nozick asks them to imagine millions of people choosing to pay Wilt Chamberlain to play basketball for their entertainment, changing the distributional pattern from D1 to D2, in which Chamberlain is a millionaire. The choices of individuals break whatever pattern of equality people might have established at D1. To maintain any pattern or any specified level of equality, Nozick (1974: 163) argues, government "would have to forbid capitalist acts between consenting adults." He concludes, "no end-state principle or distributional patterned principle of justice [such as economic equality] can be continuously realized without continuous interference with people's lives."

Propertarians then call on the government or other legal authority to be indifferent to how much property people have to all the contrived rules that establish and maintain a system in which some have enormous amounts of property and others have nothing. They call this indifference, "equality before the law" or "equality under the law" (Hayek 1960: 85–87; Machan 2006a: 315). Supposedly, this conception of equality is essential to respect for freedom and natural rights. It therefore implies a conflict between freedom and economic equality. Friedrich Hayek (1960: 87) writes:

> From the fact that people are very different it follows that, if we treat them equally, the result must be inequality in their actual position, and that the only way to place them in an equal position would be to treat them differently. Equality before the law and material equality are therefore not only different but are in conflict with each other.

Many other propertarians make similar claims. Jan Narveson (1998: 3), echoing Calhoun, writes, "private property, with all its 'inequalities,' . . . is a natural outcome of a principle of general liberty."

Most propertarian authors do not seek empirical confirmation or falsification for the claim that freedom and equality are inevitably in conflict. They seem to believe that they have fully established the existence of the trade-off by a priori reasoning, so that they feel little need to confirm their conclusions empirically. But it is a testable claim. If there are (or could be) societies that are both equal and free (in the relevant sense), the claim is falsified.

Although the claim of a conflict between equality and liberty is the only version of the inevitable inequality claim propertarian arguments require, many propertarians also suggest that inequality stems from innate differences between people or that equality is unattainable even at the sacrifice of freedom. Any effort to create a more equal society in terms of wealth or social position supposedly requires substantial inequalities of power so that it will sacrifice freedom without achieving its goal of attaining genuine equality. For example, the thrust of Hayek's (1944) *The Road to Serfdom* is an argument that creating equality requires an intervening authority that necessarily accrues unchecked power.

Murray Rothbard's (2012) essay, "Egalitarianism as a Revolt Against Nature," concludes, "[E]galitarians are acting as terribly spoiled children, denying the structure of reality on behalf of the rapid materialization of their own absurd fantasies . . . the egalitarian goal is, therefore, evil and any attempts in the direction of such a goal must be considered evil as well." Tibor Machan (2006a: 315) writes, "[T]he only relevant equality is equality under the law. . . . To strive politically for universal equality of any other kind is to strive for what is impossible and therefore wrong to pursue." These claims are nonsense because although no societies have achieved *complete* equality, no societies have achieved *complete* hierarchy either. That is, there are no societies in which every individual has a unique place, in which no two people are equals, and in which no rules apply equally to more than one person. That the two extreme points are impossible says nothing about which possible points in-between are achievable or desirable.

The claim of conflict between freedom and equality doesn't require proof of the superiority of anyone in terms of virtue, divine favor, ability, effort, or any other characteristic. It requires only cumulative effects of property rights and trade. Even if inequalities are largely arbitrary, they might be an inevitable by-product of freedom. Yet few, if any, people who claim that freedom naturally creates equality seem willing to concede that inequality is largely arbitrary.

One possible reason is that it is unpleasant to think the enormous differences between rich and poor are seldom merited even if one thinks allowing such arbitrary inequality helps preserve freedom. Therefore, propertarians tend not to stress that their theory accepts severe stratification even if some just happen to be born into deep poverty with few opportunities to get out while wealthy dynastic families live in luxury because of privileges their family acquired by dumb luck generations ago. Propertarians often ignore or dismiss such outcomes as mere theoretical possibilities, while implying or stating outright that those who end up better-off are naturally superior.

Rothbard (2012), for example, writes, "in every organization or activity, a few (generally the most able and/or the most interested) will end up as leaders, with the mass of the membership filling the ranks of the followers." He employs the Burkean conservative claim that prejudices reflect accumulated intuitive wisdom, supposing that "redheads are excitable," that men really are natural leaders, and that women are better at jobs requiring, "housewifely skills," "patience," "sex appeal," and "contact with children." This sort of reasoning is supposed to explain why some groups end up with more wealth than other groups—because they have abilities more suited to high-paying occupations.

Hans-Hermann Hoppe (1995) connects private property with a wide variety of explanations of natural inequality:

> [T]he maintenance and preservation of a private property-based exchange economy requires as its sociological presupposition the existence of a voluntarily acknowledged "natural" elite—a nobilitas naturalis.

The natural outcome of the voluntary transactions between various private property owners is decidedly non-egalitarian, hierarchical and elitist. As the result of widely diverse human talents, in every society of any degree of complexity a few individuals quickly acquire the status of an elite. Owing to superior achievements of wealth, wisdom, bravery or a combination thereof, some individuals come to possess "natural authority", and their opinions and judgments enjoy widespread respect. Moreover, because of *selective mating* and marriage and the laws of *civil and genetic inheritance*, positions of natural authority are more likely than not passed on within a few—noble—families.

Here, he repeats a eugenic error about the effectiveness of selective breeding that was scientifically discredited more than a half-century earlier. Hoppe's elites are not only better than everybody else; they also benefit everyone else. Hoppe does not believe that current elites in the world today always have superior breeding and virtue, because governments have created avenues for less virtuous people to get ahead, implying that trade always benefits the virtuous. He believes it will take the establishment of a propertarian system to realize all the benefits of natural inequality and selective breeding (Hoppe 2001: 94–121).

Some propertarians go beyond class-based elitism into downright racism (Fischer et al. 1996; Hernstein and Murray 1994). Richard Hernstein and Charles Murray (1994) have tried to explain the racial gap in income and wealth in the United States as the result of natural differences between the races. Although their analysis has been resoundingly discredited, at least Hernstein and Murray attempt to present empirical support. But their attempt runs into the difficulty that Western scientists have been trying to prove the superiority of Western elites for hundreds of years without success. They failed resoundingly and found instead so much contrary evidence that no reputable scientist believes it today.

Propertarians often equivocate on the issue of whether inequalities in their preferred system are often arbitrary, because doing so has advantages and disadvantages. The *advantage* is that it frees the theorist from having to substantiate any claims about the better-off actually having any superior characteristics. But the *disadvantage* is the unattractiveness of thinking of the people ending up with billions of times the wealth of other people without being more meritorious than them in any way. Therefore, it is tempting for propertarians to try to have it both ways, to imply or to state outright that the observed inequalities in a market economy really do reflect differences in skill, effort, natural ability, or other desirable attributes, while backing away from any responsibility to substantiate those claims on the grounds that, after all, the theory is about freedom not merit.

Nozick never uses obvious scoundrels or lucky fools as the people who get ahead in his system. He picks popular people, such as Wilt Chamberlain and Henry Ford, to make the point that "liberty upsets patterns." Wilt Chamberlain came from humble origins and childhood illness to be adored by millions of fans around the United States. Nozick could have made his point with a story of Landlord X who senses that people might be interested in saving money on rental apartments and who are uninterested in diligently researching whether lower rent in a particular building is attributable to fewer safety features. The landlord builds apartment buildings with lead pipes, lead paint, and fewer precautions against fire. Many people of lesser means choose to save time, effort, and money by moving into those apartments without paying close attention to the risk of living there. As a result, his tenants and their children get cheap apartments; some die in fires; some of their children grow up with lead poisoning; other tenants and children arbitrarily escape those problems; and Landlord X and his children become wealthy and healthy. This is an outcome we should expect in a propertarian system, and we should consider it *desirable* by the liberty-upsets-patterns logic.

Even though the Landlord X example is less attractive, it just as well allows Nozick (1974: 164) to make his points: (1) that the wealth of third parties—those who chose not to deal with that landlord—is unaffected (still fitting the original pattern), and (2) that "Any distributional pattern with any egalitarian component is overturnable by the voluntary actions of individual persons over time." It is much more pleasant to think of wealthy people being like Wilt Chamberlain instead of Landlord X but, like Landlord X, Nozick doesn't call attention to the less attractive features of the thing he sells.

Nozick (1974: 158) further argues, "[I]f almost anyone would have bought a car from Henry Ford, the supposition that it was an arbitrary matter who held the money then (and so bought) would not place Henry Ford's earnings under a cloud. In any event, *his* coming to hold it is not arbitrary." To readers who see Ford as a hard-working, far-sighted entrepreneur, Nozick's argument implies, without stating outright, that capitalism has a cleansing effect: even if the starting point is arbitrary, eventually property will get into the hands of people with desirable characteristics—and their "coming to hold it is not arbitrary."

But, of course, this claim is only true if, no matter what, everyone really would have bought a car from Henry Ford. This claim could only be true if capitalism has perfect equality of opportunity, so that, say, an impoverished black woman growing up in one of Landlord X's buildings is just as likely to become the head of a major car company as Henry Ford or one of his children. After making the implication that capitalist distribution has something to do with merit, Nozick (1974: 158, emphasis added) softens his claim, "Distribution according to benefits to others . . . does not constitute *the whole* pattern of a system of entitlements (namely, inheritance, gifts for arbitrary reasons, charity, and so on) or a standard that one should insist a society fit."

By saying it does not determine *the whole* pattern of distribution, Nozick implies it determines *a great deal* of the distribution without taking responsibility to show evidence that it determines *any part* of the pattern of distribution. Notice also that the factors that Nozick admits fail to reward benefits to others are all unrelated to market exchange, implying that trade does in fact reward merit—ignoring rentier income, the enormous inequality of opportunity, people like Landlord X, and many other factors that cause market exchange to reward things other than merit. Therefore, Nozick heavily implies that inequality is not only natural and inevitable but also benign. Yet he takes on no responsibility to prove any of these implications, even as he writes, "*one* possible explanation why certain inequalities *rankle* so; is *not* due to the feeling that this superior position is undeserved, but to the feeling that it *is* deserved and earned" (Nozick 1974: 241).

Nozick (1974: 194, emphasis added) does more than imply that his system rewards the "better endowed" when he criticizes John Rawls's egalitarian system for not offering enough to them. He relies on it as an unstated assumption when he writes "I do *not* mean to imply that the better endowed should get *even more* than they get under the [propertarian] entitlement system." For this complaint against Rawls's system to be a reason to prefer Nozick's system, Nozick must assume that the better-endowed actually do get more in his system than Rawls's system. That is, he assumes that the people who thrive under his system are *the same people* who thrive "under conditions of fair equality of opportunity" (Rawls 1971: 302). For this argument to work, capitalism has to be a natural meritocracy, directly contradicting Nozick's assertion that he has no responsibility to prove his claims about rewarding the naturally well endowed.

Nozick is trying very hard to have it both ways. He would like his readers to believe claims that people who thrive under capitalism are naturally superior to people who do not, but he wants to deny that his argument requires proof of any such claim. Thus, as much as Nozick and other propertarians attempt to rely on the claim that equality is in conflict with freedom, they very much do rely on the claim that equality is natural.

2. OTHER CONTEMPORARY SCHOOLS OF THOUGHT

One popular explanation for natural inequality is the functionalist idea that it provides some necessary value for everyone—not just for the people at the top of the hierarchy (Davis and Moore 1945). Functionalist explanations for inequality include the need to get the more capable people into the more demanding positions and to motivate everyone to work by offering differential rewards.

One functionalist explanation of inequality, inspired by Hobbes, is that the enforcement of rules requires an inequality of power. The connection between the need for political power and *inequality* is more explicit in some modern theories than it was in Hobbes. For example, Ralph Dahrendorf (1968: 172–176) uses functionalist reasoning to argue that equality is impossible, writing:

> [B]ecause sanctions are necessary to enforce conformity of human conduct, there has to be inequality of rank among men. . . .
>
> Time and time again, anthropologists have told us of "tribes without rulers," and sociologists of societies that regulate themselves without power or authority. But in opposition to such fantasies, I incline with Weber to describe "every order that is not based on the personal, free agreement of all involved" . . . as "imposed," i.e. based on authority and subordination. . . . Society *means* that norms regulate human conduct; this regulation is guaranteed by the incentive or threat of sanctions; the possibility of imposing sanctions is the abstract core of all power.
>
> . . . [I]nequalities among men follow from the very concept of societies as moral communities, then there cannot be, in the world of our experience, a society of absolute equals . . . the idea of a society in which all distinctions of rank between men are abolished transcends what is sociologically possible and has a place only in the sphere of poetic imagination.

On one hand, he leaves open the possibility of egalitarian societies if they could be based on the personal, free agreement of all involved. On the other hand, by dismissing reports of egalitarian societies as fantasies that can't be moral communities and that belong to the sphere of poetic imagination, he states unequivocally that no such communities exist. Yet, he offers no empirical evidence to back up his assertions.

J. R. Lucas (1965: 304–305) argues along similar functionalist lines and takes it to a farther-reaching conclusion that "it is foolish to seek to establish an equality of wealth on egalitarian grounds . . . because if we do not let men compete for money, they will compete all the more for power."

Melvyn Fein (2012: 27, 60, viii) uses a combination of functionalist, evolutionary, and human nature reasoning to support his claim that human beings are "hierarchical animals." He makes far-reaching empirical claims that hierarchy is natural and universal and that it must, therefore, provide evolutionary advantages to all. According to Fein, "most researchers" recognize "hierarchical arrangements are universal. Despite numerous attempts to prove otherwise, every known society, both large and small, has exhibited some form of stratification." He accuses anyone who favors "greater equality" to have "foreclosed objective explorations into the nature of human ranking systems." They merely "imagine" that "social coercion can produce greater fairness. This, however, needs to be demonstrated rather than assumed." He spends an entire chapter chiding those who believe greater equality is possible for failing to look at the facts.

Despite his complaints about other researchers' lack of attention to facts, Fein's book is not well sourced and doesn't offer much empirical evidence. He has no citations connecting his claims to his sources, and so he presents no verifiable evidence for his far-reaching claims, such as "In societies of every shape and dimension, human beings vie to determine who is superior to whom." He recognizes that at least some small-scale societies are less hierarchical than large-scale societies but makes three arguments to explain away that evidence. First, the most observed egalitarian societies are marginal (whatever that is supposed to imply). Second, no societies are completely equal. Third, relatively egalitarian societies must expend effort to maintain equality (Fein 2012: 27–60).

Chapter 4 examines the truth of these claims in detail. For now, it's important to realize how little they deliver to support Fein's conclusions. First, even if egalitarian societies are unusual (which they are not historically), as long as they exist, they disprove his claim of *impossibility*.

Second, no one argues for *complete* equality. The questions involve whether stratification is necessary for all human societies and whether the prospect of substantially *greater* equality than defenders of natural hierarchy want to see is possible.

Third, the need to expend effort to maintain equality does not prove that equality is impossible or that people prefer to be dominated by others than to be equal to others. Reversing Fein's arguments shows their weakness: all hierarchical societies expend enormous effort to establish and maintain inequality with strong enforcement of coercive laws that grant power over resources to some and lesser or no such power to others, indirectly giving those who control resources power over other people as well (Widerquist 2013). If we can't do anything that requires effort, we can't have any laws, rules, or norms. We can't have either equality or inequality.

Far-right authors take these ideas a little further. "Far right" (now sometimes called "alt right") is a twentieth-century term, sometimes retroactively applied to authors who strongly support natural inequality usually with an element of classist, nationalist, or racist explanations of inequality whether based on scientific, religious, or philosophical reasoning. Oswald Spengler (1934: 50–51) expressed the sentiment in 1934: "society rests upon the inequality of men. That is a natural fact. . . . 'Equal rights' are contrary to nature."

Julius Evola (2002: 136–142) justified inequality very differently than Spengler but agreed about its naturalness. He declared, with very little argumentation, "The principle according to which all human beings are free and enjoy equal rights 'by nature' is truly absurd;" "the hierarchical idea in general, derives from the very notion of a person;" "Where there is equality there cannot be freedom;" and he adds for good measure that ordinary people did not demand equality before they "fell under the spell of . . . subversive ideologies." Like Calhoun, Evola uses "freedom" to mean the freedom of the aristocrat. To him, the aristocrat is a real "person" while other people are just "individuals." Apparently, people are naturally so unequal that only the freedom of aristocrats is important.

It is easy to dismiss the far right, but similar ideas persist in mainstream philosophical literature.

At least one contemporary school of thought, made up of followers of Leo Strauss (1953: 134–143), has explicitly sought to reintroduce the ancient Greek conception of natural aristocracy into modern political theory, if only to make it compatible with modern, liberal democracy. Like Plato, Strauss prefers the rule of an elite group of philosophers as the highest ideal, but he is willing to accept the rule of wealthy gentlemen if, as expected, his preferred ideal is impractical. Rulers need the consent of the vulgar masses, but hopefully in a representative democracy ordinary people will come to admire the achievements of gentlemen and grant upper-class males power through a modern electoral process (McDaniel 1998; Strauss and Cropsey 1987; Tavov and Pangle 1987: 917–928).

Explanations based on both functionalism and innate differences in human ability are popular today even in liberal-egalitarian literature. Isaiah Berlin (1978: 92) considers the unequal distribution of natural gifts to be a well-known obstacle to economic equality. He endorses the inevitability of material equality, writing "in societies where there is a high degree of equality of economic opportunity, the strong and able and ambitious and cunning are likely to acquire more wealth or more power than those who lack these qualities."

Rawls's (1971, 2001) difference principle is built on the acceptance of functional inequality—arranging social and economic inequalities to be to the greatest benefit of the least-advantaged members of society. Rawlsianism accepts inequality to whatever extent (large or small) is necessary to achieve that goal by enticing more capable people to accept more responsible positions and by motivating everyone to put forth effort. Rawls makes no statement about how much inequality he thinks that will be, leaving open the possibility that inequality within a Rawlsian system could be great or small, pending the results of a future investigation. Although most Rawlsians read his work as implying that social organization needs a substantial overhaul, depending on one's opinion about the level of incentive needed to elicit effort, one can also read it as requesting a small tweaking of the system. John Tomasi (2012) for example, incorporates Rawlsian ideas into a theory supporting a version of propertarianism.

Another functionalist explanation came from Soviet sociologists, who faced the task of using an ideology that praised equality to justify a system that obviously had enormous inequalities of power and to some extent of wealth as well. They argued that capitalist inequality was based on class and was therefore exploitive, but Soviet inequality was a reflection of the natural division of labor and was therefore natural (Béteille 2003: 17). Just like Wister's narrator in *The Virginian*, they believed their new society more closely approximated natural inequality than any other system in history.

When Westerners think of a society with unnatural and oppressive inequality, they probably think of the caste system of India, but Indians have expressed similar views about Western inequality. Mohandas Gandhi believed that the Western capitalist system based on class and pitting people against each other in competition was unnatural and therefore *inherently* corrupt. Although he believed the existing caste system in India was corrupt, it was based on spirituality and cooperation which are natural and therefore good. Therefore, unlike capitalism, it was capable of being reformed. Sympathy for the caste system is much less popular in India than it was in his time, but Indians retain (at least for now) a popular skepticism about class-based inequalities associated with the growing market system in India (Béteille 2003: 17–19, 82).

Westerners might be tempted to suppose Gandhi was foolish because he failed to see the naturalness of the inequalities in market economies. If so, they would be like people in so many other societies supposing that their form of inequality was a closer approximation of true natural inequalities than other cultures' systems.

3. CONCLUSION: TESTABLE CLAIMS

The history reviewed in this chapter and the preceding one reveals both wide agreement that inequality is inevitable and strong disagreement about how, why, and in what ways people will inevitably be unequal. Dominant ideologies tend to assert that the level and type of inequality in society is close to that which is natural and inevitable. Yet few people espousing these beliefs seriously attempt to prove them, perhaps because, like *The Truman Show*, we accept the reality of the world around us.

It's *possible* that the freedom necessitates people taking superior positions in a market economy and that they really are more deserving, as Nozick implies. It's *possible* that redheads are more excitable and women are less capable of leadership as Rothbard suggests. It's *possible* that some people have the mentality of the head and other people have the mentality of the hand. It's *possible* that an all-wise providence made Calhoun the master of slaves. It's *possible* that all people have a unique position in the Great Chain of Being. It's *possible* all people really should have a place in the Hindu caste system. It's *possible* that Hawaiian chiefs really were the highest-born descendants of a semi-divine founder. And it's *possible* that Baruya men's sperm contains a magical life force without which women could not supply milk or children could not reach puberty. But almost all of these claims directly contradict all the others. Perhaps, instead, the rules enforcing inequality in each of these societies are the real causes of inequality, and the ideologies attesting to the inevitability of those rules are just window dressing.

Are contemporary Western beliefs about natural and inevitable inequality really so different from the long-discredited claims discussed above? Or do dominant beliefs in contemporary society also stem from system-justification, belief in a just world, and self-serving bias? Prudence suggest a skepticism about these claims or any like them, especially when presented without convincing evidence and used to justify enforcing rules that appear to be the cause of inequality. Yet the naturalness and inevitability of our stratified society is still being accepted with little scrutiny. We owe it to those at the bottom of the hierarchy to take the evidence seriously.

Several claims discussed in this chapter are testable with anthropological evidence from small-scale societies. The two central claims are: (1) equality is impossible to obtain (efforts to eliminate stratification either entirely fail or replace one kind of inequality with another), and (2) equality is inevitably in conflict with freedom (efforts to eliminate stratification also reduce liberty in the relevant sense, usually negative freedom). To state these claims in reverse: (1) stratification is inevitable and (2) the inevitable result (or the natural expression) of free human interaction.

We can also tentatively examine some of the explanations for inequality, such as that it is functionally necessary for the enforcement of rules; inequality of wealth, power, and position is the inevitable result of inequalities of talent, virtue, or other attributes; inequality is the inevitable result of people's natural desire to form hierarchies.

Chapter 4 examines these claims in light of evidence from anthropology and archaeology. It is important to examine claims in light of how they are used. They are used to support existing levels of inequality of social position and economic and political power and to head off arguments that society should reduce or eliminate social, economic, and political stratification. We will not find societies with complete equality or complete inequality. The question is whether we will find societies with high levels of social, economic, and political equality, or whether we will find a higher degree of equality than proponents of the thesis of inevitable inequality usually defend. Such evidence proves the possibility that at least some kind of society can exist that is equal in the way egalitarians propose. That evidence in combination with evidence from Chapters 5–6 shows that egalitarian societies can also be free societies.

Chapter 4

HOW SMALL-SCALE SOCIETIES MAINTAIN POLITICAL, SOCIAL, AND ECONOMIC EQUALITY

Recorded history provides at least some inductive support for the hypothesis that inequality is natural and/or inevitable. All of the 200 or so contemporary nation-states have substantial economic, political, and social inequality. Although some states, such as the Nordic countries in the mid- and late twentieth century, significantly decreased inequality within their borders, the states nominally most committed to radical egalitarianism (such as the Soviet Union, Maoist China, and North Korea) have failed to deliver it.

With a few exceptions, the further back one looks in recorded history the more inequality one seems to see. Despotism was the rule in all of the "cradles of civilization" (areas where states developed with little or no influence from previously established states). These include places as far apart as East Asia, South Asia, Mesopotamia and Egypt, sub-Saharan Africa, North America, and South America. Although a few states occasionally deviated from the rule, despotic governments with extreme inequalities of power, wealth, and social position eventually took hold in all of these areas (Trigger 2003).

If, after looking at recorded history, one looks at the behavior of our closest primate relatives, one finds that they instinctively form social hierarchies (see section 1) (Boehm 2001; de Waal 2005). Although the hierarchy varies by species and ecological circumstance, all social, nonhuman primate societies maintain some form of social dominance hierarchy (Gintis et al. 2015: 337).

This evidence, if viewed in isolation, makes the inevitable-inequality hypothesis appear reasonable. Yet, this version of the story leaves out the vastness of human prehistory and especially hunter-gatherer societies, which existed for hundreds of thousands of years (Washburn and Lancaster 1968). As this chapter argues below, most of human prehistory does not follow the pattern of inequality known from the historical records of state societies. Evidence from history, archaeology, and ethnography suggests that the historical pattern is U-shaped (Knauft 1991). We must have had some form of dominance hierarchy similar to other apes at some point in our evolutionary past, which amounts to some form of inequality. However, Section 2 shows that all observed, modern hunter-gatherer bands are egalitarian—politically, economically, and socially. The preponderance of evidence suggests that prehistoric people with similar foraging strategies were similarly egalitarian. Thus, at some point in human prehistory, people found a way to eliminate the baseline primate pattern of social dominance hierarchy and to live together without stratification. In this respect, some anthropologists have even gone so far as to refer to egalitarian hunter-gatherer social systems as a kind of reverse dominance hierarchy (Boehm 1993).

Section 3 shows that autonomous villages are nearly as egalitarian as hunter-gatherer bands. Section 4 argues that inequality returns in a small way in small-scale chiefdoms and tends to increase with scale. Section 5 argues that most early states developed extreme inequality in terms of wealth, power, and social position, although some seem to have maintained surprising levels of equality. Section 6 brings this evidence together to argue for an overall U-shaped pattern. Section 7 argues that the evidence presented in this chapter falsifies the claim that inequality is natural or inevitable or that it is in conflict with freedom.

1. PREHUMAN INEQUALITY

Our closest living animal relatives, nonhuman apes, including chimps, bonobos, and gorillas, live in foraging groups that have pronounced social dominance hierarchies (Boehm 2001; de Waal 2005). Even bonobos, which maintain a uniquely level social structure based on frequent non-reproductive sexual encounters between group members, still have pronounced dominance hierarchies in ways that humans absolutely do not. These dominance hierarchies were probably little different millions of years ago when the human ancestral line branched off from other ape species. The impetus to form social hierarchies seems to follow from some instinct that all nonhuman apes share, although the instinct to resist those hierarchies is also present to some degree in all ape species (Gintis et al. 2015: 337).

It takes very little observation of human behavior to see that humans also have tendencies both to dominate others and to resist dominance by others, as do our nonhuman ape ancestors and relatives. Understanding the dominance structures of nonhuman ape foraging groups helps to understand how the balance of power tipped from potential dominators to resisters in human foraging groups, transforming human social structure into the reverse dominance hierarchy documented among modern egalitarian hunter-gatherers and presumably among our hunter-gatherer ancestors. What tipped the balance?

We focus here on chimp and gorilla foraging groups. Their ranking systems are more pronounced in males than females, and the highest-ranking individual always seems to be male. High-ranking males force females into mating groups dominated by a single male. This action also effectively forces some males into permanent celibacy (Boehm 2001; de Waal 2005; Gintis et al. 2015: 337).

Unlike humans, apes forage almost exclusively for themselves and their very young offspring (Washburn and Lancaster 1968: 301). The one exception seems to be that high-ranking individuals (of either sex) exact tribute by demanding that lower-ranking individuals, who happen to have food, share some or all of it with them. But this seems to be mostly a token sign of submission. Unlike human chiefs and monarchs, top-ranking apes still have to get most of their food by foraging for themselves.

Higher-ranking males establish and maintain their positions by violence and intimidation. Their fights can end in death, but more often they end in submission. Lower-ranking males usually attempt to fight their way up the ranking system. But many eventually do give up. At this point, they have two choices. They can remain with the group and accept dominance, or they can spend some or most of their time on the fringes of the group's territory. This strategy does not give them sexual access to females but it frees them from the day-to-day demands of dominant males.

The reasons for the existence of such extreme forms of dominance hierarchy among chimpanzees and gorillas—or, viewed from another perspective, the human divergence from this pattern—are complex and debated. From an evolutionary perspective, dominance hierarchies clearly convey selective benefits to dominant males in increasing the number of offspring that they may have with a larger number of different females (Clutton-Brock 1989). It is likely that females also receive certain selective benefits from the dominance hierarchy systems, since it effectively promotes competition between prospective male suitors and ensures that offspring are sired by the fittest males. From the perspective of group- or kin-selection, it has been argued that dominant males protect their foraging groups in the context of intra-group conflict and manage inter-group aggression, thereby increasing the selective fitness of the foraging groups of females and offspring (Wrangham and Peterson 1997). Yet, as the reverse dominance hierarchy model suggests, there are also evolutionary costs associated with dominance hierarchies in terms of the limitation of male investment in parenting effort, the risk of injury resulting from mating competition, etc.

What tipped the balance between the dominance hierarchies of nonhuman ape species, presumably including our ape ancestors, and the reverse dominance hierarchies of human hunter-gatherer societies remains a bit of a mystery. One idea is that chimpanzees and gorillas tend to have much more strongly defined group territories and much intra-group conflict having to do with territoriality (Boehm 2001). Such conflict has serious consequences in terms of the access of foraging groups to food resources and, in both that sense and others, success in conflict matters for nonhuman ape foraging groups. In contrast, most human hunter-gatherers tend to have more loosely defined foraging territories and to deal with territorial concerns over food resource access through reciprocity rather than conflict (Binford 2001; Kelly 1995). It is possible that the selective benefits of dominance hierarchies at the scale of both groups and individuals declined as social systems of reciprocity and cooperation took their place.

Our main point here is that we are fairly certain that our ape ancestors maintained strong social dominance hierarchies, which were similar to those documented among living nonhuman ape species in the modern world. Then, at some point in our evolutionary past, human societies transitioned to social systems more like those described among modern nomadic hunter-gatherers, which were egalitarian in at least certain dimensions. At a minimum, it is clear that humans did not simply inherit some hierarchical instinct from our ape ancestors. The fact that we did not is one of the most salient features of human evolutionary prehistory. What egalitarianism means for nomadic human hunter-gatherers is also complicated and is the subject of the next section.

2. HUNTER-GATHERER BAND SOCIETIES

This section presents evidence that hunter-gatherer bands have successfully maintained an extremely high level of economic, political,
and social equality for a very long time. The first subsection discusses
the level of equality in observed bands. The second discusses the strategies bands use to maintain egalitarianism.

A. The Egalitarianism of Band Societies

The evidence discussed in this section pertains to "hunter-gatherer
band societies," i.e. nomadic foraging groups that obtain all of their
food by foraging, do not store food, and have a loose membership
that, at any given time, tends to be between 15 and 50 people including children and the elderly (Fried 1967: 113; Leacock and Lee 1982:
7–9; Lee and Daly 1999: 3). Bands are also called "immediate-return
societies" because they consume what food they have soon after they
obtain it (Woodburn 1982: 431). Bands are nomadic, usually within
a fairly defined range (Bird-David 1994; Turnbull 1968: 135). They
tend to have fluid membership with individuals or families easily able
to split off to camp by themselves for a while or with related bands
nearby (Bird-David 1994; Boehm 2001: 72–73, 86–87; Gardner 1991:
547–549; Johnson and Earle 2000: 32–33, 58, 62, 80, 112; Leacock
1998: 142–143; Roscoe 2002; Turnbull 1968; Woodburn 1968b).

There is ethnographic and historical evidence about hunter-gatherer
bands on all inhabited continents and many islands, in all climates
and geographies from the Arctic regions to the tropics (Layton 2001;
Leacock and Lee 1982: 7–9; Lee 1988: 256; Tacitus 1996). Without
exception and though variable, all observed band societies are highly
egalitarian politically, economically, and socially. Mobile, egalitarian
hunter-gatherer societies were ubiquitous across all geographic regions
and climates in historic times, and egalitarianism was likely the dominant social system for hundreds of thousands of years (Bird-David
1990; Boehm 2001: 31; Gardner 1991: 547–549; Lee 1979; Lee and
Daly 1999; Lee and DeVore 1968a; Renfrew 2007; Woodburn 1982).
Although sedentism, food storage, and social inequality all emerged
among hunter-gatherers within the last 15,000 years or so, there is no
denying that fact that egalitarian social systems existed among hunter-
gatherer band societies as a prevalent social system over most of the
time and space in which our species has existed.

Economic equality

Band societies have no economic stratification. Food is shared to the point that no one in the band goes hungry unless everyone goes hungry (Lee 1988: 267). Everyone in the same band has a virtually identical economic standard of living. They consume the same varieties of food, live in the same types of shelters, use the same types of tools, and have the same types of ornaments or consumption goods. All observed bands share large game equally between all people present (including visitors) at the time that the game is divided or consumed—no matter who catches the game (Barnard and Woodburn 1988: 16; Hill and Hurtado 1996: xii; Woodburn 1998).

The requirement to share applies to durable goods as well. People are also obliged to share tools or any other goods if they have more than they need at any given time (Barnard and Woodburn 1988: 16; Hoebel 1954: 69). No one who wishes to remain with the band can accumulate noticeably more personal wealth (i.e. more durable goods) than anyone else (Lee 1990). The social pressures discussed below are so strong that the distribution of goods winds up being conspicuously equal. According to Lee (1990: 244), "The obligation to share food and the taboo against hoarding are no less strong and no less ubiquitous in the primitive world than the far more famous taboo against incest."

To find miniscule differences in standard of living between people in the same band, ethnographers have been forced to count calories. Surprisingly, given the requirement to share, the best hunters and their immediate family members do tend to consume more calories than others in the band (Enloe 2003; Wood and Marlowe 2013). The requirement to share applies only when the hunter has more than their immediate family can eat right away. If they have less, they are free to consume it themselves (Johnson and Earle 2000: 78, 89, 116–117). The extra calories apparently come from these less-successful hunts (Enloe 2003; Woodburn 1968a: 52).

It is fair to say that people have the same living standard when the search for economic differences comes down to counting calories among people who share the following characteristics. They eat virtually the same diet. They are roughly equal in health. They have access to virtually the same durable goods. They share tools and food whenever they have enough to go around. They live in virtually the same housing. They have no economic hierarchy or stratification. Clearly band members are far more equal than people who use claims about natural and inevitable inequality want to see.

Band members are completely equal in terms of their most valuable material wealth. They all have exactly the same access to resources. Fruitful land, clean water, and a clean atmosphere are open for every band member's use without restriction. And access is sufficient to enable people to meet their basic needs.

To the extent that bands assert land rights, the group rather than the individual is the owner. But even these rights are extremely limited with nearby bands able to gain access to the land when necessary (Bird-David 1990), and the group's "ownership" is distinctly decentralized with no public or private authority controlling access to it.

Bands material culture is so different from that of contemporary states that it is impossible to apply culturally specific terms such as ownership or governorship. The land, water, and atmosphere can just as well be described as jointly owned or equally *unowned*. Everyone has direct, individual access to resources (Woodburn 1982), but they cannot take possession of them to the exclusion of other members of the band. No one has to pay rent, taxes, or tribute to one of the people who claim exclusive rights to control land, and as a direct result, no one is homeless. No one has a smaller dwelling because someone else controls the resources necessary to build dwellings. No one has to ask a boss's permission or follow a boss's orders to gain access to resources with which they might produce consumption goods. No one is forced to live in a crowded, polluted neighborhood with unsafe water access.

Political equality

Political power is also very nearly equal in band society. No individual has power over another individual in a band. No one gives orders. If one person tried to command another, they would not obey, and no other member of the band would expect them to obey. All interested band members get together and talk out political decisions, from important ones, such as whether to punish one member of the band for harming another, or seemingly trivial ones, such as where to camp next. Even then, decisions often are not fully binding on those who refuse to accept them. People who don't like the next campsite don't have to continue with the band. Hunting or gathering are not usually coordinated activities; one person might say they're going and ask who wants to join. Even when conflict breaks out between bands, members do not take orders like soldiers. They decide for themselves whether to participate and if and when to disengage (Endicott and Endicott 2008: 63–67; Freuchen and Freuchen 1965: chapter 7; Fried 1967: 62–63, 83–84, 91, 104–105; Gardner 1991: 457–549; Ingold 1986: 223–224; Silberbauer 1982: 25; Woodburn 1968a: 52).

Of course, some people have more influence in the sense that their recommendations are more likely to be adopted by the group. The most influential people are not always the most successful hunters and warriors (as one might expect from observations of larger-scale societies with achievement-based social competition) but those with a better ability to motivate and persuade others (Gintis et al. 2015: 327, 337–338; Johnson and Earle 2000: 178; Katz et al. 1997; Wiessner 2005).

Influence often comes from tact and the understanding of group dynamics, traits that aren't necessarily coordinated with hunting ability. And the most consistently influential people tend to be more senior members of the band. Deference to seniority is a form of inequality, but it is not stratifying because less senior members who live long enough obviously become senior members in their turn (Endicott and Endicott 2008: 63–67; Katz et al. 1997; Lee 1982: 53; Silberbauer 1982: 29; Wiessner 2005).

The power to influence people is very different from political power, as power is most commonly understood. Political power is the ability to make others do things whether they want to or not. Less influential band members who do not like the group's decision on any issue short of a judgment of death are free to ignore it. Differential *influence* is unlike the differential *power* that proponents of the inevitable inequality hypothesis seek to justify. It would be a very bad argument to say all societies have inequality of influence; therefore, our society must have inequality of power.

The respect for each individual's freedom from taking orders reflects a commitment to social equality (as well as economic and political equality). Each individual is fully autonomous, and anyone who wants her or his cooperation must obtain it voluntarily. Even the deference shown to more senior members of the band and the influence the senior members wield has to be obtained voluntarily. Many aspects of social interaction within bands reflect the commitment to equal status. Individuals do not brag about their achievements or their influence. If they do, they will find themselves quickly put down or even deserted, perpetuating a culture of humility and of conspicuous equality of social position (Boehm 2001; Endicott and Endicott 2008: 49; Flannery and Marcus 2012: 24).

Gender equality

Bands have significant but not complete respect for gender equality. Women and men tend to specialize in different tasks. In most band societies, women tend to do more gathering, childcare, and food preparation. Men tend to do more of the hunting. But this tendency is not a clear rule, and it does not usually translate into inequalities of power, wealth, or position. Women participate equally in decision-making and are probably less subject to male domination than in most past state societies and even some present ones (Endicott 1988; Endicott and Endicott 2008; Lee 1990: 243–244; Lee and Daly 1999: 5; Winterhalder 2001: 13, 31). Eleanor Leacock (1998: 145) writes, "[N]othing in the structure of egalitarian band societies necessitated special deference to men. . . . This was even true in hunting societies, where women did not furnish a major share of the food."

Band societies can and do have sexist practices. Within the family, men often dominate women and domestic violence exists (Boehm 2001). But some anthropologists argue that, although no society has eliminated such crimes, women in band societies were freer and better able to protect themselves or escape a dominating man than they are in most other societies (Barnard and Woodburn 1988: 19; Dubreuil 2010; Leacock 1998). Anthropologists suggest several reasons why this might be so.

Like everyone in band society, women have equal and unconditional access to resources. This freedom gives them the same power to control their social and political affiliations as men, and a much greater potential to free themselves from an abusive spouse than women in many contemporary state societies (Leacock 1998: 140–147).

Women have access to extended families and social networks, not only within the band but across neighboring bands. These ties can help create social pressure against abuse and give women a place to escape. For example, among the Ju/'hoansi, divorce initiated by female partners is very common (Scelza 2013), with domestic abuse being a major reason behind it (McCall and Resick 2003), and social networks of relationships of reciprocity provide options for alternative residences (Wiessner 2002).

Within the band, individuals live in very close quarters with little privacy, and they pay very close attention to everyone else's activity (Hill and Hurtado 1996: xii). They do not have houses or walls capable of blocking much sound. These characteristics make it easier for others to intervene, for shame to have a positive effect, and for women to seek aid. Gender equality often extends also to the transgendered (Flannery and Marcus 2012: 70–71). Increased spouse abuse might be in part an unfortunate by-product of privacy.

Male dominance tends to be greater in small-scale societies that have more frequent conflicts with neighboring groups, that store food, that have greater population density, that are relatively larger in scale, and that require men to spend longer periods away from women and children such as on extended hunting trips (Johnson and Earle 2000: 170, 172; McCall 2009).

Equality assessed

In summary, observed hunter-gatherer bands do not have the markings of rank and hierarchy observed in nonhuman ape foraging groups and some autonomous villages or the stratification observed in state societies and some chiefdoms. There is no dominance structure. No one fights to get to the top of that dominance structure. No one gives tribute to higher-ranking individuals. Women are not forced into single-male mating groups or pushed out of the political decision-making process. There is no class of wealthy or politically connected people. No one works for a boss, pays a landlord, or obeys an official. No one has noticeably superior wealth or adornment than others. No one goes without food, shelter, or other necessities because they cannot afford to "buy" the resources necessary to secure them. No small-scale, nomadic, human, foraging society has been observed with these kinds of social practices. Bands achieve approximate equality of wealth, power, and status.

In short, nonhierarchical, unstratified, egalitarian societies exist. They have been well observed in anthropology, ethnography, and history.

B. Strategies Band Societies Use to Maintain Egalitarianism

As we've argued previously (McCall and Widerquist 2015), there are two main sets of dynamics that result in egalitarian social systems: First, there is what we call "weak egalitarianism," i.e. the aspects of egalitarianism that are simply the outcome of foraging group mobility and flexible group membership. Second, there is what we call "strong egalitarianism," i.e. the assertive mechanisms mobile foraging groups use to maintain an egalitarian social structure. Band societies are nearly universal in exhibiting the weak forms of egalitarianism derived from mobility and flexible group membership, though there is tremendous variability in terms of the manifestations of the assertive leveling mechanisms of strong egalitarianism.

Why do mobility and flexible group membership result in so many features of egalitarian social structure? The short answer is that, if individuals begin to feel as if they are being dominated or treated unfairly with respect to sharing norms, etc., they can simply leave the group and move elsewhere. All individuals have equal access to the means of economic production and no individual has the power to force any other individual to do something that they don't want to do; or what Widerquist (2013) has called "the power to say no." In the early literature on hunter-gatherer egalitarianism, Turnbull (1968: 136) observed the crucial importance of what he called "flux," or the tendency of foraging groups to fission or fuse, and for families or individuals to leave or join groups according to their satisfaction with social dynamics, or to simply live by themselves for a time. Many anthropologists have confirmed such observations (Altman and Peterson 1988: 93; Endicott 1988: 112; Johnson and Earle 2000: 32–33, 58, 62, 78, 80, 89, 112, 116–117). Peter Gray (2009: 486) goes so far as to identify the ability to quit the group as *the* essential element that makes the other leveling mechanisms work.

We have argued in the past (McCall and Widerquist 2015) that weak egalitarianism is the oldest form of social structure known among humans and our ancestors, going back at least to the earliest modern human hunter-gatherers some number of hundreds of thousands of years ago, and perhaps to our earlier hominin ancestors some number of millions of years ago. In this respect, it is no surprise that signs of significant, persistent human inequality are absent from the archaeological record prior to the first permanently settled villages within the last 15,000 years or so. Sedentism laid the groundwork for storage, accumulation, wealth, status, and power; and thus for debt, obligation, and subordination.

The assertive mechanisms of "strong egalitarianism" include ridicule, criticism, disobedience, expulsion, desertion (noncooperation), demand sharing, tolerated theft, appeals to egalitarian religious beliefs, and in the most extreme cases execution (Boehm 2001: 84). While some combination of these leveling mechanisms manifests in virtually all egalitarian hunter-gatherer societies, the use of these mechanisms varies widely from one case to another. Although all observed band societies employ social strategies of weak egalitarianism, some use few if any of the assertive leveling mechanisms of strong egalitarianism.

It is not important for our argument that the use of these mechanisms is ubiquitous, only that human societies have successfully taken advantage of some means by which to maintain significant social, political, and economic equality. Many anthropologists have found confirming evidence that a large number of band societies have done so (Barnard and Woodburn 1988: 12, 21; Bird-David 1990; Blurton-Jones 1987; Cashdan 1980: 117, 120; Endicott 1988: 116–121; Flannery and Marcus 2012: 59–60; Gison 1988: 78, 87; Ingold 1986: 223–224; Kelly 1995: 21–22, 164–166; Kuper 1994: 223; Lee 1979: 458–461; Lee 1982: 55–56; Lee and Daly 1999: 4; Peterson 1993: 860–874; Wilson 1998; Winterhalder 2001; Woodburn 1982: 431–451).

Why do band societies so often develop the assertive mechanisms of strong egalitarianism? Before answering this question, let us personally attest to the reality and the force of the social pressure involved in the assertive mechanisms of strong egalitarianism. One of the authors of this book, McCall (2000), began his career working with Ju/'hoansi in the Kalahari and knows first-hand the constant discourse and social pressure involved in assertive leveling strategies. The reason for the development and persistence of assertive leveling mechanisms has to do with the necessity of level social structure in maintaining strong sharing practices (McCall and Widerquist 2015). If individuals begin to feel that they have statuses elevated over others in the group, then they also feel that they can selectively ignore sharing norms and other elements of the reciprocity systems in which they are involved. Once cracks start to emerge in these sharing systems, they break down quickly, since individuals cannot rely on their sharing partners to fulfill their obligations in the future. This is precisely why strongly egalitarian societies are so quick and forceful in punishing "cheaters" through shaming and ostracism, and why many band societies maintain constant discourse about the propriety of the actions of foraging group members.

Strong egalitarianism might be more recent than the weak form. We have tentatively argued that many of the trappings of strong egalitarianism, such as reciprocity networks marked by symbolic gift-giving and shamanic religious practices aimed at relieving the enormous social tension, caused assertive leveling mechanisms, and emerged among Later Stone Age and Upper Paleolithic hunter-gatherers late in the Pleistocene, mostly within the last 40,000 years or so. We have also argued that the emergence of strong egalitarianism may have paradoxically set the stage for the emergence of social inequality, since strong egalitarianism is an all-or-nothing proposition. Once individuals make the decision to begin ignoring the norms of strong egalitarianism, and once separated from their social systems of sharing, individuals must then rely completely on accumulation as their personal risk-reduction strategy. Likewise, strong egalitarianism is essentially a long list of things one *shouldn't do* in accumulating wealth, status, and power. Once individuals lose the "power to say no" conferred by mobility and flexible group membership, the norms and taboos of strong egalitarianism turn into a road map for would-be aggrandizers (McCall and Widerquist 2015).

C. Conclusions

The regularity with which people *can* desert dominators and *do* desert them contradicts Fein's (2012) conclusion that humans are "hierarchical animals." The need for assertive mechanisms to maintain equality in a band does not make it less natural. All societies require norms and sanctions to maintain social structures and practices. Stratified societies require forceful mechanisms to keep people who want no part of their hierarchical structures from abandoning them, and even when the lower orders are unfree to abandon the dominators, stratified societies require coercively enforced laws, police, courts, military, and so on. If Gray's observation is correct, egalitarian bands require less force—little more than the power to refuse cooperation with the would-be dominators.

Similarly, the evidence here addresses Dahrendorf's (1968: 172) argument that the need for sanctions ensures that "there has to be inequality of rank among men." Band societies have sanctions, but they enforce them very effectively without the need to empower any particular person or group as the enforcer.

3. AUTONOMOUS VILLAGES

Autonomous village societies, which we define as those living in permanently settled villages but lacking a centralized political authority such as a chief or king, have existed for about the last 15,000 years and include both complex hunter-gatherers and small-scale farmers (Boehm 2001: 3–4; Lee 1990: 236; Renfrew 2007: 142; Wilson 1988: 3). In a sense, autonomous village societies are the most poorly defined and problematic of Service's (1962) types, since they are more defined by what they are not (i.e. bands and chiefdoms) than what they are, which is tremendously variable. As with band societies, some autonomous village systems have persisted into the twenty-first century on the fringes of modern nation-states (Roscoe 2002).

Observed autonomous villages are in many ways nearly as egalitarian as hunter-gatherer bands. Stratification is absent. Economic arrangements assure almost identical living standards for everyone in the village. In all known autonomous villages, there is virtually no trade or specialization. All people (including headmen and religious leaders) produce their immediate family's consumption (Fried 1967: 129–132, 177). There are usually no fixed property rights in land; all members of the village are entitled to access to land for farming, but not necessarily a particular plot (Bailey 1992: 92; Sahlins 1974: 93–94). As in band societies, no one in the village starves unless everyone is starving. No one has to get a job taking orders from a boss to earn the right to gain access to the natural resources they need to survive. No one has to pay rent to a landlord to gain the right to farm, forage, or build a shelter.

The most obvious inequality in most autonomous villages—in addition to the kinds of sexism noted above—is the existence of rank as people vie to become a "big man" or the "headman" (Henrich et al. 2015; Sahlins 1963). It's uncertain the extent to which these gender-specific terms reflect observations of sexism or observations by sexist ethnographers (Strathern 1988). The main functions of big men are to mediate disputes and assign people plots of land on which to farm or build their shelter. A high-ranking person will usually collect favors from people by doing favors for them. Big men can usually command gifts of food, which they then give back, usually in the form of feasts and festivals.

The superior position of the headman in an autonomous village is almost entirely in terms of prestige rather than wealth or power (Boehm 2001). In reference to both band and autonomous village societies, Bruce Trigger (2003: 668) writes, "Smaller-scale societies often lacked even the concept of obedience, in the sense of one person's being thought to have the moral right to tell another person what to do." Headmen might voice orders, but they are often ignored. More often they lead by example. People who do not like a headman's resolution of a dispute or some other decision can appeal to the group as a whole, and in the extreme, if a village is in an area with low population density, dissatisfied individual(s) can pick up their things, walk a few miles away, and start their own village.

Membership in autonomous villages, though more stable than membership in band societies, is still fluid. Ethnographic evidence suggests that the fissioning of autonomous villages is fairly common (Bandy 2004: 322–333). Although there is no technical barrier preventing most village societies from sustaining populations in the thousands, their tendency to fission is so strong that they are seldom observed with populations more of than a few hundred and almost never with populations approaching one thousand. Limiting factors seem to have to do more with how hard it is for people to get along and how easy it is to pick up and leave than with the number of people a village can sustain (Carneiro 1970; Sahlins 1974: 98).

Many village societies practice swidden (or slash-and-burn) agriculture, which requires them to move at least every few years (as we will discuss further in Chapter 12), and therefore creates opportunities for fissioning. But most of them have crops in the ground, semi-permanent homes, and stored food, all of which make fissioning more difficult for villages than for bands. Depending on the particular circumstances, there might be only a short interval each year when moving can be done relatively easily. These commitments probably help explain the larger population size at which they tend to fission and perhaps also their greater acceptance of inequality of rank.

In general, small-scale farming societies have larger populations than forager bands and that population packing limits the available options in terms of alternative residences. In addition, arable land is at least somewhat limited and there is often hostility between neighboring villages, both of which make fissioning more difficult and

potentially dangerous. Yet, even these limited opportunities to abandon dominators remain useful. Like bands, autonomous villages use
fission as a mechanism to keep anyone from taking too much power
over the village. Any individual attempting to establish dictatorial
rule over the village will find it empty before long. Individuals who
cannot be stopped from leaving the village to farm where they wish
cannot be made into subordinate laborers to a self-declared landlord.
Thus, although rank and some wealth inequality exist, stratification
of power, wealth, or social position is absent.

4. CHIEFDOMS

Archaeological evidence indicates that the first truly hierarchical societies came into existence within approximately the last 10,000 years
when the first chief succeeded in bringing multiple villages under one
rule. Although chiefdoms vary considerably in terms of their social
and economic organization, they are the oldest and smallest-scale
form of social organization to show signs of economic specialization
and of persistent political, economic, and social inequality (Renfrew
2007: 152, 164, 173–176; Thomas 1999: 229).

In some cases, chiefs may hold relatively little political power and
may not be considerably wealthier or higher-ranked than their subjects.
The Iroquois Confederation, for example, kept significant economic
and political equality for centuries despite relatively large-scale political
integration (Boehm 2001: 98; Trigger 1990a: 119–145).

At the other end of the spectrum—for example, the Hawaiian
chiefdom that we discussed previously—there were also extremely
powerful paramount rulers who ruled large populations through a
network of vassals, who accumulated enormous power, wealth, and
prestige, and who held the power of life and death over their subjects.
Most often, political consolidation beyond a single village coincided
with increased stratification and sexism, even if outright despotism
might only become commonplace in larger chiefdoms or small states
(Boehm 2001: 255; Lee 1990: 239).

With some exceptions, economic, political, and religious powers
were usually all held by a chief or a group of chiefs, who tended to be
surrounded by a group of elites who protect and manage the chiefs'
possessions. Their children would usually display signs of their elevated social status and hereditary power was often justified by descent
from mythical or semi-divine ancestors. Chiefs sometimes manage

large joint projects such as irrigation, flood control, and temple or monument building (Earle 1997, 2000, 2002), which emphasizes their potential similarities to the rulers of the first states.

Many features of chiefdoms, including strategic appeals to religion and brute force, help chiefs maintain power, but the key factor seems to be the difficulty of dissatisfied individuals to pick up and move. Unlike bands and autonomous villages that habitually underutilize available resources, chiefdoms tend to control territory and tend to be largely circumscribed by other chiefdoms also controlling territory. A dissatisfied group could not simply pick up and move nearby without fearing attack by some chief's warriors. To be free from that, they might either have to accept the rule of another chief or make a long and uncertain journey to unfamiliar territory.

5. STATES

By 4,000 years ago some chiefdoms became so large and complex that they could be called states or empires (Trigger 2003). Although all early (or archaic) states were still primarily agricultural, even the earliest states had complex economies with specialist warriors, administrators, rulers, priests, professionals, and cities. Most early states for which there is sufficient available information eventually became extremely hierarchical—politically, economically, and socially (Trigger 2003: 44–45). But some might have been relatively egalitarian. Architecture in some very early states in the Indus Valley, South Asia seems to be unusually uniform, which might indicate economic inequality, but there simply isn't enough information to say whether these states were significantly less stratified than any other archaic state (Possehl and Raval 1989). Graeber and Wengrow (2018: §5) argue that there is evidence of some significantly egalitarian early states:

> [I]n the more established heartlands of urbanisation – Mesopotamia, the Indus Valley, the Basin of Mexico – there is mounting evidence that the first cities were organised on self-consciously egalitarian lines, municipal councils retaining significant autonomy from central government. In the first two cases, cities with sophisticated civic infrastructures flourished for over half a millennium with no trace of royal burials or monuments, no standing armies or other means of large-scale coercion, nor any hint of direct bureaucratic control over most citizen's lives.

Graeber and Wengrow (2018) cite the Central American city of Teoti-
huacan, which around 200 CE appears to have turned its back on the
pyramid-temples that make it famous today, reconstructed itself as a
collection of roughly equal-sized villas, and remained so for perhaps
400 years. They write, "Even in Cortés' day, Central Mexico was still
home to cities like Tlaxcala, run by an elected council whose members
were periodically whipped by their constituents to remind them who
was ultimately in charge." They conclude, "Egalitarian cities, even
regional confederacies, are historically quite commonplace."

Although Graeber and Wengrow might be right that such evidence
is mounting, we cannot say that there is enough of it yet to establish
the existence of egalitarian state societies as commonplace. What we
can say is that extreme inequality eventually appeared in most archaic
states about which we know enough to say. These stratified states
include most states in each of the widely dispersed places where state
societies developed independently. Extreme social stratification might
not have been ubiquitous, but it was more common and longer-lived
than state egalitarianism. Stratification was often more extreme in the
cities and less so in rural areas that weren't dependent on any centralized project such as large-scale irrigation. Many rural communities
within states operated in ways similar to autonomous villages that
were expected to adhere to certain regulations and pay some minor
tribute to the rulers of the state (see Chapter 13).

Most archaic states for which significant evidence exists were ruled
by kings with the aid of a small, powerful elite group. The upper
classes were no more than a few percent of the total population, but
they controlled most surplus wealth (above subsistence), lived luxuri-
ous lifestyles, made all of the important decisions about policy and
administration, and justified their position by claiming special supernatural origin (Trigger 2003: 145–153). Compared to chiefdoms, the
inequality was much more apparent in the economic realm. Upper-
class people in early states consumed a more varied diet, had far better
housing, and had much more access to luxuries, and so on.

Inequality was not confined to the economic realm. Lower-class
agricultural laborers, who were generally barred from social mobility,
made up the bulk of the population and faced not even the pretense of
equal protection of the laws. Some early states held slaves, but slave-
holding was not as common in early states as it was in later antiquity
in Greece and Rome (Trigger 2003: 155–160, 239, 264–265). Long

before then, thousands of years of experience had made inequality appear natural and inevitable.

Trigger (2003: 668) finds, "only by making hierarchical relations pervasive in everyday life could unequal relations be made to appear sufficiently natural that they operated effectively at the societal and hence the political level." The heritage of this history seems to be behind the many claims of inequality discussed in Chapters 2–3: the pervasiveness of inequality in a given society makes it appear natural and inevitable, despite the violence and force used to maintain it.

Early states set up political, economic, and social power structures to maintain inequality. Their religion gave it a stamp of legitimacy. The legal system established a structure of control of resources and the goods people make out of them to maintain their power relations. Many states and empires that established authority over former chiefdoms and autonomous villages allowed them to maintain a measure of autonomy and equality among themselves especially in lightly inhabited areas. But further integration into states was synonymous with taking a position in a hierarchical society.

Circumscription—the inability of low-ranking individuals to flee—was critical to the maintenance of hierarchy in archaic states. As our previous book discussed, there has been a long history of people escaping from states into mountains, swamps, or underpopulated areas to live outside of the control of hierarchical authority, but these individuals were the adventurous or lucky few. Some might not even have known of the existence of non-state societies. Although escape to some non-state region was seldom impossible for everyone, it was often unrealistic for most people (Widerquist and McCall 2017). Circumscription was not everything; the wealth of states did attract people from non-state societies (Maisels 1990: 214–216).

Circumscription should not be thought of as a binary condition. The more difficult for a person to move (either because there is nowhere to go or because they have property, social ties, and family in a state), the more difficult it is for that individual to move or refuse cooperation with the people who impose a hierarchy over them, and therefore, the easier it is to maintain a stratified state society. The ability to refuse cooperation without departing is also important. The existence of a commons or opportunities for subsistence agriculture within states continued to empower many rural people until recent times (see Chapters 13–14).

6. THE HISTORICAL PATTERN OF INEQUALITY

The history we have traced from nonhuman primates through human bands, autonomous villages, chiefdoms, and early states indicates that the historical pattern of social inequality seems to have been U-shaped (Boehm 2001; Knauft 1991). At some point, likely between about 2.5 million and 200,000 years ago, our hominin ancestors got rid of the dominance hierarchies that had characterized the foraging groups of their ancestors. Whether this change occurred gradually or rapidly is unknown.

Although we cannot be sure what the social organization of Pleistocene foragers was like, the preponderance of evidence indicates that many small-scale, nomadic foraging peoples successfully maintained egalitarianism the entire time that humans have been on this planet. Their foraging strategies were similar to bands. They had access to all or most of the mechanism modern band societies use to maintain a reverse dominance hierarchy, and they had just as much intelligence to put it into practice. Although many anthropologists are skeptical of any firm conclusions about social relations in the deep past (Graeber and Wengrow 2018; Kelly 1995: 339), what evidence we have tends to support the conclusion that egalitarian societies existed for hundreds of thousands of years and have been the predominate form of social organization among modern humans for most of prehistory (Boehm 2001; Flannery and Marcus 2012; Johnson and Earle 2000).

The stratification of chiefdoms and states that has become almost ubiquitous around the world is a historical anomaly.

There have been promising trends toward equality in recent centuries, such as movements toward democracy, universal suffrage, equality before the law, the abolition of slavery, the freedom of religion, the emancipation and liberation of women, and so on. These trends might suggest that the U-shaped pattern is beginning to look like a sine wave, with a little downturn at the right end of the U. But these trends have to be measured against still-growing economic inequality, the final destruction of most of the world's egalitarian indigenous societies, and the existence of extremely unequal dictatorships, such as North Korea, which might be as unequal as any society that has ever existed. There is reason to be hopeful, but even if there is a worldwide trend toward greater equality, we still have a very long way to go to establish true democracy and genuine equality before the law.

To show that it happened this way is not to show that it could only have happened this way, but these forms of social organization are real, and this pattern is well-established history. Significant inequality was only gradually established around the world by the conscious effort and the aggressive enforcement of small but powerful groups of people.

7. THE INEVITABLE-INEQUALITY HYPOTHESIS EVALUATED

The evidence presented above proves the possibility of egalitarianism and even its historical prevalence, but it does not imply that egalitarianism is any more natural than any other social condition. Human beings are capable of maintaining both highly egalitarian and highly hierarchical societies for long periods of time. Social, political, and economic equality are possible, but they "will always be threatened by the forces of despotism" (Gintis et al. 2015: 340).

This evidence is enough to falsify the inevitable-inequality hypothesis as the claim in the extreme form in which it is usually stated—that *no* society can exist without significant levels of inequality. Therefore, it falsifies claims discussed in Chapters 2–3 made by Burke, Adams, Calhoun, Huxley, Hayek, Rothbard, Dahrendorf, Lucas, Fein, and many others.

The evidence in this chapter alone is not enough to falsify the most common modern characterization of the hypothesis: that inequality is the natural and inevitable result of a free society. But combining the evidence here with evidence presented in Chapter 6 falsifies that hypothesis as well.

There is no conflict between freedom and equality. Chapter 6 demonstrates that the most egalitarian societies known (bands and autonomous villages) were in fact more respective of freedom (in its most liberal, negative sense) than modern state societies.

In combination with evidence from our earlier book, the evidence from this chapter falsifies another reformulation of the inevitable-inequality hypothesis: that inequality necessarily exists in any society that anyone would want to live in. That book argues that life in band and village societies is very difficult, but the least advantaged people in modern, industrial state societies have reason to prefer life in band and village societies than their lot in industrial state societies (Widerquist and McCall 2017). When that option was more available, substantial numbers of people fled the authority and inequality of state societies to establish or assimilate into far more egalitarian non-state societies

(Scott 2009). There is little doubt that if the option were still available, many people today would flee as well. We actually have to make society more equal to make it a place that everyone—including the least advantaged—would want to live in (Widerquist and McCall 2017).

The evidence presented in this book alone cannot definitively falsify the following reformulation of the hypothesis: inequality is inevitable in all states or large-scale complex societies. To falsify this hypothesis by observation, one would have to conduct a large study of various historically recorded state societies and evaluate the extent of their equality or inequality. Although we're unlikely to see state societies practicing egalitarianism as strong as that practiced in band and autonomous village societies, some contemporary states have maintained greater socio-economic equality than adherents of the inevitable inequality hypothesis usually like to see, and some early states apparently maintained significant egalitarianism for long periods of time. These observations aren't definitive, but they cast significant doubt on that formulation of the natural inequality hypothesis.

The ubiquity of egalitarianism in observed band societies does not prove that all nomadic, immediate-return, hunter-gatherer societies are always egalitarian, but it does indicate that something about band lifestyle is very favorable to egalitarianism. In the same way, the near ubiquity of stratification in state society does not prove that egalitarianism is impossible in state society, but it does indicate that something about state society is favorable to inequality. Large-scale societies have to work harder to maintain equality and freedom.

The promising moves toward greater equality mentioned above might indicate that our societies are gradually learning how to overcome the difficulty of establishing greater political, economic, and social equality within a state society. There is little reason to doubt that states are capable of greater equality than any of them have so far achieved. In addition, it might be a mistake to overemphasize the specialness of large-scale states. Small-scale societies are made up of people like us with similar desires, ambitions, virtues, and vices. Large-scale societies can do many things that small-scale societies cannot do, but small-scale societies have done things that large-scale societies have not yet matched. Perhaps we can learn to adapt some of the strategies small-scale societies have used to maintain freedom and equality. Chapter 16 discusses this issue further.

Part Two

The market freedom hypothesis

Chapter 5

THE NEGATIVE FREEDOM ARGUMENT
FOR THE MARKET ECONOMY

The negative freedom argument for the market economy is the most common argument for propertarian capitalism (i.e. a market economy with liberal private property rights and little or no taxation, regulation, and redistribution) or for ethical limits on government authority to tax, regulate, and redistribute property within a less extreme version of the market economy.

Negative freedom is the absence of interference (i.e. coercion) by other people (Berlin 1969: 121–122). The negative freedom argument is any argument for the market economy and/or strong private property rights based on the premise that it promotes negative freedom greater than any other system. In Hayek's (1960: 11) words, "We are concerned . . . with that condition of men in which coercion of some by others is reduced as much as possible in society."

Most—if not all—propertarians stress significant if not overriding moral priority of negative freedom (Boaz 1997: 64–65; Hayek 1960: 87; Kirzner 1989: 7–10; Lomasky 1987: 123; Machan 2006b: 270–279; Narveson 1988: 99–101; Nozick 1974: 183–231; Rothbard 1982: 35–43). It is the reason they call themselves "libertarians." And they claim to deliver real, substantive freedom. For example, David Boaz (1997: 59, 291) in *Libertarianism: A Primer*, writes, "[W]e have an infinite number of rights contained in one natural right. That one fundamental human right is the right to live your life as you choose so long as you don't infringe on the equal rights of others." And, "do you make the decisions that are important to your life, or does someone else make them for you? Libertarians believe that individuals have both the right and the responsibility to make their own decisions."

Loren Lomasky (1987: 102) endorses negative liberty as "the fundamental moral imperative," and he endorses Rawls's description of what it means to promote freedom, "Each person is to have an equal right to the most extensive basic liberty compatible with a similar liberty for others." The claim of *equal* liberty is important. One social arrangement only counts as being freer than another if it makes *everyone* freer. The focus, therefore, has to be on the least free individuals, not the freest.

The negative freedom argument is popular not only with propertarians, but also with conservatives and supporters of less extreme versions of the market economy. Even some critics of propertarian capitalism concede the negative freedom argument, relying on some other definition of freedom or some competing value to justify deviations from the presumably freedom-maximizing propertarian capitalism. As before, this book focuses on propertarians because they spend much more time expounding the negative freedom argument, but its implications apply to anyone who endorses or concedes the negative freedom argument.

The negative freedom argument is not without controversy, and it is an argument that can be meaningfully explored in pure theory. However, this chapter argues it also has an important and under-explored empirical dimension. This chapter discusses the negative freedom argument to show that it involves an empirical claim we call "the market-freedom hypothesis": a market economy with strong private property rights is more consistent with negative freedom than any other system. This claim can by investigated by comparing the market economy and any other system, even something as different as the hunter-gatherer band economy. This argument sets up Chapter 6, which argues that the negative freedom argument actually supports a hunter-gatherer band economy rather than propertarian capitalism, and that that conclusion invalidates arguments based on the claim that taxation, regulation, and redistribution of property necessarily decrease freedom.

Section 1 argues that the establishment and maintenance of the private property system involves an empirical trade-off that most versions of the negative freedom argument ignore. Section 2 considers and rejects the attempt to resolve that trade-off in pure theory by employing a rights-based conception of freedom. Section 3 considers other possibilities for resolving the trade-off in pure theory and concludes that it must be addressed empirically. Propertarians using pure a priori theory have so far failed to demonstrate that their system delivers greater freedom from interference and coercion than any other system. Section 4 explains why a particularly useful way to examine that trade-off is to make an empirical comparison of the freedom experienced by people in the market economy and the hunter-gatherer band economy.

1. THE TRADE-OFF OF LIBERTIES IN THE NEGATIVE FREEDOM ARGUMENT FOR THE MARKET ECONOMY

Most propertarians portray the negative freedom argument as the primary reason for supporting their system. To some, any other benefits of the market are merely a "happy accident" (Murray 1997). Many propertarians argue that negative freedom should have a strong moral priority, such that even if welfare capitalism or some other system might be better at securing some other value (such as equality, fraternity, welfare, opportunity, or another conception of freedom), negative freedom is more important, therefore we must have propertarian capitalism (Boaz 1997: 64–65; Hayek 1960: 87; Kirzner 1989: 7–10; Lomasky 1987: 123; Machan 2006b: 270–279; Narveson 1988: 99–101; Nozick 1974: 183–231; Rothbard 1982: 35–43).

We use the terms "negative freedom" and "negative liberty" synonymously, but we tend to use "freedom" as a more general term and "liberty" as a more specific term. For example, a person has more freedom if they have not only the liberty to do X but also the liberty to do Y.

Negative freedom can be described in many different ways, such as the freedom from coercion, from interference, from force, from aggression, from involuntariness, and from noncontractual obligations. These terms are not necessarily interchangeable, but they are all negative in the sense that they conceptualize freedom as the absence of some action by other people. They have nothing directly to do with people's abilities, their interaction with nature, or the presence or absence of opportunities provided by other people; they have to do with one person or group inhibiting others.

Although not all philosophers agree that the distinction between positive and negative freedom is meaningful, we believe it is possible to draw a meaningful distinction using a simplified version of Gerald C. MacCallum Jr.'s (1967: 314) formula: the freedom of agent X, from constraint Y, to do action Z. A conception of freedom is negative if constraint (Y) is imposed by other people.

Consider a person who can't get out from the bottom of a hole. If she was pushed by another person, she is negatively unfree, because the constraint was imposed by another person. If she fell, she is not unfree even if she is equally unable to get out because the constraint is a part of nature. Relieving people from limitations caused by the action of other people enhances their negative freedom. Reducing natural limitations on human actions does not increase negative freedom; neither does extending greater opportunities for action.

Negative freedom imposes negative duties (duties of forbearance) on others, but it does not directly impose positive duties (active duties) For example, "don't stop me from doing this" is a negative duty; "help me do this" is a positive duty. The concern that the distinction is not meaningful appears because negative duties often indirectly imply positive duties: "don't be here" implies "do go over there." As discussed below, indirectly imposed duties can be substantial.

Propertarians often oversimplify the distinction between negative and positive duties by looking only at some interference and not others. G. A. Cohen (1995: 55) demonstrates that the basic observation behind the negative freedom argument for the market economy is a "banal truth." If A holds property, and the government taxes, regulates, or redistributes that property for the benefit of B, it has to force A to comply. This truth is banal because, "if the state prevents me from doing something [*anything*] that I want to do, then it places a restriction on my freedom" (Cohen 1995: 55).

Consider a stoplight: the banal truth that red lights inhibit negative freedom (stopping people from crossing at certain times) does not mean that stoplights decrease freedom overall because green lights increase negative freedom (freeing people from the interference of cross traffic as they cross at certain times). Stoplights involve a trade-off of one liberty for another. If a priori reasoning can't establish that one liberty is more valuable than the other, the only way to know whether stoplights increase or decrease freedom is to examine empirically whether people have more chances to cross unimpeded with or without the stoplight in place.

A commons is like an unregulated intersection. Anyone can use it, but they might have to navigate through the interference of cross-traffic, and they have a responsibility to share the way with other users.

Private property is like a stoplight. If you own land, resources, or anything people make out of them, you have a green light to use that asset as you want without any responsibility to make room for anyone else to use it. Wealthy people own lots of green lights. People without property face nothing but red lights.

The establishment and maintenance of the property rights system involves interference with people—putting up stoplights. Redistribution of property means more red lights (more interference) for property owners but it also means more green lights (less interference) for the propertyless. The banal version of the market economy ignores the empirical trade-off inherent in the maintenance of the property rights system. It ignores half of the comparison necessary to determine whether the property rights system they envision actually increases negative freedom overall.

Although the legal structure interferes with A when it taxes her property for the benefit of B, it also interferes with B when it forcibly establishes and maintains A's ownership of resources by imposing duties on B. Cohen (1988, 1995: 57, 1998, 2011) argues that the freedom propertarians actually cherish—the freedom of the property owner to do what she wants with the resources she controls—comes necessarily by coercively granting the "owner" that control and by interfering with everyone else who might want to use those resources.

Propertarians often incorrectly portray redistribution of property as imposing an active duty on property owners. Lomasky (1987: 95–102), for example, argues that people have a greater interest in "liberty rights" (the right to be undisturbed in what one has) but not necessarily in "welfare rights" (the right to be provided things by others), because liberty rights tend to be less burdensome on others than welfare rights. This argument might apply to a request for human services to be provided for the disadvantaged, but a propertyless person's request for access to resources is just as much a demand for negative liberty—for a "liberty right"—as the property owner's request to be left alone to use the resources they claim to "own."

Whenever two people want to be in the same place or use the same resource at the same time, they are both equally asking for a negative duty on the part of the other, both equally asking for negative freedom. The propertyless person asking for access to resources or compensation for lost access to the commons is just as much asking for negative liberty as the property owner is when asking for freedom from taxation.

The establishment and maintenance of the private property rights system almost certainly enhances freedom for those with a significant

amount of property, but it might not for those with little or no property. With all the land privately owned they are under the duties: don't
be here; don't be there; don't be just about anywhere except for streets
and public parks. The only way they can gain access to resources
they need to survive is to follow the orders of someone who controls
resources. In this way, an excessive amount of negative duties effectively adds up to an active duty. If you have a negative duty not to
consume resources essential to your survival unless you get a job for
someone who owns resources, you effectively have an active duty to
take orders from at least one resource owner (Widerquist 1999, 2008,
2009a, 2010b, 2013).

Taking orders is not necessarily freedom-reducing in negative terms
as long as the subordinate freely accepts their position as a "contractual obligation." But if one group of people interferes with another
group of people in a way that gives them no other choice but to accept
becoming a laborer, their "choice" to take orders is forced. The indi-
rectness of the force makes it no less onerous, no less effective.

Effectively forced service is exactly what happens when the legal
system closes the commons without compensating the propertyless
sufficiently to make the choice to accept a job unforced (Widerquist
1999, 2008, 2009a, 2010b, 2013; see also Chapters 10–14). People
who make similar observations include Daniel Attas (2005: 7), Jeffery
Friedman (1997: 428), Allan Gibbard (2000), Alan Haworth (1994:
45–46), Michael Otsuka (2003: 19), Paine (2012), and Jeremy Waldron (1988: 132, 172, 411, 1993a: 20–21, 309–338). This argument
calls the entire distribution of property into question because all property (any external asset) is made at least partly out of natural resources
(Cohen 1988: 301–302).

This loss of liberty is substantial and it affects everyone who can't
afford to live off their assets—basically everyone in the middle and
lower classes. That's a big trade-off in liberty attributable to the
establishment and maintenance of the private property system both
as we know it and as propertarians want to see it. For the negative
freedom argument, for the market economy to survive the recognition of the existence of this trade-off it would need much more support than mere reliance on a banal truth. Yet, many propertarians
rest their statements of the negative freedom argument on little else.
For example, consider the arguments below by Nozick, Narveson,
and Rothbard.

Nozick (1974: ix, 149–150, 160–164, 163, 169, 235, and 273–274) argues that government should do little else but enforce the property rights system with defense, police, and courts on the grounds that other actions involve "continuous interference with people's lives." Nozick describes the market distribution in his version of propertarian capitalism as a "freely-arrived-at set of holdings." He connects virtually all other government action with coercion, arguing "the state may not use its coercive apparatus for the purpose of getting some citizens to aid others." He declares, "Taxation of earnings from labor is on par with forced labor." He summarizes his conception of distributive justice as, "From each as they choose; to each as they are chosen." But to get to that point, he admits he is "[i]gnoring acquisition." That is, he ignores all but the banal truth.

The banality of Nozick's (1974: 168) argument is clear in his portrayal of a state protecting strong private property rights as "minimal," which requires him to assume readers are ignorant of the history of violence and aggression that is necessary to establish and maintain that system (see Chapter 14). Nozick's state might be "minimal" in its interference with the people it designates as property owners but it might well prove to be "maximal" in its interference with the people it makes propertyless.

Narveson (1988: 19, 22, 30, 34, 316, 329 and Narveson 1998: 3–4) connects negative freedom with the absence of aggression, coercion, force, threats, interference, and being prevented from doing what one wants. His reason for being concerned with freedom—what freedom is supposed to deliver—is that individuals' ways of life should not be disrupted by others who might be tempted to impose their way of life on them. According to Narveson, "Libertarians do not allow anybody to be sacrificed for anybody else's benefit." Yet, he argues that unequal private property "is a natural outcome of a principle of general liberty." He does not go beyond the banal truth to weigh the freedom the property bestows on the owner of a resource against the interference it imposes on nonowners.

Rothbard (1982: 41–43, 52, 162) claims he attempts to identify, "the society of free and voluntary exchanges . . . the 'free society' or the society of 'pure liberty,'" which is one that respects self-ownership, non-aggression, and voluntariness. He credits a system of anarcho-capitalism with delivering equal rights and equal liberty, "the society of natural liberty is the *only* society that can apply the same basic rule to every man." His criticism of the state is based on the belief that it inherently obtains income coercively while private property holders obtain their income voluntarily.

Many other libertarians argue long these lines (Hasnas 2003: 115–128; Mack 2002b: 254–255, 2006: 110–112; Shapiro 2002: 1–35).

Although the negative freedom argument has been controversial as long as it has existed (Cohen 1988: 193, 294; Paine 2012: 168–169; Rousseau 1984), Cohen (1995: 57, 2011) argues that many opponents of propertarian capitalism also accept the negative freedom argument for it. They do so by (explicitly or tacitly) accepting idealized capitalism as the presumptive embodiment of negative liberty and justifying deviations from it either with reference to some other value (including other conceptions of freedom) or with the recognition of a particular market failure.

For example, although Fabienne Peter (2004: 7) is skeptical about the extent to which propertarians succeed, she concedes, "Libertarian political philosophy values freedom, understood negatively as the protection from interference by others, above everything else." Similarly, Richard J. Arneson (2003: 139) tacitly concedes when he writes, "Against the libertarian view, this essay argues that coercion aimed at bringing about a more equal distribution across persons can be morally acceptable."

Berlin (1969: 124–125), in one of the most influential essays in twentieth-century political philosophy, explicitly concedes the negative freedom argument for the market economy, writing: "To offer political rights, or safeguards against intervention by the state, to men who are half-naked, illiterate, underfed, and diseased is to mock their condition; they need medical help or education before they can understand, or make use of, an increase in their freedom." He argues that society must nevertheless clothe, educate, feed, and heal people who have those needs, because individual freedom is not everyone's primary need. But he believes it would be a pretense to claim this action increases freedom, writing,

> [L]iberty is liberty, not equality or fairness or justice or culture, or human happiness or a quiet conscience. If the liberty of myself or my class or nation depends on the misery of a number of other human beings, the system which promotes this is unjust and immoral. But if I curtail or lose my freedom in order to

lessen the shame of such inequality, and do not thereby materially increase the individual liberty of others, an absolute loss of liberty occurs (Berlin 1969: 124–125).

In recent decades, some political theorists have come to realize that these authors concede too much. Berlin fails to address the far-reaching nature of negative freedom. Waldron (1993a: 303) best sums up the issue,

> When a person is needy, he does not cease to be preoccupied with freedom; rather, his preoccupation tends to focus on freedom to perform certain actions in particular. The freedom that means most to a person who is cold and wet is the freedom that consists in staying under whatever shelter he has found. The freedom that means most to someone who is exhausted is the freedom not to be prodded with a nightstick as he tries to catch a few hours' sleep.

Waldron (1993a: 304, 306) concludes, "The familiar claim that, in the negative sense of 'freedom,' the poor are as free as the rest of us . . . is simply false. . . . [H]omelessness consists in unfreedom."

If one wants to say that impoverished people—who are poorly clothed, illiterate, underfed, diseased, and (we add) lack adequate shelter—are not unfree in the negative sense, one must claim that *only* their natural inabilities prevent them from meeting their needs. It is to say that they simply lack the ability to clothe, educate, feed, heal, or shelter themselves or each other; interference or coercion by other people and by the legal system would have to have *nothing* to do with it.

However, most impoverished people around the world are not unable to do these things, to acquire the necessary skills to do so, or to educate and heal each other as their hunting and gathering or subsistence-farming ancestors did. Nor are they unable to start businesses or cooperatives. They lack access to the resources necessary to do these things for themselves. That is, other people will *interfere* with and *coerce* them if they try to use the resources of the earth to meet their own needs as their ancestors did for hundreds of thousands of years.

The reason people lack access to the resources necessary to keep them out of poverty is that they have a *noncontractual* and *nonreciprocal* obligation: the legal structure endows some individuals but not others with "property rights," and it forces people without such "rights" to refrain from using natural resources without the permission of the group privileged to hold these "rights." Under these circumstances, it might be better to call them "property privileges." It is, of course, possible to create a private property regime in which each person has some resources of their own, but no state we know of has yet done so.

Poverty *is* the lack of access to resources and the things we make out of them; an individual can only lack access to resources because other people interfere with her when she attempts to use them. The demand for free access to resources by impoverished people is as much a demand for noninterference as the demand by privileged people for exclusive access to the resources they hold. It requires only a negative duty to say, "leave me alone to use these resources to meet my needs." Impoverished people simply ask the legal system for a green light or for the unimpeded common access their ancestors enjoyed for 200,000 years.

This section has shown that a market economy with strong private property rights involves an empirical trade-off in freedom. It puts up green lights for some and red lights for others. We consider whether propertarianism has arguments capable of rejecting the significance of the trade-off theoretically before Chapter 6 attempts to assess it empirically.

2. THE RIGHTS-BASED CONCEPTION OF NEGATIVE LIBERTY AS A RESOLUTION TO THE TRADE-OFF

Many propertarians and contemporary conservatives rest the negative freedom argument on a "moralized" or "rights-based" conception of negative liberty. Under this conception, freedom means only the absence of *unjustified* interference, coercion, and force rather than the absence of *all* interference, coercion, or force. Propertarians thereby build their property rights theory into their definition of what is and is not called "coercion." This strategy attempts to resolve the trade-off by recognizing its objective existence but denying its ethical significance.

Many propertarians allude to or explicitly endorse the rights-based conception of negative freedom. Rothbard (2006: 50) states it explicitly, "Freedom is a condition in which a person's ownership rights in his own body and his legitimate material property are not invaded."

Machan (2006a: 270) equates negative liberty with freedom from property rights violations as does Nozick (1974: 262) when he writes, "Other people's actions place limits on one's available opportunities. Whether this makes one's resulting action non-voluntary depends upon whether these others had the right to act as they did."

This move might initially appear plausible. Certainly no one supports *unjustified* interference; one person has to interfere with another to prevent them from committing murder, rape, assault, and so on, but morally speaking should that count as interference? Such liberties are not what a reasonable freedom-seeking, freedom-respecting citizen should want. But one doesn't need to resort to a rights-based conception to determine that the freedom from rape provides greater equal freedom for all than the liberty to rape. It is obvious that freedom from rape gives people greater control of their lives than the freedom from interference while committing the act of rape. By contrast, it is uncertain whether a highly unequal property rights system gives all parties greater overall freedom from force and greater control of their lives than a more equal system.

The main problem with the rights-based conception is that it cannot be used in the negative freedom argument without circular reasoning. It counts interference with existing (unequally held) private property rights as *unjustified* coercion and the interference necessary to establish and maintain private property rights as *justified* coercion. The rights-based conception of negative freedom assumes what it is supposed to prove. The *justification* for propertarian rights is supposed to be that they promote freedom. But if freedom is no more than the name propertarians give to the exercise of their historically idiosyncratic system of rights, supporters cannot meaningfully appeal to freedom to justify those rights. Waldron (1988: 321) argues that once we incorporate the presumed morality of the existing property system into the conception of justice, "We cannot even extol our property system as the basis of a 'free' society, for such a boast would be nothing more than tautological." Many critics of propertarianism recognize that the rights-based conception of freedom necessarily falls into circularity, tautology, or begging the question, including Attas (2005: 29), Cohen (1988, 1995, 1998, 2011), Friedman (1997: 432), Haworth (1994: 80), and many others (Attas 2005: 37 n39).

Many propertarians have recognized problems with the rights-based definition. Lomasky (1987: 113) writes, "It seems impossible to frame acceptable principles for the allocation of property rights by reference to the standard of noninterference. That is because what will count as interference is itself a function of rights to property and so cannot noncircularly be employed to establish those rights." Narveson (1998: 10) writes, "Nozick . . . proposes to define freedom as doing what you have a right to do – which is circular and thus useless."

Yet, it is difficult to find propertarians who consistently stick to a neutral definition of freedom. Even Narveson (1988: 76–78, 1998: 14 n28) resorts to it on occasion, "Predicating common ownership of hunter-gatherers at 500 square miles per person is thin stuff for arguing possession." Under a neutral definition of freedom, the question of whether anyone has established "possession" is irrelevant. Ownership and possession are rights-based concepts. The only questions are whether stopping people from what they would otherwise do involves interference, coercion, force, and so on, or whether it involves a demand for more than negative duties from others. No matter how low the population density of hunter-gatherers might be, appropriators have to interfere with them to take that land and make it anyone else's property.

The rights-based conception has five problems in addition to the circularity. First, rights-based negative liberty is in fact, positive liberty, because as Waldron (1988: 321) argues, "It was precisely the identification of freedom with virtue (and the inference that a restriction on vice was no restriction at all) that most troubled [early] liberals about theories of positive liberty."

Second, the rights-based conception leads to absurd moral judgments. Suppose an oil company appropriated land in Peru. With the help of legal authority, they force indigenous hunter-gatherers who had been using the land without establishing a private property right in the land to leave it. The indigenous—and all neutral observers—are supposed to understand not only that the company is justified in forcing them off the land, but also the "force" the company applies isn't really "force" at all in any moral sense of the term. The act is also not "interference," "coercion," or "aggression" in any moral sense. The indigenous people and their descendants might not have any other choice but to take subordinate positions in the market economy, but their inevitable participation should not be considered involuntary or forced in any ethical sense. These judgments are absurd.

Third, despite the appeal of the idea that only the freedom to do what one has a right to do is useful, rights-based conceptions of freedom are more easily manipulated than neutral conceptions. Rights-based conceptions are as good or bad as the list of rights incorporated into the definition, but lists of rights can easily incorporate privileges or cultural biases. Anyone can play the game of declaring their system the freest possible by manipulating the set of rights. Supporters of welfare capitalism or socialism can say that no one has the right to property without paying their taxes; therefore, only a system that taxes property means "absolute freedom" for everyone. A duke can say to a peasant, "I have the right to be a duke and all the liberties it implies. You have the right to be a peasant and all the liberties it implies. Therefore, only our royal system means absolute freedom for both of us." One theme that runs through both of our books is that the conception of strong, unequally held private property as a "natural right" incorporates a great deal of privilege and one-sided coercive power into the legal system.

Fourth, once one commits to a rights-based definition, one has to embrace the possibility that other systems offer people far greater neutral freedom, far more meaningful control over their lives, than the "justified" system. Yet, many propertarians seem to think they have proven that capitalism objectively delivers people control of their lives simply by showing that it defined their extremely limit choice set as "moral" (Rothbard 1982: 41 for example).

Fifth, propertarians face a dilemma: either the rights-based conception of liberty is important *or* the freedom to control your own life is important—not both. Without recognizing this dilemma, many propertarians seem to be unclear whether they endorse the rights-based conception or its opposite—the neutral, empirical, or non-rights-based conception of freedom. The rights-based conception of freedom disavows any concern with the freedom of people to control their lives. Consider the following illustration.

We cannot in pure theory rule out that a propertyless person might have no other choice than prostitution or some other difficult, demeaning act to obtain the money they need to access the resources they need to survive. A propertarian might use empirical reasoning to argue that that situation is unlikely, but they would have to abandon the rights-based conception of freedom to admit that the liberty from being indirectly forced into prostitution is relevant to being free. A person truly committed to the rights-based conception has to say that it's perfectly fine if many people have no other choice to survive but to become prostitutes. If that happens, they simply have no right to keep living if they refuse to be prostitutes. People who sincerely believe in the moral priority of rights-based liberty have to believe that there is nothing ethically troubling about indirectly forced rape.

Certainly, an individual demanding freedom wants what John Stuart Mill (1859) called for, "The only freedom which deserves the name is that of pursuing our own good in our own way." Propertarians want to be seen as delivering such substantive freedom. Hayek (1960: 11) is concerned that the "coercion of some by others is reduced as much as possible." Boaz (1997: 291) appeals to the liberty to "make the decisions that are important to your life." If we want to know whether any system actually delivers such control, we have to use a neutral definition of freedom and we have to face the empirical trade-off involved in setting up one legal system of rights versus another.

Some critics suggest a way for propertarians to get out of the circularity. They could drop the pretense that their argument has anything to do with liberty and concentrate on justifying property rights by some other means (Attas 2005: 40–41; Waldron 1993b: 321–322). This strategy involves dropping the argument from liberty, and so the rights-based conception of negative freedom doesn't concern this essay any further.

3. OTHER ATTEMPTS TO RESOLVE THE TRADE-OFF

All or most propertarians want to believe the empirical claim that their theory can reduce coercion even for the disadvantaged. Few of them want to their theory to be nothing more than the use of definitional fiat to throw the label "moral" on onerous noncontractual obligations that prevent people from having substantive control over their lives. Quotes above from Hayek, Boaz, Narveson, and Rothbard all indicate belief in the substantive value of the freedoms they offer. Many other propertarians make similar statements. Machan (2006a: 271) writes, "one is going to emphasize being free from interference because the central condition that an adult needs to flourish is not to be oppressed by other persons—that is to say, not to have others constrain them." Eric Mack (2002a: 76) wants a system that is consistent with "the moral inviolability of persons—an inviolability that is manifested in the wrongfulness of unprovoked acts of killing, maiming, imprisoning, enslaving, and extracting labor from other individuals." Nozick's (1974: 33) words are similar, searching for a system that reflects the "Kantian principle that individuals are ends and not merely means: they may not be sacrificed or used for the achieving of other ends without their consent. Individuals are inviolable."

The concern for individual inviolability and the freedom from constraint are a priori moral principles, but once we demonstrate that the maintenance of the private property rights system involves force against the most vulnerable, it becomes far more difficult to establish that a system dedicated to protecting private property also promotes those concerns. Is there any way that doesn't fall back on the rights-based definition of liberty that can demonstrate by pure theory whether a private property regime actually delivers the substantive freedom it promises?

One such argument is that propertarian rights achieve a sort of moral minimalism, because supposedly this set of rights requires duties that are less demanding on people who might disagree about issues of justice. Lomasky (1987: 95–102) argues along these lines, but admits that there could be some welfare rights that were not excessively burdensome in comparison to individuals and thereby admits the empirical nature of the question. He offers only casual observations to support his conclusion that "each has reason to value [the] liberty to acquire and use goods . . . not equality in holdings but equal liberty to acquire holdings" (Lomasky 1987: 123).

If the "liberty" to *acquire* holdings were about the liberty to *appropriate* resources, the argument might clearly be one about equal freedom from interference. The maintenance of a commons requires interference with any would-be appropriators, just as the recognition of a right of appropriation involves interference with would-be foragers who would like to use the same resources.

No argument about the freedom to appropriate can support the market economy, because capitalism makes people no freer to appropriate property than the common property regime, public property regime, or any other system. A person born into the contemporary market economy is as unfree to appropriate land as a person born to a common property regime or a public property regime that allows no private landownership. The right to appropriate *scarce* resources, as economists define the term (i.e. anything with a monetary value), is inconsistent with a system of equal freedom from coercion. The propertyless today are not and cannot be equally free to appropriate.

Lomasky's (1987: 123) "liberty to acquire" holdings actually means the "liberty" to purchase goods. That's not a liberty at all. That's a positive opportunity. The goods you are expected to buy are made out of resources you have forcibly been excluded from using yourself. The chance to take orders from one resource owner so that you can "earn" the right to buy goods from other resource owners might be useful, but it is not freedom from some form of coercion that exists in societies with a common property regime (Cohen 1995; Otsuka 2003; Waldron 1988).

Opportunity-based arguments are the kind that propertarians usually dismiss offhand when applied to government investments. The government proposes to interfere with people to create greater opportunities for all. Propertarians usually reply that no increase in opportunity can justify that interference. If we must apply this reasoning to the taxation of those privileged to hold property, we must apply the same logic to the establishment and maintenance of a private property regime relative to a common property regime.

Despite the potential inconsistency with other propertarian arguments, there could be something extremely valuable about the freedom one can secure specifically with private and strong property rights (as opposed to access to common property, a share of public property, or some weaker form of property available in a welfare market economy). If so, the coercive legal structure necessary to establish and maintain a private property regime might end up giving people greater control of their lives and greater ability to avoid coercion on balance.

Jeremy Waldron (1988) traces arguments based on the usefulness of ownership as far back as G. W. F. Hegel. It seems to be what Nozick (1974: 167) meant when he argued, "Patterned distributional principles do not give people what entitlement principles do, only better distributed. For they do not give the right to choose what to do with what one has." Rothbard (1978: 42–43) expresses similar ideas. They are correct to recognize that *strong* property rights necessitate *unequal* property rights. Property rights could be both weak and unequal (as private property often is in monarchies), but property rights cannot be both strong and equal, because trade, gift, and bequest in the context of strong property rights increase inequality.

Nozick argues that more equal property rights systems "do not give people what entitlement principles do, only better distributed" (Nozick 1974: 167). This statement is true, but it is equally true that democracies do not give to each individual the same political power that monarchs hold only better distributed. Monarchy is the logically strongest power one person can have over the law, just as full, liberal ownership is "the logically strongest set of ownership rights over a thing that a person can have" (Vallentyne et al. 2005: 204). In both cases, sharing the power more widely inherently weakens the power. The taxation, regulation, and redistribution necessary to establish more equal access to resources inherently delivers weaker property rights in those resources to each individual, but it will deliver those rights to more people, and therefore it might well deliver greater over-all equal freedom from coercion.

Waldron argues that the security of property comes only when someone succeeds in coming to own a significant amount of it. For everyone else, "an opportunity to become free is not freedom." Waldron (1988: 5, 411, 425) concludes that any argument based on the good it does for people once they become owners can only ground an actual right to property, not merely the right to work for owners in hopes of eventually obtaining a significant amount of it. Securing the right to property for all requires some taxation, regulation, and/or redistribution of property. Waldron (1988: 425–445) admits that more equal property rights are weaker, but argues that weaker, more equal property rights imply greater freedom. The independently wealthy would face more interference, but the middle and lower classes might face less, and the concern is for the highest *equal* freedom.

Propertarians usually respond to this sort of reasoning by tacitly falling back on the rights-based conception of freedom, ignoring the coercion involved in moving from a common property regime to a private property regime, or by ignoring the common property regime altogether. These might be effective rhetorical strategies to distract people's attention from the problem, but none of them logically establishes that capitalism provides greater equal freedom than a common property regime.

The argument that remains open is an empirical one. Suppose trade worked out such that even the least propertied people in market economies with strong private property rights somehow experienced less interference, coercion, and aggression than people in all other societies including those with common property regimes. If so, propertarian capitalism would reduce coercion as much as possible, even if people have to take advantage of the positive opportunity to buy property to reach their positions. That argument involves an empirical claim about the relative freedom of people in different property rights regimes.

If we can disprove the often-presumed-but-seldom-argued assertion of a connection between the market economy and negative liberty, we disprove the claim that policies to promote economic opportunity, equality, and so on necessarily come at the expense of the greatest equal liberty. If we can show that the maintenance of propertarian capitalism comes at the *expense* of the negative freedom of the poor and propertyless or perhaps anyone in the middle and lower classes, redistributive programs should not be looked at as some kind of mandatory charity but as compensation for lost freedom. If the target beneficiaries of redistribution are actually made unfree by the prevailing property rights regime, negative freedom does not stand in the way of redistribution; it requires redistribution.

4. THE HUNTER-GATHERER BAND ECONOMY AS THE FOCUS OF COMPARISON FOR THE INVESTIGATION

The market freedom hypothesis is obviously a universal claim. If it's true, propertarian capitalism preserves negative liberty better than all other forms of socio-political organization, including the hunter-gatherer band economy. It is a claim about small-scale societies from prehistory to the present, even if people making the universal claim never mention or think about those societies. This much explains why we can make this comparison but not why we should bother. Good work has been done comparing the negative freedom-promoting aspects of contemporary alternative systems (Cohen 1988, 1995, 1998, 2011; Waldron 1993a). This subsection explains how this particular comparison advances understanding of the negative freedom argument in the present political context.

One reason to make this comparison is that hunter-gatherer band economies have a common property regime, which contrasts starkly with the two forms of property rights usually considered in the debate: private and public property.

Another reason to make this investigation is that it is possible to draw some firm conclusions about the relative level of freedom in these two economies. Freedom is notoriously hard to measure. Any legal system makes people free to do some things and unfree to do others. Therefore, the net effect of propertarian rights on freedom is theoretically indeterminate (Cohen 1995: 57; Friedman 1997: 428) but not necessarily empirically indeterminable. At least two kinds of empirical arguments have the potential to demonstrate that one system has greater equal freedom than another.

The first is to appeal to the central importance of certain liberties. The *number* of liberties available does seem trivial compared to the *value* of some liberties. Most people would prefer to be out of prison with a finite number of things they can do than to be in prison with an infinite number of games they can play by themselves in their cell. Chapters 6 argues that people in capitalist societies lack important liberties that people in band societies have.

The second way to make the comparison is to argue that the negative freedom of one system *dominates* that of another. That is, one system imposes forms of coercion that another system lacks without also relieving them of forms of coercion that the other system has. In other words, one system has all the specific liberties another system has and additional specific liberties the other lacks. Chapter 6 argues that the negative freedom of people in band societies dominates that of middle- and lower-class people in contemporary capitalist societies.

The comparison with hunter-gatherer bands is also important because propertarian justice is "historical; it depends on what actually has happened" (Nozick 1974: 152). And this historical theory is largely based on the idea of first come, first served (Epstein 1978–1979: 1221–1244; Kirzner 1989: 16–18; Locke 1960 [1689]: §46; Narveson 1988: 11; Rothbard 1982: 58).

The hunter-gatherer band is not some theoretical alternative. It and other forms of socio-economic organization with common property regimes are real systems that preceded capitalism on all six habitable continents. History favors the common property regime in propertarian terms, and the example of band economies shows how free people can be with a common property regime. As Chapters 10–14 show, private resource ownership did not simply "develop" out of the common property regime; state societies forcibly and aggressively imposed it on smaller-scale peoples around the world.

For propertarian capitalism to be justified under its own freedom-based historical theory of justice, the forceful imposition of private property rights would have to be freedom-enhancing overall.

If Chapter 6 can show that the imposition of private control over resources is freedom-limiting (relative to what existed before), the justification for unequal entitlements to resources falls apart. If we can show that the targets of redistribution are those made most unfree by the forcible imposition of private control over resources, the freedom-based argument against redistribution no longer holds. If so, anyone truly committed to the overriding priority of freedom over opportunity has to prefer the hunter-gatherer band economy to the propertarian market economy and perhaps to any form of industrial state society. The justification of the market economy would have to allow some amount of opportunity to override freedom.

This comparison also has at least three important implications for the freedom-based justification of the market economy relative to all other systems. First, some amount of redistribution is owed to disadvantaged people not only for the above reason but also as compensation for the violent way the noncontractual obligation to respect others' property rights was imposed on them (see Chapters 13 and 14). Second, because of the need for compensation, a significant amount of redistribution, possibly in non-monetary form, is freedom-enhancing overall. The claim that taxation, regulation, and redistribution are necessarily freedom-reducing is false. Therefore, very different systems might be more consistent with freedom. Third, if, in the end, supporters of the market economy have to appeal to opportunity or welfare to justify it relative to the band economy, they can no longer use the priority of negative freedom to justify the market economy relative to other systems.

5. CONCLUSION

This chapter has demonstrated that the negative freedom argument for the market economy requires an empirical claim we call "the market-freedom hypothesis" and that it can be tested by comparing the market economy and the hunter-gatherer band economy.

To make an empirical version of the freedom-based argument for the market economy, propertarians would have to take seriously the freedom-inhibiting aspects of the private property rights regime and weigh them against whatever freedom from coercion the private property regime delivers to the propertyless. We have been unable to find any propertarian literature that does so.

If there is more than a banal truth to the negative freedom argument for the market economy, this comparison would show that people face as little or less coercion and less interference with their lives than in the band economy. All the freedom lost in the history of violent aggression to establish the private property rights system and the interference needed to maintain it would be compensated by the freedom it bestows on everyone including the least advantaged people.

The market freedom hypothesis would be true, if—say—weak individuals in a band society were subject to constant bullying by strong individuals under a common property regime, and if private property ownership freed everyone—even the least advantaged—from it. Therefore, the negative freedom argument cannot be dismissed offhand on a priori grounds. But if the negative freedom argument actually supports the market economy, we can expect to see that propertyless people are freer in the following ways and others.

- They would be coerced less often or in less important ways.
- They would be less constrained overall.
- They would be freer from taking orders if they didn't want to.
- They would be less likely to have labor extracted from them.
- They would have fewer noncontractual obligations.
- They would be less often sacrificed to achieve the ends of others.
- They would have more control over the decisions that are important in their lives.

These claims provide testable hypotheses for Chapter 6.

Chapter 6

THE NEGATIVE FREEDOM ARGUMENT FOR THE HUNTER-GATHERER BAND ECONOMY

Chapter 5 established that the negative freedom argument for the market economy requires the empirical claim that the market economy reduces coercion more than all other systems, calling this claim the market-freedom hypothesis. Its truth or falsity cannot be established by a priori reasoning or definitional fiat. It can only be established by an examination of the effects of different forms of social organization on the coercion of individuals. It also established the relevance of testing this claim with a comparison of the market economy and the hunter-gatherer band economy.

This chapter makes that comparison, presenting an empirical argument that the hunter-gatherer band economy is more consistent with negative freedom than the market economy. Although freedom is difficult to measure, this chapter argues that the freedom of people in band societies dominates the freedom of the least free people in capitalist societies. There is no form of coercion, interference, force, noncontractual obligation, involuntariness, or aggression to which people in band societies are subject and from which lower- and middle-class people in capitalist societies have been freed. Lower- and middle-class people in capitalist societies are subject to forms of coercion, force, and so on, that do not exist in band societies. The independently wealthy might have more liberties than people in band societies, but, if so, their additional liberties come at the cost of fewer liberties for middle- and lower-class people. Therefore, the market economy—as usually conceived—fails to deliver the highest equal freedom. The potential advantage of large-scale societies is in opportunity not freedom.

1. NEGATIVE FREEDOM IN BAND ECONOMIES

This section summarizes observations of the extensive negative freedom experienced by people in hunter-gatherer band economies as observed by both anthropologists and by propertarians.

A. Anthropologists' Observations

The extensive negative freedom of people in hunter-gatherer band economies is well-documented and uncontroversial. Anthropologists who have written about it include but are not limited to Nurit Bird-David (1994: 591, 597), Boehm (2001: 72–73), Richard Daly (Lee and Daly 1999), Karen L. Endicott, Kirk Endicott (1988, 2008: 43–45, 50), Morton Fried (1967: 58, 62–63), Peter M. Gardner (1991: 547–550), Ernest Gellner (1995: 33–34), Marvin Harris (1977: 69), Tim Ingold (1986: 222–223, 1999); Robert L. Kelly (1995: 296), Richard Lee (1982: 53, 1999: 4, 1968b), Robert Redfield (1967: 21), Colin Renfrew (2007: 148), Colin M. Turnbull (1968), and James Woodburn (1968a: 52, 1968b: 103, 1982: 434).

Leacock (1998: 143) writes, "What is hard to grasp about the structure of the egalitarian band is that leadership as we conceive it is not merely 'weak' or 'incipient,' as is commonly stated, but irrelevant." Some of the pithiest observations come from Fried (1967: 8), an often-controversial mid-to-late-twentieth-century anthropologist who, on this issue, is solidly within the professional consensus. He writes,

> It is difficult, in ethnographies of simple egalitarian societies, to find cases in which one individual tells one or more others, 'Do this!' or some command equivalent. The literature is replete with examples of individuals, saying the equivalent of "If this is done, it will be good," possibly or possibly not followed by somebody else doing it. More usually the person who initiates the idea also performs the activity

That is negative freedom: to be under no one else's command, free from following orders from an authority. Hunter-gatherers in band societies experience this freedom throughout their adult lives (and parents begin to respect it in children surprisingly early).

Fried (1967: 62–63, 66) adds, "Cooperative labor parties, whether for hunting or gathering, take place with very little apparent leadership." No one has the power to say, *it's time for the hunt, you must come.* Furthermore, "the prestige which even the mightiest hunter enjoys is not transferable to other areas and does not constitute a firm basis for political power." These generalizations hold true even during military action against other bands (Fried 1967: 104–105).

Many anthropologists confirm these observations (Endicott 1988: 212; Endicott and Endicott 2008: 43–44; Gardner 1991: 547–549; Harris 1977: 69; Lee 1982: 53). Woodburn (1968a: 52) writes, "Hunting is not a coordinated activity. Men hunt individually and decide for themselves where and when they will go hunting." According to Harris (1977: 69),

> In most band and village societies . . . the average human being enjoyed economic and political freedoms which only a privileged minority enjoy today. Men decided for themselves how long they would work on a particular day, what they would work at—or if they would work at all. Women, too, despite their subordination to men, generally set up their own daily schedules and paced themselves on an individual basis. . . . Every man and woman held title to an equal share of nature. Neither rent, taxes, nor tribute kept people from doing what they wanted to do.

To the extent that there is any significant controversy on this topic, it is over the meaningfulness of the term "hunter-gatherer band." Some anthropologists prefer to generalize by economic activity rather than scale, thus considering *all* hunter-gatherers together regardless of the size of the communities they live in, of their food storage practices, or of their nomadic status. This grouping makes it harder to generalize on this issue, because many larger-scale, food-storing, settled hunter-gatherer communities, such as the chiefdoms of the northwest Pacific coast of North America, had a slave class and fairly strong centralized leadership. The claim we make about the groups we call bands do not generalize to all hunter-gatherer communities that do not share the relevant definitional characteristics.

Remember, we use the term "hunter-gatherer band" for communities that share four characteristics: (1) nomadic groups of (2) less than 100 people (3) who get all of their subsistence from foraging, and (4) do not store food. Whatever name (if any) you might want to use for them, observed communities that meet this description seem always to place great respect on the freedom and independence of all individuals. This statement is supported by observations of bands living across Eurasia, Africa, the Americas, Australia, and many islands, in all types of climates and geography, from the Arctic to the tropics, in the mountains, deserts, forest, and so on. This statement is also supported by many historical accounts of encounters with bands that were incorporated into larger-scale societies without being observed by ethnographers. Whether it generalizes universally for all bands in all times and places is not necessarily relevant for all formulations of the negative freedom argument. The correlation with freedom is far better established among all observed band societies than it is among all historically observed states and/or market economies (Gardner 1991: 550).

Like all other societies, bands have social norms that restrain behavior, but these restraints are voluntary in the sense used in theories of negative liberty. That is, they are "contractual obligations"— obligations that one has freely chosen to take on. Every norm, rule, and social convention in band society comes into effect with the tacitly understood qualifier, *if you want to camp with us*. An individual, a family, or a group of families who do not like the way their band does things are free to go off on their own and do things another way (Endicott 1988: 121; Johnson and Earle 2000: 120; Leacock and Lee 1982: 7–9; Lee 1982: 55; Woodburn 1982: 434, 445). Therefore, the extent to which band members have explicit duties to each other is the result of an informal agreement that can be dissolved at a moment's notice by breaking camp.

The ability of people to exit the band—either individually or with a subgroup of their choosing—is not merely a formal right, but a real substantive power secured by individuals' direct access to resources. Land and other resources are not only common property but also habitually underutilized, making it possible for people to go off on their own with relative ease and without encroaching on others' ability to provide for themselves. As discussed further below, this basic liberty protects the negative freedom of individuals in the personal, economic, and political realms (Carneiro 1970: 735; Gardner 1991; Gray 2009: 481, 485–486; Ingold 1986: 222–223; Lee and Daly 1999: 4; Woodburn 1982: 434, 445).

Under the band society's version of a common property regime, no person can put any other person under a duty to refrain from using resources. The most extreme examples are provided by groups such as the Hadza of Tanzania (Woodburn 1968a: 49–55) and the Inuit of the Canadian Arctic for whom "the very notion of exclusive rights in land or hunting and fishing territory—whether private, familial or communal—is nonexistent" (Fried 1967: 58). According to Fried (1967: 58),

> In no simple society known to ethnography is there any restriction on access to the raw materials necessary to make tools and weapons. This statement can be made flatly about resources in the habitation area of a given unit, and with moderate reservations it may be extended to resources located in alien areas.

Leacock (1998: 144) writes, "the direct relation between production and consumption was intimately connected with the dispersal of authority. Unless some form of control over resources enables persons with authority to withhold them from others, authority is not authority as we know it."

Although bands can make rules as a condition of camping with the group, they tend to avoid making rules as much as they can. Bands have seldom if ever been observed to make some members accept subordinate positions or take orders from others. Observed bands are explicit about their respect for each other's freedom, independence, and rights to pick up and go. They pride themselves on their respect for individuals' right to be free from the coercion or even the direction of others (Kelly 1995: 296; Lee 1982: 53).

Endicott and Endicott's (2008: 63) description of the Batek (an indigenous group in Southeast Asia) is typical:

> The Batek had no formal political organization coordinating their activities. Decision making about all economic and social matters resided ultimately with individuals and conjugal families. Yet most decisions were not made in isolation. . . . Before a move, people discussed informally or in a meeting where to go and what to do. All interested parties, male and female, expressed their views, and those conjugal families that decided to do the same thing in the same area would move there together, while other families might go somewhere else.

Band societies carry their respect for individual freedom to such an extreme that they tend to lack all trappings of political authority, power, or even corporate identity (Ingold 1999: 399, 406, 408; Lee 1990: 254–255; Steenhoven 1962: 58).

B. Propertarians' Observations

Importantly for the discussion here, the extensive freedom of people in hunter-gatherer bands is uncontroversial not only among anthropologists but also apparently among propertarians, who also remark on their freedom. An article by Thomas Mayor (2012), entitled "Hunter-Gatherers: The Original Libertarians," provides an excellent example. Despite some glaring errors about anthropology as a science, Mayor gets a surprising amount right about the freedom of people in band society. He recognizes that people in hunter-gatherer bands are extremely free in the negative sense and (for the most part) how they maintain that level of freedom.

Mayor rightly recognizes many ways in which hunter-gatherers are free in the sense that propertarians claim to promote: "Bands have no effective government or formal laws;" bands have a high "degree of decentralized authority;" band institutions "indicate compatibility with individualism;" people in bands experienced, "a level of individual autonomy in decision making that far exceeded anything experienced since the introduction of extensive agriculture" (Mayor 2012: 486, 490, 491). Notice that this last quote indicates that people in band societies are *freer* than people in capitalist societies. Mayor doesn't explore that implication.

Mayor (2012: 498) correctly (if perhaps only partially) recognizes why band societies have so much negative liberty: "Hunter-gatherer societies were free primarily because each individual possessed effective economic mobility. In the face of attempted political or economic exploitation, the hunter-gatherer always had the opportunity to pick up and move without paying a significant price for doing so." For hunter-gatherers *in band societies*, this statement is exactly right, although it is not necessarily true for complex hunter-gatherers in larger-scale societies. As mentioned above, people in band societies recognize this right and prize it (Kelly 1995: 296; Lee 1982: 53).

As section 2 discusses in greater depth, Mayor doesn't effectively explore the word "effective." He leaves out what is most important to a band members' "economic mobility:" wherever they might move, they have direct access to resources they need to survive, and they know how to use those resources to maintain themselves. Leaving the territory isn't necessarily important. People breaking off from a band can often forage in the same range of common land as long as they don't camp and hunt in the same area at the same time (Carneiro 1970: 735; Gardner 1991; Gray 2009: 481, 485–486; Ingold 1986: 222–223; Lee and Daly 1999: 4).

Because no one interferes with the use hunter-gatherers might make of the land, they "are not dependent on *specific* other people for access to basic requirements" (Woodburn 1982: 434, original emphasis). Although hunter-gatherers in most geographical conditions can survive for some time on their own, they do eventually need the help of others, but importantly they don't need any *specific* group of others. That is, they are not attached to any power structure, be it the power of private landlords, employers, governments, or chiefs, because none of these groups comes between them and the resources they need to survive. The freedom to reject *all* authority is the essential element that gives hunter-gatherers the power to remain so consistently free of coercion throughout their lives. As discussed in Chapter 3, it is individuals' freedom from dependence on any power structure that maintains their freedom from coercion. People in band societies can walk away from anyone who tries to give them orders (Endicott 1988: 121; Johnson and Earle 2000: 120; Leacock and Lee 1982: 7–9; Lee 1982: 55; Woodburn 1982: 434, 445).

If you could join a hunter-gatherer band today, you would probably notice the absence of coercion and freedom from authority. But you would also notice the limits of your opportunities. Only one career path would be open to you: forager/caregiver. You would also notice significant social pressures. People won't tell you what to do, but they will ask you a lot of personal questions and constantly comment on the propriety of your behavior. And if you want to camp with the band you will have to share: they won't recognize what you bring to camp as being your exclusive property. These limitations on what you could do will affect you, and they might be a considerable trade-off against the freedom from authority you have gained. They might even make you feel unfree in important ways, but these limitations on what you can do are not limitations of your negative freedom as propertarians define it because they are contractual obligations that therefore do not involve coercion. Lack of opportunity is not coercion and the social pressure you feel is a contractual obligation. You knew when you camped here that people paid close attention to each other's business and that anything you brought back to camp would be shared. As a "band member"—or more accurately as a "person camping with this group at this moment"—you knew these expectations when you made camp. You are free to go and live by your own rules alone or with whatever group is willing to join you. You don't need seed money or a legal permit to start your project, and you don't need the neighboring society to give you an entry visa.

Hunter-gatherer bands and autonomous villages practice something like the "framework for utopia" that Nozick (1974: 297–334) and other propertarians have lauded in theory. Nozick imagined people being able to live in communities in which virtually all of their obligations would be contractual and in which the people would be free to set whatever rules they want. Those who did not like the rules could leave. But in Nozick's framework, people who leave one community would have to buy in to the next community. That is, people in Nozick's framework had one centrally important noncontractual obligation: they had to respect the property "rights" of people who happened to own land and other resources. That means that everyone but the wealthiest would find landlords and employers with the power to interfere with the use they might make of resources. Therefore, bands and autonomous villages free people from forms of force and coercion than do the communities envisioned by Nozick. In market economies, everyone but the independently wealthy will find the rent, taxes, and rules of employers keeping them from building whatever framework for utopia they might envision, unlike in band societies in which "Neither rent, taxes, nor tribute kept people from doing what they wanted to do" (Harris 1977: 69).

2. COMPARISON WITH MARKET SOCIETIES

Before we can compare the respect for negative freedom in the two forms of social organization, we need to elaborate a little more on the differences between market and band economies. As much as Mayor praises hunter-gatherer bands for being "the original libertarians," he ignores how different their institutions (e.g. norms, rules, and conventions) are from propertarian institutions. He accurately praises band societies' respect for liberty but barely mentions that they have no respect whatsoever for the institution most central to propertarian capitalism: private property. As discussed above, Mayor's "original libertarians" did not believe private property was useful in the promotion of liberty. All band societies known to anthropology treat land as a commons, and with some qualification, we can say that they treat food and durable goods as common resources as well (see Chapter 11).

Mayor (2012: 487) mentions the absence of private property rights to land and natural resources in band society, but quickly sets it aside, writing simply, "With very few people and abundant natural resources, creating property rights in those resources yields no advantage." Although he recognizes that people lost their "basic freedoms as soon as settled agriculture became the predominant mode of production," he fails to draw any connection between stratified *ownership* of land and resources and that loss of freedom (Mayor 2012: 498).

Mayor treats people who do not use the institution of private land-ownership as if they simply haven't developed it; as if they would gladly adopt it like dutiful propertarians as soon as a wannabe landlord found it to their advantage to stake the ground. Observed hunter-gatherer bands and autonomous villages universally oppose the imposition any such institution, as do many people from state societies that haven't imposed the institution on everyone (see Chapters 11 and 14). The violent history of agricultural peoples' slow and steady colonization of hunter-gatherer territory and the accompanying history of band and other small-scale societies' resistance to it over the last several thousand years (both discussed in Chapters 13 and 14) reveals the falsity of any implication that people in band societies are propertarians-in-waiting (see also Scott 2009). Their norms and conventions are diametrically opposed to the *raison d'être* of propertarianism: the justification of elite ownership rights without taxation, regulation, or redistribution.

Now that we have shown that the band economy and the market economy are two very different socio-political systems (separated significantly by their property regimes), we are in a position to show how the market economy fails to deliver as much negative freedom. Examining this argument requires addressing Boaz's (1997: 291) rhetorical question as a serious empirical question, "do you make the decisions that are important to your life, or does someone else make them for you?" To answer that question in the context of attempting to promote freedom equally to everyone requires us to compare the situation of people in band societies to the least free people in industrialized, capitalist societies—the propertyless, the homeless, and the people who work long hours for low wages to keep themselves from becoming homeless.

With that in mind, we compare the market economy with the hunter-gatherer band economy in terms of several kinds of negative freedom: status freedom or "effective economic mobility," political freedom, sexual freedom, and freedom from gender and group-based oppression. We distinguish them using the formula (MacCallum 1967: 314): the freedom of agent X, from constraint Y, to do action Z. All of these conceptions of freedom are negative in the sense that the constraints involved in (Y) are imposed by other people. Finally, we compare the two systems in terms of negative freedom in general.

A. Status Freedom or Effective Economic Mobility

Section 1 concurred with Mayor's observation that people in hunter-gatherer band economies "were free primarily because each individual possessed effective economic mobility" (Mayor 2012: 498). This subsection argues that that type of freedom is central to an individual's status as a free person, that it helps protect virtually all other liberties, and that the contemporary market economy denies this freedom to all but a wealthy few.

One of the authors of this book elsewhere defines status freedom as "effective control self-ownership," "independence," or at the risk of oversimplification "the power to say no." Effective control self-ownership is the freedom of an individual from constraints (directly or indirectly) created by other people to exercise the effective power to accept or refuse active cooperation with other willing people (Widerquist 2006a, 2010b, 2011, 2013). This definition is negative because any agent (X) with the physical and mental abilities to turn resources into consumption only needs the freedom from constraints imposed by other people (Y) to have this effective power (Z).

The band economy helps to secure status freedom, because, as Mayor (2012: 498) recognizes, it gives individuals "effective economic mobility" or "the opportunity to pick up and move without paying a significant price for doing so." In a discussion of nomadic hunter-gatherers' social existence, the psychologist Gray (2009: 484, 485–486) argues,

> The most basic freedom . . . is the freedom to quit. . . . It prevents leaders from enforcing rules that are not agreed upon by all. People who are unhappy will quit, and if too many quit play will end. . . . One implication is that players must not dominate or bully other players. People who feel dominated will quit. Another implication is that players must attempt to satisfy the needs and wishes of all the other players, at least sufficiently to keep them from quitting. . . . If players were compelled to stay in the game, then the more powerful players could dominate, and the autonomy, equality, sharing, and consensual decision making would be lost.

This section argues that except for the independently wealthy, people today do not have the relevant kind of freedom to quit. They can quit any *one* job, but everywhere they go they need to work for the same power structure. They cannot quit all jobs or all landlords or all public officials. They cannot live off their own efforts or by their own rules as band members and the wealthy can. While all people living in hunter-gatherers bands have direct access to their means of production, virtually all people living in industrial capitalist societies do not.

Jean-Jacques Rousseau (1998) recognized the essential nature of the freedom to quit when he wrote, "it is impossible to make any man a slave, unless he be first reduced to a situation in which he cannot do without the help of others." Attas (2005: 7), Cohen (1988, 1995: 57, 1998, 2011), Friedman (1997: 428), Gibbard (2000), Haworth (1994: 45–46), and Otsuka (2003: 19) make similar arguments about the loss of negative freedom a property rights system imposes on propertyless people.

Contemporary propertarians tend to deny that propertyless individuals are dependent wage laborers, but in doing so they deny the stated intentions of the people who created the institution of private property. Chapter 14 discusses how the replacement of rural common access rights with the modern property rights system (called the "enclosure movement" in Britain) was explicitly designed and justified in part as a way to force commoners to become full-time laborers and to accept the wages property owners were willing to pay (Carson 2011).

Freed slaves recognized the importance of this kind of freedom. Garrison Frazier, the freed slave who spoke with General Sherman at the meeting that produced the famous unfulfilled promise of 40 acres and a mule, defined freedom as, "placing us where we could reap the fruit of our own labor [and] take care of ourselves." He argued that "The way we can best take care of ourselves is to have land, and turn it and till it by our own labor" (Townsend 2007; Widerquist 2013: 25–26). It was understood at the time that someone with 40 acres could take a job if they wanted to, but they would also be free to work only for themselves, giving them the protections that Gray (2009) discussed above.

Of course, the freed slaves did not get that land, and at the wages they were paid few of them could save enough to buy it. The legal system effectively coerced them to take subordinate positions working for their former masters, because by designating all land as the property of their former masters it interfered with any efforts the former slaves might make to take care of themselves. The had the legal right to quit, but the legal system coercively took away their effective power to quit. This effective power, we argue, is the key difference between the lives of people in band economies and the lives of people in market economies from Frazier's time to the present. People in band economies and any other economy with a sufficient commons have the power to quit that makes economic mobility effective.

Instead of "effective economic mobility" lower- and middle-class people in market economies today have what we can call *ineffective economic mobility*. Although even a minimum-wage worker might be able to raise the funds to move 3,000 miles from Miami to Seattle— much farther than all or most hunter-gatherers could conceive of moving—a minimum-wage job in Seattle isn't much different than one in Miami. Wherever they go, they are subject to the same economic and political power structures, and they fight themselves in the same place in the hierarchy. The move doesn't do much to relieve them from "attempted political or economic exploitation" (Mayor 2012: 498). To make economic mobility effective, people would need the power to refuse not just any one but all subordinate positions—a power that people who are free to access a sufficient amount of common resources have naturally.

The last substantial commons in the contiguous United States was closed with the defeat of the Apache in 1886. The Homestead Act made it possible for some people to become self-sufficient farmers for a few more decades, but it required people to move to remote areas and, therefore, wasn't a realistic option for everyone. In any case, options like that are long gone for most of the world's population.

The remaining commons is not much more than the streets and the parks. Unless one is wealthy, the decision to refuse all jobs means being homeless, which exposes one to a great deal of suffering and coercion.

Jeremy Waldron (1993a) has an excellent discussion of how the homeless are comprehensively unfree in the most negative sense of the term. The homeless are unfree to do some of the most basic human functions, unfree to urinate or have sex in a private place, unfree to sleep unmolested, and so on. He argues that the homeless are not *unable* to do these things. They are unfree to do them; they face coercion keeping them from satisfying their own needs by their own efforts. Homeless people find themselves constantly moved on by the police with no private place they can legally be long enough to perform many basic functions—such as get a good night's sleep.

We can extend Waldron's argument by pointing out that the propertyless are no less able to learn how to hunt, gather, fish, or scavenge than their ancestors were. They are not any less able to learn how to procure their own food or build their own shelter out of materials they can gather in nature without the aid of property owners. Nor are they any less able to learn farming, mining, or manufacturing. Homeless people today don't bother learning the skills their self-sufficient ancestors knew because they know they are unfree to use them. The skills they need in their social context involve pleasing a boss, attracting charity, satisfying governmental eligibility criteria, or finding relatively safe food in other people's garbage—the one foraging option that remains open in most countries today. Many homeless people take advantage of that option at great risk to themselves.

For non-wealthy people today, the only possible way to avoid homelessness is the not-always-effective solution of taking a job. That is, to take orders from someone who controls enough property to pay a wage that can sustain a person. Some people become eligible for disability benefits, but many people spend their lives taking orders in subordinate positions. Few "working-age" people ever "earn" the right to be free from those orders or gain enough property to be free from the restrictions of a landlord.

As long as anyone is without the amount of property they need to maintain their status freedom, the possibility of obtaining it remains an opportunity not a liberty. As Waldron (1988: 411) argues, "an opportunity to become free is not freedom. . . . So long as the opportunity remains unconsummated, the person who possesses it and who is even actively pursuing it, remains in a negative sense unfree."

People who become free from the necessity of doing so are called "independently wealthy," a term that reflects the dependent nature of everyone else and the rarity of individual accession to that lofty position in the contemporary capitalist hierarchy.

The threat of homelessness affects not just people on the margins, but all lower- and middle-class people. The alternative to any one job is another job, but the alternative to all jobs is homelessness for everyone but the independently wealthy. We're not meaningfully free to quit, not free to exit the prevailing social, political, and economic power structure the way people in band societies are. As argued above, without that "most basic freedom . . . the more powerful players could dominate, and the autonomy, equality, sharing, and consensual decision making would be lost" (Gray 2009: 484, 486).

In the band economy, any potentially oppressed person or group can get up and walk away from the person, group, or power structure and have *the same access to natural resources* as they had while working with the group. They can camp and forage with whom they want, where they want, and they use this tool effectively to maintain nearly constant freedom from coercion.

Today's *ineffective economic mobility* means that middle- and lower-class people can walk away from any one person who might coerce them, but to do so means *losing virtually all access to natural resources*. While people in band economies are free to camp where they want; people in contemporary market economies are forced to meet the conditions of a landowner or a bank to obtain a safe, private place to sleep.

The issue is not simply that people need people. In the long run, hunter-gatherers need other people as much as anyone in any other economic system, but they are not dependent on a *specific* group of people. Fewer than ten nomadic hunter-gatherers can start a viable band, if they don't like the way other bands are doing things. They wouldn't need any seed-money to get started. They would have no one to please but each other, and they would hardly notice the difference in living standard by foraging with the smaller group.

That is effective economic mobility.

But 10, 20, or 1,000,000 disgruntled middle- and lower-class people are not allowed to support each other; they cannot simply break off from all employers, landlords, banks, and government officials. They don't need the wealthy to provide a service for them: they need the wealthy's permission. That is, they need the wealthy to exercise their government-maintained power to decide who gets to use resources. They have an *artificial need* for bosses and landlords. It is created and maintained by the legal system. The history recounted in Chapter 14 shows how governments divided people into dependent workers and independent owners. Dependent workers are not legally allowed to make their living by hunting, gathering, fishing, farming, or starting their own business or coop. Wherever they go, their legally created need for bosses and landlords remains.

That is *ineffective* economic mobility.

Freely chosen employment does not threaten status freedom because it is a contractual obligation. But forced work does, even if the force is indirect and many employment options are available (Widerquist 2006a, 2010b, 2011, 2013).

This empirical comparison refutes the argument that the ease of obtaining and the value of holding private property ensures that the market economy leads to greater overall freedom from coercion. Whatever value full private property rights have in protecting people from coercion once obtained, it is simply too difficult to obtain enough property in the existing market economy for that system to protect people from exploitation or coercion as well as the band economy does.

This loss of freedom is significant not just for the least advantaged but for people well into the middle class. A system that ignores the unfreedom of masses of people being forced into a position where they have no choice but to spend a lifetime taking orders from members of another group of people (many of whom are free from taking similar orders) has little or no claim to minimize equal freedom from coercion or maximize equal freedom for people to control their own lives.

The following subsections discuss how this artificial dependency affects other forms of freedom.

B. Political Freedom

We use the term "political freedom" for the freedom from all constraints (Y) for individuals who live under the law (X) to participate equally in the making of it (Z). Political freedom is not obviously negative because it is about participating in a group decision, but the aspect that makes it negative is that one cannot impose laws on another without interfering with them in some way.

Bands would seem to have the maximum possible political freedom: they have few laws, make political decisions collectively, and allow anyone who doesn't agree to live by their own rules nearby. We do not see how political decision-making could have wider participation. Some people might be more persuasive than others, but that would happen in any society. The power that people are able to hold over others seems to be least effective in a band society (Endicott 1988: 121) and tends to increase with scale and as options for noncooperation decrease (Widerquist and McCall 2017).

The twentieth-century trend toward political democratization could be seen as a revival of some of the political freedom that band societies have had, perhaps, for a very long time. But even the most democratic nations today cannot claim to share influence over the political process as widely or evenly as band societies. The outsized influence of privileged people, corporations, and lobbyists is undeniable as is the marginalization of others. And even apart from systemic unfairness, the size of most states inherently creates a gap between citizens and leaders. Even if the trend toward greater democracy continues, large-scale democracies will have a hard time matching the political freedom of band societies.

One thing democracies can do to increase political freedom is to concede as much power as possible to disadvantaged people. We've discussed how the power of noncooperation is essential to the political freedom of people in a band society. Greater power of noncooperation for the disadvantaged could be as important as curbing the power of the money in politics.

C. Sexual Freedom and Freedom from Gender and Group-Based Oppression

The freedom from gender, sexual, and group-based oppression is the freedom of an individual (X) from constraints created by other people (Y) to live as an equal, control their private interactions, and exercise their identity in a group (Z). These freedoms are negative because it is difficult to oppress people in any of these ways without interfering with them in some way. Most forms of group-based oppression are rare in band society. Their small-scale and flexible membership forces them to accept people with different outlooks and orientations. Group-based animosity between different bands is unfortunately common.

In a society in which no person is thought to have the right to tell another what to do, sexual freedom tends to be high. For example, many Native American societies recognized "two-spirit people" who were essentially transgendered. Two-spirit people could marry any one-spirit person, achieving a form of same-sex marriage (Flannery and Marcus 2012: 70–71). This system was not full marriage equality, but it was closer than most nations have today, and it came without social stigma or loss of status.

Although sexism of some form exists in all societies, observed band societies tend to have great gender equality relative to most known larger-scale societies (Widerquist and McCall 2017). Gardner (1991: 547) goes so far as to describe it as "extreme gender egalitarianism." Even if the term "extreme" goes too far, it is fair to say that women in band societies take full part in decision-making and have the same freedom from authority and effective economic mobility as any man.

According to Leacock (1998: 140, 145), women,

> held decision-making power over their own lives and activities to the same extent that men did over theirs. . . . [N]othing in the structure of egalitarian band societies necessitated special defer-ence to men. There were no economic and social liabilities that bound women to be more sensitive to men's needs and feelings than vice versa. This was even true in hunting societies, where women did not furnish a major share of the food.

Lee and Daly (1999: 5) concur but use more qualified terms,

> Women in hunter-gatherer societies do have higher status than women in most of the world's societies, including industrial and post-industrial modernity. This status is expressed in greater freedom of movement and involvement in decision-making and a lower incidence of domestic violence against them. . . . [But] nowhere can it be said that women and men live in a state of perfect equality.

The strong respect for autonomy, the ethic of nonviolence, the free-dom to leave the group, and the close scrutiny between members of the group while camping together seem to be the key factors protecting women from domestic violence in band society. We don't know of any studies comparing domestic violence levels in band and capitalist societies, but many anthropologists have made this observation. For example, Endicott and Endicott (2008: 50) write "Women and men alike were protected [in Batek society] from abuse, spouse beating, and other acts of physical violence that are committed—and often accepted—in many societies." They attribute the Batek's successful gender egalitarianism to three things: the economic independence of women, the wide distribution of authority and power, and strong belief in nonviolence.

Significant gender oppression has been observed in some small-scale stateless societies, such as the Yanomamo, who live in communities only about two-to-four times the size of bands. "But because the Yanomamo are crowded in their landscape ... a fundamental and far-reaching transformation has taken place: they can no longer avoid resource competition simply by moving elsewhere, and brave, aggressive men are now treated as valuable allies rather than as dangerous outcasts" (Johnson and Earle 2000: 170). That is, some of the central mechanisms for maintaining freedom discussed throughout this chapter are less available to the Yanomamo.

By comparison, women in contemporary market economies—especially economically disadvantaged women—often find themselves economically dependent on husbands, employers, and other men, exposing them to domestic violence, rape, and sexual assault and harassment. The opportunity to someday become full private property owners simply has not fulfilled Hayek's (1960: 11) promise of reducing coercion of women as much as possible or Boaz's (1997: 291) promise of giving women the power to make the decisions that are important to their lives.

D. Negative Freedom in General

We have said that virtually all obligations within a band qualify as voluntary in propertarian terms; we can also say that even those obligations tend not to be enforced by coercion if it can be avoided. For example, people in the band are effectively obliged to share what they have, but the enforcement mechanism is mostly criticism and ridicule. Tolerated theft comes only as a last resort (Widerquist and McCall 2017).

Extremely widespread anthropological agreement exists about the extensive freedom of observed immediate-return hunter-gatherers and about the role of noncooperation and the ability to exit the group in maintaining that level of freedom. As mentioned above, band members, "decided for themselves how long they would work on a particular day, what they would work at—or if they would work at all" (Harris 1977: 69). A comparative level of freedom for lower- and middle-class people in the contemporary market economy is inconceivable.

In a negative sense, a person who owns land is free to do some things a person who lives on a commons does not, and vice versa. If common resources are privatized to others but not you, you get no new liberties, only new forms of coercion. As argued above, contemporary market economies maintain a property rights system in which virtually all middle- and lower-class people have far less property than they would need to maintain the level of individual power afforded by access to a common property regime.

Some of the ways in which the existing property rights system make people unfree are so familiar that they go unnoticed: people with less money are less free to use the resources of the earth than people with more money. Some of the uses they make out of resources trickle down to benefit everyone, but many do not. An enormous portion of the earth's resources are devoted to serving the wants of the most advantaged people who often use those resources in ways that deplete the environment for everyone. Breathing, drinking, and eating other people's pollution is unfreedom in the most negative sense of the term.

The enormous inequality of resource control feeds back to the status freedom issue discussed above to the point at which equality before the law doesn't really exist. We are born in a world where a small group of people owns most of the earth's resources. Their full liberal ownership rights give them power to decide arbitrarily who gets access and who doesn't. We are all equally subject to the whims of the previous generation of property owners. They will bestow great wealth on some of us. They'll give others of us a lifetime of low wages and unattractive working conditions.

The freedom of people in band society is also evidenced by the strong expressions of contentment that people in band society have made to ethnographers and others (Bird-David 1992; Hill and Hurtado 1996: 78–79; Kelly 1995: 16; Lee and Daly 1999: 4; Tacitus 1996; Turnbull 1968: 136) and by the unwillingness to be incorporated into larger-scale societies that stateless peoples (including people in band societies) have consistently displayed. The resistance of stateless peoples to the imposition of private property rights systems has been documented in places as diverse as highland Southeast Asia, the Philippines, Indonesia, the Middle East, Central and Eastern Europe, Brazil, Columbia, and many more (Brown 2007; Marshall III 2002, 2005; Scott 2009).

Wealthy economies like the pre- and post-colonial United States were no exception. Many European Americans and African Americans joined native communities or started their own stateless communities on the periphery of U.S.-controlled territory in places such as Florida, North Carolina, Virginia, the Great Lakes region, and the far west (Scott 2009).

The demise of such societies exhibits a worldwide pattern: they tend to integrate into states when forced—either directly through conquest or indirectly through degradation of territory (Scott 2009: 132–133, 208–211; see Chapter 14 of this book). Government authorities usually tell themselves that such areas were inhabited by criminals and violent people, and for at least some of them that must have been true, but no reasonable observer can ignore how many people fled to the hills to avoid servitude and domination (Scott 2009: 186, 218). It is difficult to uphold the claim that the private property rights system somehow reduces coercion overall when its establishment and maintenance require so much coercion (see Chapters 13–14).

This chapter has considered whether there is a significant liberty secured for all under a private property rights regime that cannot be secured for all under a common property regime, and we have found that none of the candidates usually touted by propertarians fills the role. That is, contemporary market economies secure no significant liberties for everyone that are not also secured by hunter-gatherer band economies. And we've found that hunter-gatherer band economies secure extremely significant liberties that are denied to middle- and lower-class people in contemporary market economies.

This evidence supports the conclusion that the freedom of people in band societies *dominates* that of propertyless people in capitalist society (as we currently know it or as propertarians propose it). The advantages conferred on propertyless people by the market economy (to get a job, to buy property, to have more property available) are all positive opportunities, and they remain unfulfilled for most economically disadvantaged people. If the negative freedom argument for the market economy were valid, the establishment of capitalism would have to *relieve* people from some form of coercion that exists in band society. Instead, it increases the forms of coercion that most people are subject to and relieves them of no significant liberties that we can find or that ethnographers have managed to observe. Therefore, freedom in the hunter-gatherer band society dominates freedom in the market economy. Capitalism, relative to band society, increases the overall level of coercion in society. The negative freedom argument does not support the market economy; it supports the hunter-gatherer band economy. The following section explores the implications of that finding.

3. IMPLICATIONS

People who invoke the negative freedom argument for the market economy often give freedom overriding moral priority so that whatever economic system best promotes negative freedom is the one we must have no matter how well other systems might promote other laudable values (Boaz 1997: 64–65; Hayek 1960: 87; Kirzner 1989: 7–10; Lomasky 1987: 123; Machan 2006b: 270–279; Narveson 1988: 99–101; Nozick 1974: 183–231; Rothbard 1982: 35–43). Supposedly, that liberty-promoting system is propertarian capitalism.

It is not.

This chapter has demonstrated that the establishment and maintenance of the private property regime that capitalism requires increases opportunities for some (especially those with the most property) by exposing others (especially those who have little or no property) to greater coercion than anyone would be subject to under a common property regime.

The most freedom-promoting regime known is the hunter-gatherer band economy. Some autonomous villages with common property regimes might be equally or nearly as free. Perhaps some populations in large-scale societies with common property regimes have experienced near that level of freedom. If you believe negative liberty is an overriding value that must be followed wherever it leads—even at the expense of other worthy values—then you must choose the hunter-gatherer band economy over the market economy.

Because the level of opportunity in band and autonomous village societies is so low, few people in state society will insist that the hunter-gatherer band economy is the only ethically acceptable form of socio-economic organization. Propertarians might like to tell themselves that making this opportunity-based concession is merely a technicality—a not-worth-mentioning deviation from their support for liberty. They would like to think that with one negligible loss of liberty, everyone shares in the enormous increase in work and consumption opportunities.

This strategy is no technical concession. It reveals fundamental flaws in the negative freedom argument for the market economy, and it is incapable of rescuing arguments for propertarian capitalism not only against the band economy but against alternatives involving greater taxation, regulation, redistribution, and public or common ownership of resources.

The loss of freedom involved in the establishment and maintenance of the unequal property rights system cannot be dismissed as negligible. The claimed moral minimalism of propertarianism is false. Lomasky (1987: 94–95, 146, 151), for example, argues that the negative duties involved in respecting other people's property rights are less burdensome than the supposedly more active duties of property owners when they pay their taxes and comply with trade regulations.

Many propertyless people have duties such as "don't eat," "don't build a shelter," "don't drink clean water." Although these duties are negative, they are also life-threatening, and to avoid them, middle- and lower-class people have to "get a job" (Machan 2006a: 273). That is, they must take a subordinate position often involving a lifetime of taking orders when they might prefer to be left alone with enough access to resources to be their own boss as most of their ancestors were for the last 200,000 years. These noncontractual obligations effectively force people to take subordinate positions serving the interest of at least one member of the property-owning group.

The belief that the legal system can interfere with people in a way that effectively forces them to "get a job" is inconsistent with delivering the values propertarianism supposedly promotes. It is inconsistent with the greatest equal freedom from coercion or with treating people as inviolable beings who "may not be sacrificed or used for the achieving of other ends without their consent" (Nozick 1974: 30–31). No system can be said to promote negative liberty if it forces people who are capable of living without taking orders into the position where they must take orders from superiors to survive—not to mention that the willingness to take orders is no assurance that a propertyless person will get out of poverty or homelessness.

This chapter has shown that alternative economic arrangements exist that subject *no one* to this level of coercion. People under the alternative arrangements are free to meet their basic needs without hearing an order throughout their entire lives. These alternative arrangements predated capitalism, survived for hundreds of thousands of years, and were replaced by capitalism in most places on Earth because of a long series of aggression, force, and coercion (see Chapters 10–15).

The market economy does not deserve the presumptive place it has been given in Western political dialogue as somehow more consistent with freedom than more equal systems. Some amount of taxation, regulation, and redistribution toward those most unfree in contemporary market societies increases negative freedom overall by compensating them for the coercion they are experiencing and restoring some of the freedom they have lost.

Propertarians usually deal with problems related to the coercion involved in the establishment and maintenance of the private property system by distracting attention as they switch from promoting freedom to promoting opportunity. For example, Nozick (1974: 175) sacrifices freedom for welfare writing, "the things I do with the grain of sand I appropriate might improve the position of others, counterbalancing their loss of the liberty to use that grain."

Mack (2002b: 247) writes, "one person's private acquisition need not involve diminished access for use by another." The market might provide her with goods "in more accessible form," than she could have obtained before the process of privatization began. But of course, "It will cost Sally something to rent (or buy) the [goods]; but it would have cost her something (in time and effort) to lay hands on the original material." Because Sally would have to expect "time and effort" to work as her own boss with direct access to resources, she might as well be forced to expend "time an effort" as the subordinate to a boss who can give her permission to access resources. Sally's loss in liberty goes unnoticed by this "libertarian" author.

The *only* gain these propertarians offer the disadvantaged (relative to the band economy) is not the negative freedom supposedly characterizing the market economy but the values of welfare and opportunity that propertarians almost universally reject as justification for interference with property owners.

If opportunity is what propertarianism is about, fine, but liberty is liberty, not equality or fairness or justice or human happiness or opportunity (paraphrasing Berlin 1969: 5). Freedom-as-increased-opportunity is not negative liberty.

Once propertarians appeal to opportunity as a justifying value of the market economy—no matter how much they distract attention from it—they cannot use negative liberty as a trump card to reject opportunity-promoting policies involving taxation, regulation, and redistribution. If it's morally acceptable to interfere with the most disadvantaged people in society to create opportunity for property owners, it must also be morally acceptable to interfere with property owners to create opportunities that compensate nonowners for that initial interference.

The opportunity-claim has another problem: it isn't true. Wealthy people in state societies have long had enormous opportunities that are unavailable in stateless societies, and in the last century or so most countries have gotten to the point at which the average person has the opportunity to live better than their brethren in small-scale stateless societies. But as our earlier book argued, the least advantaged people in contemporary state societies have opportunities that leave them worse-off than people in hunter-gatherer bands (Widerquist and McCall 2017).

Although band societies offer extremely limited opportunities, they offer two extremely attractive opportunities that capitalist states only offer to the wealthy few: the freedom from forced propertylessness and the opportunity to be one's own boss. Propertyless people in the market economy have to accept subordinate positions and save their money for years to "earn" the right to be their own boss. And only the lucky few make it. Many never get out of poverty or the fear of homelessness if they miss a few paychecks. Many die younger than necessary because of complications of poverty. People in band society are always their own boss. And they greatly value that ability. It is, therefore, hard to say whether contemporary capitalist economies or hunter-gatherer band economies offer more valuable opportunities overall. If we reformed the contemporary economy to have greater equal opportunity, it could easily surpass the opportunities available in the band economy. Unfortunately, all or most state societies have failed to do so (Widerquist and McCall 2017).

This comparison between the negative freedom arguments for the market and band economies reveals that propertarian arguments against redistribution fail. A significant amount of redistribution within industrial society is freedom-enhancing, because it relieves the least free group in the market economy from the onerous level of coercion they face. It reduces the noncontractual obligations imposed on lower- and middle-class people. It restores some of the access to resources that people lose when a private property regime replaces a common property regime. Therefore, it can free people from forced subordination and create greater equal freedom than capitalism without redistribution.

This chapter has not compared the band economy to all conceivable theoretical alternatives, but it has given some indication about the difficulty of exceeding the band economy in terms of negative freedom.

Although band society provides an extremely low bar for comparisons of *individual welfare* (Widerquist and McCall 2017), this chapter has shown that band society provides an extremely high bar for comparisons of *individual freedom*. Band (and other small-scale) societies coerce their members so little that it is hard to envision an alternative with less coercion. A successful alternative would have to allow individuals to go through their lives, successfully maintaining themselves, without obeying the orders of others if they did not want to. It is possible that some large-scale alternative might exceed the hunter-gatherer band in opportunity and equal it in negative liberty. However, such an alternative is likely to be very different to the well-known options of capitalism, welfare-state capitalism, and socialism, all of which involve significant supervision of disadvantaged people.

If we want to reduce coercion in society, we have to concede power to the least privileged individuals. The final chapter of this book discusses that issue further.

Part Three

The individual appropriation hypothesis

Chapter 7

CONTEMPORARY PROPERTY THEORY: A STORY, A MYTH, A PRINCIPLE, AND A HYPOTHESIS

People arguing for unequal private property rights usually tell a fictional story set in the Stone Age. Locke's (1960 [1689]: "Second Treatise," chapter 5, §24–51)[1] version has been repeated since 1689. Before any government comes into existence, an individual goes into a virgin wilderness, clears a piece of land, plants crops, and thereby appropriates full ownership of that piece of land. From that starting point, property is traded, gifted, and bequeathed in ways that lead to something very much like the current distribution of property in a market economy.

Propertarians tell this story along with a set of moral principles that would justify the titles of anyone with an unbroken chain of just transfers connecting their title to the original appropriator. Then they admit no such chain exists; the story is fiction; but the private property system is justified anyway. Why is it justified anyway? What does this story have to do with the actual justification? Is this story purely for illustration? If so, what does it illustrate exactly? Which of the hypothetical claims in the story function as premises in the argument, and are those premises true? If the story has nothing to do with it, why has it been retold for 350 years? Apparently, the story is meant to do something, to be—somehow—relevant for the ethical justification of strong, individual private property rights.

This chapter uses textual analysis to argue that the story illustrates a moral principle and an empirical hypothesis, which play important

---

[1] Further reference to Locke's *Two Treatises* are to the "Second Treatise" and are identified by their paragraph number with the symbol, "§".

roles in the propertarian argument for strong private property rights. These claims are used even by propertarians who prefer not to repeat the story. We summarize this argument as follows.

1. **The appropriation principle**: People have a natural right of "appropriation": some method, by which individuals (alone or in groups) can create morally binding property rights over previously unowned external assets—land, natural resources, and the things people make out of them.
2. **The individual appropriation hypothesis**: If people were allowed to appropriate resources, in the absence of interference, an unequal, individual property rights system would develop.
3. Therefore, government or collective taxation, regulation, or redistribution is an infringement on private property rights.
4. Therefore, ethical limits exist on the use of such powers.

Proposition 1, "the appropriation principle," is a normative value. Proposition 2, "the individual appropriation hypothesis," is an empirical claim. This chapter and the next two argue that this hypothesis is necessary to support Propositions 3 and 4: although many different versions of the appropriation hypothesis exist, there is no way to go from Proposition 1 to Propositions 3 and 4 without some empirical claim about the origin and development of property. Propertarians who try to distance themselves from Lockean theory, the appropriation story, and claims about the origin of the property system either resort to special pleading or fall back on some version of the hypothesis. The belief that government or collective action necessarily infringes private property requires the empirical claim(s) that private entities *do* and collective entities *do not* appropriate full or partial property rights in their territories.

As Chapter 9 argues, the appropriation story does not work as a metaphor for anything that modern appropriators do. It plays both a substantive role and a (hopefully unintentional) propagandistic, mythmaking role. Its substantive role is to illustrate and to suggest the plausibility of an essential empirical premise in the natural rights defense of private property. The story is repeated as neither literal truth nor metaphor, but as an indicator of what propertarians claim is likely and unlikely.

The appropriation story's mythmaking role is to induce people to ask *how could it be otherwise?* "Land can only be appropriated, runs the usually tacit assumption, by individuals" (Carson 2011: 3). The history in Chapters 10–14 reveals many ways it could be otherwise. Collective and possibly even monarchical appropriation are more likely than private appropriation.

Yet, over the past 350 years, the story has shielded the appropriation hypothesis from recognition and, therefore, from scrutiny. Although the appropriation story and the appropriation principle are well known, the appropriation hypothesis has no name and no clear specification. Propertarians, who explicitly endorse the appropriation *principle*, tend to be less clear about whether they affirm the appropriation *hypothesis* or whether they believe there is some way to go from Proposition 1 to Propositions 3 and 4 without relying on an empirical claim. Often, they jump from explaining the principle to telling the story, giving it an ambiguous role, seeming either to affirm the empirical truth of the hypothesis or to deny the need for one.

The absence of attention to the hypothesis allows people to think either that it's obviously true or that it's not a necessary premise in the argument at all without being clear which of those two very different things they believe. The lack of clarity might be rhetorically powerful, but it's sloppy philosophy. Propertarian use of the appropriation principle, story, and hypothesis is so sloppy that this book needs three chapters to show that propertarianism requires some version of the empirical claim we call the individual appropriation hypothesis.

Therefore, the appropriation hypothesis (rather than the story, myth, or principle) is the focus of our analysis. This chapter shows how the hypothesis typically appears in the rights-based justification of unequal private property rights (sections 1 and 2) and discusses what forms that hypothesis might take (section 3). Chapter 8 summarizes the history of people tacitly or explicitly using the appropriation hypothesis from its modern origins to the present. Chapter 9 addresses attempts to rule out collective ownership of land in pure theory.

Therefore, the natural rights justification of private property is not a pure, a priori normative theory. It is an applied theory. Propertarianism has to stand on the premise that, although propertarian principles cannot rule out the possibility that other property systems might develop from appropriation, any such development is empirically so improbable that it can be safely ignored. This hypothesis involves far-reaching empirical claims about what is likely and unlikely to happen across all cultures and across time from our earliest prehistory to the present. Far-reaching claims require strong evidence. Chapters 10–15 address the evidence to demonstrate that the appropriation hypothesis is false. This finding has important implications, not only for propertarian extremists, but for anyone who believes taxation, regulation, and redistribution of property involve even a minor infringement on natural rights.

1. FOUR PRINCIPLES OF PROPERTARIAN JUSTICE

Under propertarian theory, if a territory-holding corporation collects rent from occupants of the land it controls and imposes rules for what they can do on that land, the corporation is presumed to be justly exercising its property rights. The interaction is, therefore, labeled voluntary. If the corporation's history is corrupt in a relevant way, it might be unjustly exercising a property claim, but one central belief of propertarianism is that individuals, partnerships, and corporations can hold such property rights consistently with individual freedom and any relevant principles of justice.

Under the same theory, if a territory-holding government collects taxes from occupants of the land it controls and imposes rules for what they can do on that land, the government is presumed to be unjustly interfering with private property rights. The interaction is, therefore, labeled involuntary. No one needs to prove a specific allegation of corruption; one central belief of propertarianism is that any such action by a government or any other collective entity necessarily infringes relevant principles of justice and reduces human freedom overall.

Why is the corporation presumed to *exercise* its rights, while the government is presumed to *infringe* others' rights, when both do very much the same thing (Widerquist 2009a)?

Propertarians present detailed theories of property, but we intend to show that they don't usually address this question clearly. Often, they ignore it entirely, presume the answer, or resort to special pleading. The most straightforward answers rely on the individual appropriation hypothesis.

This section outlines propertarian theory using Nozick's (1974) "historical entitlement theory" as a guide. Not everyone who uses rights-based justifications of private property is a Nozickian, but his thorough exposition makes an excellent reference point for a discussion of variations of the idea throughout this book.

Nozick (1974: 150–153) explains three normative principles of justice in the distribution of property or as he calls it, "justice in holdings." These are "original acquisition" (more commonly called "original appropriation"), voluntary transfer, and rectification. We argue below that propertarianism is logically committed to a fourth, often tacit, principle we call "statute of limitations" (Widerquist 2009a).

Some propertarians discuss other principle(s) of justice, called "nonaggression" or "noninterference." In operation, all they imply is that the other rights have no exceptions. To say that rights violations constitute interference or aggression provides a description of rights violations but adds nothing to the operation of the theory (Christmas 2018; Zwolinski 2016). Therefore, we focus on the four principles that are operationally determinant. However, even a purely descriptive role for the noninterference or nonaggression principle(s) might have importance. They might describe an underlying motivation for the other principles: perhaps people should care about appropriation, voluntary transfer, rectification, and statute of limitations because they reflect a deeper desire for noninterference and nonaggression.

Nozick (1974: 151) argues that "historical entitlement theory" of justice in holdings is "not patterned," meaning that a society has to follow these principles wherever they lead—whether they lead to basic equality or extreme stratification. Justice has nothing to do with the pattern of the distribution of property rights; justice is entirely in the history of how the current distribution came to be. These principles, "exhaustively cover the subject of justice in holdings" (p. 157).

What is wrong with a property-owning government—or a property-owning people—holding full or partial ownership of their territory, and the accompanying rights to tax, regulate, or redistribute their territory as other landlords do with theirs? Nozick (1974: 322) writes, "A face-to-face community can exist on land jointly owned by its members, whereas the land of a nation is not so held." If the theory is truly unpatterned, how do we know "the land of a nation is not" and can never be "so held?"

If the theory is truly historical, one would expect that any effort to rule out government ownership rights would involve an empirical, historical investigation, but Nozick's argument remains theoretical and hypothetical. It seems difficult for four unpatterned historical principles to conceptually rule out the possibility of any landholding entity including a property-owning government. Yet, clear, straightforward answers to that question are hard to find in propertarian literature (see Chapters 8–9).

Consider Nozick's four principles in light of this question: he explores appropriation most thoroughly. In simple terms, the appropriation principle allows people to unilaterally establish morally binding rights over a previously unowned resource. Any appropriation principle requires an appropriation criterion: the thing(s) the appropriator has to do to establish a property right. The criterion accounts for most of the variation in the retelling of the appropriation story as theorists change it to fit their appropriation criterion(s) (Attas 2005: 81).

Locke's (1960 [1689]) criterion, usually called "first labor" or "labor-mixing," is the most popular: the first person(s) to transform an unowned resource by labor appropriates it. Usually the transformation is understood to improve the value of the resource, but it might not always be so. Mining, for example, often devalues land. The story involves appropriators laboring themselves, but the theory allows them to use hired labor. Nozick (1974: 174–178), Rothbard (1982: 34, 49, 56–58), and Boaz (1997: 65–74) retell Locke's story and at least tentatively endorse his criterion.

Israel Kirzner (1989: 16–18, 152–155) replaces first labor with discovery and/or a finders-keepers ethic. His stories involve people finding seashells on the beach or leading voyages of discovery. Narveson (1988: 11) endorses something like first use, first claim, or first occupancy. Richard Epstein's (1995: 60–62) principle of relative title essentially adapts these into prior use, claim, or occupancy. Lomasky's (1987: 130) appropriation criteria (in which someone appropriates a thing by coming to possess, use, and value it) is close to relative title or prior claim. Edward Feser (2005) endorses any and all criteria in his article, "There is No Such Thing as an Unjust Initial Acquisition."

Nozick (1974: 178–182), like most propertarians, includes a side constraint along with his appropriation criterion. Nozick calls it "the Lockean proviso." It is satisfied if everyone living under the property system is at least as well-off as they would be if land remained a commons (accessible to all but owned by none). This proviso was the main subject of our earlier book (Widerquist and McCall 2017), but it plays little role in the discussion here.

Neither Locke nor Nozick specifies exactly what rights people obtain in the assets they appropriate, but the usual presumption is "full liberal ownership," which (see Chapter 1) includes the right to possess, the right to use, the right to manage, the right to income, the right to capital, the right to security, transmissibility, absence of term, the duty to prevent harm, the liability to execution, and residuary character (Honoré 1987: 161–175).

"Classical liberals" (such as Locke) believe that people agree to some limited infringement of full ownership as part of the social contract. Contemporary propertarians tend to believe all or most such powers are serious violations of ownership rights. Owners create individual property and give it value before collectives come along and steal some of it, or so the story goes.

The principle of voluntary transfer follows directly once the appropriator assumes full liberal ownership. The rights to sell or give away property follow from the right to manage, the right to income, and transmissibility. The right to bequeath property follows from these incidents combined with property's residuary character and absence of term.

Nozick does not specify the rectification principle, merely noting that there must be some process by which violations of the appropriation and transfer principles are corrected. We also spend little time on this principle, because although it is important to determining who owns what, it is not relevant for the justification of the system.

These three principles alone are not capable of justifying any current or future property holdings, because they literally work only for someone with an unbroken chain of voluntary transfers and/or justified rectifications connecting their ownership to original appropriation. Little or no property in the world today can be traced back in such a way. The history of most property involves rights violations that are not rectifiable with the information available today because no one can know who are the heirs of the disappropriated. If there were literally only three principles by which one could obtain property, most of the land of the world would be off limits to all living human beings. It would forever wait for the appearance of the rightful heirs to past wrongs.

Therefore, propertarians are logically committed to some "statute-of-limitations principle," by which we mean some way in which the legal system can justly decide *not* to rectify past wrongs (Widerquist 2010a). It can take several forms including a time limit on rectification of past wrongs, relative title, adverse possession, or abandonment and reappropriation (Epstein 1995: 64–67; Lomasky 1987: 145–146;

Rothbard 1982: 63; Widerquist 2009a). Our term, "statute of limita-tions," is a bit idiosyncratic because not all of these principles involve a specific time limit as statute-of-limitations laws usually do, but it's an adequate summary term.

Nozick does not explicitly mention a statute-of-limitations prin-ciple. He might have thought it was covered by rectification, yet the two ideas are different. One principle says how to repair past wrongs; the other says when to ignore them. Some of Nozick's (1974: 158) statements imply tacit endorsement. His Henry Ford example clearly appeals to it, mentioning the possibility that, "the operation of the system washes out any significant effects from the initial set of hold-ings," but he does not fully endorse that conclusion. Nozick's (1974: 160) slogan "from each as they choose, to each as they are chosen," is meant to summarize his entitlement theory, but he prefaces it by saying "ignoring acquisition and rectification," implying that his the-ory is really about letting contemporary transactions happen without regard to the distant history of assets. He discusses the problem of missing historical information, suggesting that something like a short-run Rawlsian difference principle can serve to justify property in the absence of the necessary historical information to properly rectify past wrongs (Nozick 1974: 230–231), implying some statute-of-limitations principle (see section 2).

Propertarian literature contains many explicit or tacit versions of the statute-of-limitations principle. Feser (2005: 79) argues that most past injustices simply aren't rectifiable. Kirzner (1989: 154, 4–6) at one point seems to rule out the legitimacy of the statute-of-limitations principle, but at another point he employs it in effect by setting aside the question of whether current property rights are justly constituted or justly held. Rothbard (1982: 63) endorses an idea similar to aban-donment and reappropriation, writing, "where the victims are lost in antiquity, the land properly belongs to any non-criminals who are in current possession."

Epstein (1995: 64–67) thoroughly describes several possible statute-of-limitations principles and argues that some such principle is necessary for any property system to work. He offers an important specification of relative title: A cannot claim property against B because B (or B's ancestors) stole it from C. Only C (or C's heirs) can make that claim. If B's title is older than A's, B's claim beats A's.

The statute-of-limitations principle (however specified) is important to propertarian theory, because it is the reason that this "historical" theory can ignore the actual facts of history. It is part of the reason the theory jumps from a story set in the Stone Age to an endorsement of a specific property rights system. If that system is the one that would develop in the absence of unrectifiable rights violations, the people who have worked in good faith to obtain property within it shouldn't be dispossessed. But our question remains: does propertarian capitalism at all resemble the system that would have developed in the absence of rights violations?

2. THE NEED FOR AN EMPIRICAL PREMISE

Nozick (1974: 293) backs up his vision for the property rights system with "hypothetical histories." He describes this methodology:

> How should hypothetical histories affect our current judgment of the institutional structure of a society? . . . If the actual history of an existing society is unjust, and *no* hypothetical just history could lead to the structure of that society, then that structure is unjust. More complicated are the cases where the actual history of a society is unjust yet some hypothetical just history could have led to its current structure. If the hypothetical just history is "close" to the actual history, whose injustices played no significant role in bringing about or maintaining the institutional structure, the actual structure will be as just as one can expect to get.

This passage explains why propertarians have repeated the Lockean appropriation story since 1689. It's a hypothetical history purporting to demonstrate the plausibility of the individual appropriation hypothesis—the counterfactual claim that a just history *could have* led to a propertarian structure. The passage also implies the need for a statute of limitations for "cases where the actual history of a society is unjust yet some hypothetical just history could have led to its current structure" (Nozick 1974: 293).

If this is how hypothetical histories are used, then they have substantial empirical content. Nozick assumes readers can determine whether hypothetical stories are "'close' to the actual history" and, if not, whether they "could have led to [the] current structure." To do that, readers must instantly recognize what could and could not have happened—to separate plausible and implausible counterfactual stories about events that occurred hundreds or thousands of years ago in very unfamiliar circumstances. That sounds difficult. Let's try.

Nozick (1974: 10–25, 276–294) begins with the Lockean appropriation story. We call it "Hypothetical History 1": before any state society comes into existence, primordial individual appropriators mix their labor with that land and obtain full ownership of it. This story provides a plausible-sounding account of how a private-property-based economy might come into existence without violating propertarian principles. Next, Nozick tells another in which a propertarian state, which he calls a "minimal" state, arises justly out of a private protective association. He pronounces it plausible. He then tells two more stories in which a more-than-minimal state arises unjustly or with implausible assumptions.

Nozick's (1974: 10–25, 276–294) three hypothetical histories about government all begin with full liberal ownership rights in place via Locke's appropriation story. With this starting point, the government's assertion of territorial ownership rights unsurprisingly infringes existing property rights. Therefore, the individual appropriation hypothesis is doing all the work. All four stories rely on the empirical claim that private appropriation happens before collective territorial claims come into existence. Without that claim, Nozick's stories cannot connect his three principles with his limits on government.

Yet, Nozick (1974: 10–25, 276–294), like most propertarians, calls little attention to this premise in his argument and provides no empirical support for it. Without referring to any historical evidence, he asserts the empirical premise that the Lockean appropriation story is "'close' to the actual history," or at least that such a history is counterfactually plausible and "could have led to" a propertarian structure even if "the actual history of [it] is unjust."

If propertarianism were the only just structure that could plausibly develop from appropriation, one could draw the inference that the statute of limitations should be applied only to property claims that maintain this structure—i.e. to private property claims but not to collective, communal, or governmental property claims. Chapter 8 uses this interpretation as it examines the history of the appropriation story and hypothesis. Chapter 9 examines whether propertarians have another way to make their case.

A discussion of four hypotheticals is certainly not an exhaustive search for plausible alternatives. Does *evidence* indicate that propertarianism is the only structure that could develop from appropriation?

Whether one hypothetical history is more plausible than another is an empirical question. Yet, like most propertarians, Nozick (1974: 174–178, 293–294) suggests no investigation, expecting readers to share his presumptions. Real history drops out of his effort to rule out a pattern of holdings with one big national landlord using an unpatterned, "historical" theory that supposedly "depends on what actually has happened" (Nozick 1974: 152).

Nozick (1974: 178) challenges people who support other forms of property to "provide a theory of how such property rights arise." In that case, consider what we call Hypothetical Histories 2 and 3 (Widerquist 2009a).

Hypothetical History 2: An individual appropriator, following relevant provisos, chooses not to transfer any rights to a protective association. She sets herself up as both owner and governor of her estate. In the absence of any higher government, the power to do so follows from the eleven incidents of full liberal ownership—most especially the rights to possess, use, manage, income, and capital. She might begin with a small estate as a family farmer. She might start with a large estate by paying laborers to irrigate arid land, to build dykes around a low-lying area, or to join her on a voyage of discovery. She attracts tenants to her land for the same primary reason any other landlord attracts tenants: because she has land and they don't. She bestows on them a form of limited, quasi-ownership she calls "title" with the understanding that titles are held at her pleasure and are subject to her fees and rules. She gradually enlarges her estate through strategic marriage alliance, primogeniture, and rectification after defensive wars until one day her estate is the size of England. By then, she has decided to call herself "the Queen" rather than "owner" and to call everyone else "subjects" rather than "tenants," but the nature of her ownership and her tenants' quasi-ownership have not changed (Widerquist 2009a).

The Queen is essentially a landholding monarch: her power is justified neither by divine right nor by social contract but by her appropriation-based property rights over her country, which is really just a very large private estate. She might eventually give or bequeath her estate to a democratic assembly representing her subjects. She might aggress against her subjects' self-ownership—such as it is for the propertyless (Widerquist 2013)—causing a group of subjects to fight a defensive war and jointly gain control of her state in rectification for that crime. Or, she and her heirs might remain property-owning monarchs with a just title to the land forever.

Hypothetical History 3: A group of willing people gets together and jointly discovers, uses, occupies, mixes their labor with, or does whatever else is necessary under propertarian theory to appropriate a piece of land, with the intention of holding it collectively. They follow any relevant provisos. People who do not want to participate in the act of appropriation have as much and as good left in the wilderness as people who do not appropriate property in the more familiar Lockean story. In accordance with the common understanding of joint ownership, anyone (including individual heirs of the original appropriation group) who later wishes to use this group's land must accept the group's terms just as any tenant (including a shareholder) must agree to any landlord's terms. The group chooses not to join any protective association and constitutes itself as a self-protecting polity. It is a corporate landownership association, which calls itself a "government" and calls its shareholders "citizens."

The citizens are essentially a landowning polity—that is, a government whose powers stem not from social contract but from appropriation-based property rights over their land, which is really just a large jointly owned estate. The polity might grow by merging with similar polities or by gaining territory through rectification after defensive wars. Eventually, the group parcels out some of its land to individuals, creating a quasi-ownership called "title," with the understanding that these "titles" confer limited ownership, subject to the groups' ultimate ownership and the taxation, regulation, and redistribution that go with group ownership, under the polity's contract they call a "constitution."

These two examples carry all the way through from original appropriation to nationwide community ownership of property, but a simpler aspect of Hypothetical History 3 might be more important: individual property does not necessarily begin as full liberal and individual ownership; full liberal ownership might begin in the community's hands, leaving it up to the group whether to privatize it on a full or limited basis.

Propertarians accept the possibility of joint tenure and weaker forms of ownership, in which different parties own different incidents. But they presume that original appropriators establish full liberal ownership. It is up to them to decide whether to divide it, and few, if any, titleholders have signed any incidents of ownership over to governments. Under these presumptions, the ethical debate becomes whether appropriation or some other principle is the valid way to establish property rights. This debate appears against the often unnoticed and unquestioned background assumption that appropriators and subsequent traders tend to establish and maintain full liberal and individual ownership.

Without historical investigation, no one can know whether original appropriators behaved more like the individuals in Hypothetical Histories 1, 2, or 3. In most of the world, the event in question took place in the Stone Age. Our everyday lives in capitalist economies do not give us insight into what kinds of property institutions were useful to the first people to discover, occupy, use, or mix their labor with land and resources. Their actions and intentions cannot be "obvious."

The Lockean appropriation story presents a hypothesis about appropriation as if it could not be otherwise. As a myth, it limits our thinking. It makes it difficult to pose the question: were original appropriators individuals seeking to establish full liberal ownership on an individual basis; were they individuals seeking to establish monarchies; or were they groups seeking to establish some other form of property? A fictional story—making very culturally-specific assumptions about appropriators' choices—does not answer this question.

If we carry these hypothetical histories through to the formation of government, they show it developing full state powers as a landholding institution, similar to a corporation. In neither case does the government violate the principles of propertarian justice in holdings—appropriation, voluntary transfer, rectification, or statute of limitations.

A property-owning government can hold whatever portion of its land publicly as a commons or as some other joint enterprise. It could confer full liberal ownership on individuals; but forcing a property-owning government to establish a private property system—against the will of its citizens—would be an act of aggression in violation of their rights as property owners.

Of course, these hypothetical histories aren't literally true. Contemporary governments can't trace their territorial claims in an unbroken chain of voluntary transfers and just rectifications to original appropriation. But neither can private titleholders. *Both* must appeal to a statute of limitations. Indeed, Hypothetical Histories 2 and 3 should be taken as literally (and conversely as figuratively) as the Lockean story.

Unless propertarians can find some principle to rule out a property-owning government, they need the premise(s) that Hypothetical History 1 is plausible but 2 and 3 are not—i.e. they need the appropriation hypothesis. As the next two chapters show, propertarians tend to deal with that issue by ignoring it or by not taking it seriously. They focus instead on theoretical justifications of unequal patterns of strong *private* holdings without seriously considering whether the same justifications might also support the pattern in which a community jointly holds full or partial ownership of territory. They treat the government as a non-property-holding institution trying to alter a pattern of private titles voters might dislike rather than as a big landholding institution that reflects a pattern of private titles propertarians dislike. Critics seldom call them on it.

Perhaps philosophers on both sides of the issue are distracted by their own myths. The founding myth of the state is not about appropriation; it's about the signing of a social contract to bring peace where there would otherwise be chaos.

We don't *think* of these stories as myths. We think of them as "illustrative examples." But the myths with real power are the ones we don't notice—the ones that affect our thinking in ways we seldom recognize and therefore seldom challenge. The most effective myths keep people from asking the right questions.

We don't *think* of states or peoples as institutions capable of possessing appropriated rights. That's the private property owners' story. We *think* of the state as something that attempts (or pretends) to be a neutral rule-keeper in accordance with an imaginary contract, policing property rights that are inherently private. We don't *think* of titleholders as the community's tenants. That's not one of the classic just-so stories of political philosophy.

To fully consider the connection between propertarian principles and the private property system, the question cannot simply be *who* appropriated property. It must be *what* kinds of property institutions did the original appropriators establish, and *how* did those institutions transform into the existing property system?

3. IDENTIFYING THE INDIVIDUAL APPROPRIATION HYPOTHESIS

Propertarians seldom, if ever, specifically define the appropriation hypothesis. The appropriation story provides minimal help. Consider the hypothetical empirical claims it contains.

1. **Although foraging tends to precede agriculture, farmers are the first to significantly transform land.** More simply, farming transforms land; foraging does not.
2. **Original appropriators are individuals acting as individuals establishing individual private property rights.** That is, they are

not groups acting as collectives or commonwealths to establish common or collective property rights; they are not individuals acting as monarchs to establish themselves as both owner and sovereign.

3. **Individual appropriation happens in "the state of nature,"** outside of and usually before the appearance of any political entity with territorial sovereignty.
4. **Property remains private as it is transferred over time.** Trade, bequests, and gifts of external assets produce private rather than collective or common ownership.
5. **Governments or collectives establish territorial claims after appropriation and by means other than appropriation.** Government is usually thought of as arising by conquest or by social contract.

That's a lot of hypotheticals. The story is presented as if it helps explain why the private property system is justified even without a literal connection to appropriation. Even propertarians who don't tell this story claim that the justification of the property system has *something* to do with appropriation (Lomasky 1987: 130). Therefore, we need to know which of these claims are relevant, what they illustrate, and whether the things they illustrate are true.

Although this story has been retold for 350 years, our review finds no significant attention to any of these claims—neither to clarify which ones are and are not important nor to investigate whether the important ones are true or false. Supporters and opponents alike usually ignore them entirely, assume they're true, or assume they're irrelevant (usually without explaining how a story can be relevant when none of its claims are). We hope this discussion helps clean up this sloppy philosophy. The lack of clarity forces our investigation to address alternative formulations of the hypothesis. We find a basket of empirical claims that might—alone or in various combinations—connect propertarian ethical principles and conclusions.

The following three versions of the hypothesis are good summaries of the propertarian outlook, but they're too vague to be investigated empirically.

- Private property rights are natural; collective and communal rights are not.
- Only private property develops naturally; collective or common property does not.

John Hasnas (2005), David Schmidtz (1994), and others take natural-istic approaches that we used to specify more testable versions of the hypothesis (see Chapter 10):

- People who are free from aggression almost always establish property rights systems based on full liberal ownership.
- Collective property-holding institutions do not tend to come into existence or to remain in existence long without violating the appropriation and transfer principles.
- In a world free from violations of the appropriation and transfer principles, only the private appropriation and accumulation of property rights is plausible (i.e. collective, communal, or government accumulation of property rights is implausible).
- Private property rights tend to arise spontaneously (i.e. without centralized decisions or hierarchical enforcement) in response to collective action problems, such as the tragedy of the commons. They tend not to be created and allotted by polities making centralized decisions to solve collective action problems.

If "natural" means "without violations of the principles of appropria-tion and voluntary transfer," these statements are equivalent to the following claim:

- Private property develops naturally and collective, public, com-mon, or government property does not.

However, not all natural rights justifications of property necessarily share a unified conception of the word "natural."

A time-based version of the appropriation hypothesis is specific enough to be testable:

- Before governments or any other collective institutions appear, individuals acting as private individuals to establish private property rights appropriate all or most resources.

This version is probably the most common, but it might be over-specified, because timing might not be the most important factor.

Carson (2011: 3), a critic of the hypothesis, drops timing from the definition:

- "Land can only be appropriated . . . by individuals."

This statement is vague. We interpret it to mean:

- Even if collective property *claims* come first, only private individuals acting as private entities perform appropriative acts (i.e. discover, occupy, use, claim, or mix their labor with unowned resources).

Equivalently,
- The people involved in collective entities consistently fail to meet the appropriation criteria necessary to give their claims ethical legitimacy as property *rights*.

Although we call it the *individual* appropriation hypothesis, the distinction between individual and group appropriation is not as important as the distinction between private and collective, public, or government appropriation.

- Only people acting as private entities perform appropriative acts.

This claim implies four others:

- Individuals intending to set themselves up as private owners perform appropriative acts.
- Individuals intending to set themselves up as monarchs don't perform appropriative acts.
- Groups intending to establish private corporations or partnerships (might) perform appropriative acts.
- Groups intending to establish collective-, public-, or government-held property rights do not perform appropriative acts.

Although we call it the *appropriation* hypothesis, it is as much about subsequent transfers:

- Transfers of titles are likely to maintain the private character of property rights (e.g. private traders never obtain enough land to become viable monarchs).
- Even if collectives perform appropriative acts, subsequent transfers (in the absence of rights violations) eventually produce private property rights.

If any of these specifications is correct, empirical investigation into the origin of property rights will show a pattern in which property tends to begin privately or to become private, and it tends to remain private unless force is asserted over it. Of course, historical investigation will show rampant rights violations (under almost any theory of rights). But, if the hypothesis is true, investigation will reveal a pattern of continually thwarted attempts to establish and maintain private property and few if any attempts to establish collective rights except as a means to assert control over existing private rights.

How governments or other collective entities are established is not as important as what existed before. At some point, historical investigation would have to show monarchs, governments, or collectives asserting control over resources that are held *privately* not just over resources held by other collective institutions. Investigation would be likely to find the relevant appropriative acts being performed by individuals, acting as individuals. It would be unlikely to find those acts performed by individuals acting as petty monarchs or by groups acting collectively as bands, tribes, villages, clans, peoples, ethnic groups, or governments. Or it would find that such collective appropriators begin to see themselves as business owners rather than as collective polities. They would then begin to treat their land as a commodity and get it into market circulation.

If this historical pattern exists, it indicates private property is a universal value and that collective property comes only at its expense. If so, the hypothesis successfully connects propertarians' ethical premises with their conclusions about the just pattern of ownership.

If such evidence is absent, the appropriation hypothesis should be rejected as unproven. In that case, the normative principles say nothing useful about existing rights in the world.

If evidence indicates that groups performing appropriative acts tend to establish collective property rights, and/or that individuals acting as monarchs tend to perform appropriative acts, and/or that private property rights tend to originate in acts of force rather than acts of appropriation, propertarian ethical principles imply something very different than most property rights literature presumes. If so, propertarian principles actually support collective, public, or government ownership of significant territorial rights. Private property rights might not put any ethical limits on government powers to tax, regulate, and redistribute private property.

These patterns are the main things to look for in the investigation in Chapters 10–14, but we can also look for evidence for some of the related claims that come up in the theoretical discussion throughout this chapter as well as Chapters 8 and 9. These include:

- Unappropriated resources are useless or nearly useless.
- Farmers (and perhaps some commercial landowners) are the first to significantly transform land (i.e. foragers do not).
- Private property rights tend to arise without aggression against groups holding land collectively (i.e. their establishment is not usually a method to take power and wealth from indigenous peoples).
- First possession has held a unique position in all past times as the organizing principle of most social institutions (Epstein 1978–1979: 1241).
- The history of the limited private property rights system that exists today will show continuously thwarted attempts to establish systems based on full liberal ownership without the limits implied by collective rights to tax, regulate, or redistribute titles.

Many of these claims are important only to certain specifications of appropriation theory, and some of them are not essential to any version—merely lending support to one of its premises. Chapters 10–15 deal with these claims as they come up, showing that all of them are false.

4. CONCLUSION

Most propertarians seem to believe either that the appropriation hypothesis is obviously true or that it is irrelevant because their theory somehow rules out the possibility of the peoples' ownership of full or partial property rights in their territory on a priori grounds. This ambiguity probably helps protect the hypothesis from more serious scrutiny. If evidence points against the hypothesis, imagine the argument as a priori; if the a priori argument seems weak, imagine that the necessary empirical premises are obviously true.

Once the conceptual possibility of a property-owning government is established, it becomes apparent that propertarians are trying to use an unpatterned theory to justify a pattern of ownership. They want to justify a pattern in which certain human-created institutions—such as corporations, partnerships, or marriages—can and do own property but other human-created institutions—such as governments, polities, nations, collectives, or ethnic groups—cannot or simply do not own property. How do they establish this pattern with only four normative premises to draw on?

If your answer is that the Lockean story is plausible and Hypothetical Histories 2 and 3 are implausible, you are willing to rely on the empirical truth of the appropriation hypothesis. You can skip the next two chapters and go on to our consideration of evidence in Chapters 10–15. If you need more convincing that the argument requires an empirical claim, Chapters 8–9 are for you.

Chapter 8

THE HISTORY OF AN HYPOTHESIS

This chapter reviews the history of the individual appropriation hypothesis from its seventeenth-century origins to the present to show how it became a background assumption in contemporary political theory. The history of appropriation theory and the appropriation story are intertwined with the history of the hypothesis.

1. ORIGINS OF THE APPROPRIATION HYPOTHESIS

The concept of individual appropriation goes back at least as far as Roman law (Epstein 1995; Gaius 1904: 160). Montesquieu (2001) attributes the time-based version of the hypothesis to "Cicero [who] maintains that . . . the community was established with no other view than that every one might be able to preserve his property." But more often ancient and medieval philosophers based justifications of property on virtue ethics. The origin and development of property rights only became important to the discussion in the early modern period (Waldron 2012).

Thomas More, Hugo Grotius, and Samuel von Pufendorf all contributed to the development of the appropriation principle, story, and hypothesis. According to Carole Pateman and Charles Mills (2007: 47), "More . . . described occupied and uncultivated land as 'worthless,' as waste, vacant, empty, virgin, wilderness—as *terra nullius* [nobody's land]—that may rightfully be appropriated for productive use." Pufendorf also argues that the good things on Earth are useless until people acquire property rights in them—a claim that is often used as a justification for appropriation. Grotius briefly discussed appropriation as a way to attain property in the state of nature, but it might not give rise to any legal right. Both of them apparently attributed the origin of property to a mix of appropriation and social agreement (Olivecrona 1974: 213–217).

147

2. JOHN LOCKE

Locke's (1960 [1689]) appropriation story begins in "the state of nature," which, importantly for him, is not only a place without government but also a time before government. Natural rights, including the right of appropriation, exist in Locke's state of nature. Chapter 7 describes his appropriation story and his criterion usually called "first labor" or "labor-mixing." He also asserts three provisos involving charity, leaving opportunities for others, avoiding waste (Widerquist 2010a). Only the waste proviso plays a significant role in this discussion (see below).

Locke (1960 [1689]: §37) justified his criterion in part by drawing on Pufendorf and More's assertion that unimproved resources are nearly useless with most or all of the value of property coming from the appropriator who invests some of her self-ownership in an otherwise valueless object. Although past owners and paid laborers have contributed to the current value of an external object, the current owner is the rightful holder of that value in propertarian theory because those parties voluntarily transferred their claims to the current owner by sale, gift, or bequest.

Locke's (1960 [1689]: §42–45, §123, §134–135, §138) story continues to the establishment of government "by compact and agreement" of individuals motivated partly to protect existing unequal property holdings. In this way, the time-based version of the hypothesis appears in the story. Scholars of Locke disagree about what he intended to happen to property when government was established. Some interpretations suggest he believed property ultimately becomes subject to social agreement. But the majority opinion is that he believed pre-existing private property rights put at least some limits on governments' authority to tax, regulate, and redistribute property (Widerquist 2010a).

Although Locke (1960 [1689]) did not intend for the entire story to be taken literally, he did not explain exactly what a largely fictional story has to do with the justification of the private property system, when his theory, as stated, seems to depend on the literal truth of the story. Interpreters disagree whether the story is a metaphor for something modern owners do or whether it is a fiction meant to tell a greater truth and exactly what that greater truth is (Widerquist 2010a).

There are three reasons why some aspects of Locke's appropriation story call for empirical interpretation. First, Locke told stories in which property precedes government throughout his property chapter, and he wrote as if many of his claims are empirical. For example, he wrote, "in the beginning all the world was America"—a stateless region with land available for appropriation. It seems impossible to interpret this claim in any other way but literally. As Richard Ashcraft (1987: 145) argues,

> Since Locke specifically cites from various descriptive accounts of Indians "in many parts of America" [§102; §105] as part of his attempt to supply "examples out of history, of people free and in the state of nature" [§103], it is rather disingenuous for some interpreters to claim that Locke has no historical conception of the state of nature . . . it makes no sense at all to claim that Locke did not intend to provide the reader with historical examples of life in the state of nature, when he says explicitly in the text that this is precisely what he is doing, and when he refers throughout the *Second Treatise* to the Indians in America as "a pattern" for what life is like in the state of nature he is describing, as it existed during "the first ages of the world" [§108].

Second, according to Locke (1960 [1689]: §28, 35, 97, 100–124, 138) public property can be created by compact. Therefore, apparently, lands still unclaimed by private individuals when the compact is established are available to become public property. He did not consider whether people might first establish public property by compact (or appropriation) and then parcel out limited title to individuals. Although more than half of his chapter on political society makes an empirical argument that a just government must be established by compact, stories in that chapter all involve compacts among people wishing to preserve existing estates.

Third, he made no reference to any metaphorical interpretation of the appropriation story, and no such interpretation seems to work in his arguments. His appropriation principle is a principle of first come, first served. The limits of a government established by compact to assert control over resources, therefore, stem from prior existence of appropriation-based property rights. That is, the limits depend on the truth of a time-based version of the appropriation hypothesis. He states it as a fact and relies on it in his arguments.

The two most important ethical premises in Locke's theory are appropriation and transfer, both of which are controversial. But his empirical claims have attracted little discussion to clarify either their meaning or their role in the justification of property. Locke's story has been retold ever since. The normative claims vary only slightly. The hypothetical historical claims vary even less.

3. LOCKE'S SUCCESSORS

By the 1700s, Locke's story was a standard part of Western property theory. Francis Hutcheson, Henry Home, Lord Kames, and Adam Smith, writing in 1745, 1758, and 1762, respectively, told variations of it. For all of them, occupation and labor established property rights in the state of nature, placing limits on the later agreement to create civil society (Horne 1990: 75–83), although for Smith (1982: 14–16, 459–160) and Lord Kames, the establishment of full property rights in land may not happen until after some form of government comes into existence (Horne 1990: 105–106, 115–116).

William Blackstone (2016 [1753]: 2) portrayed private property as if it was the only possible form, writing, "There is nothing which so generally strikes the imagination, and engages the affections of mankind, as the right of property; or that sole and despotic dominion which one claims over the external things of the world, in total exclusion of the right of other individuals in the universe."

James Otis, Jr.—in a 1761 speech that John Adams credited with sparking the American Revolution—gave a straight Lockean account of appropriation in the state of nature. According to a summary Adams wrote years later, Otis asserted that every man in the state of nature was an independent sovereign:

> His life, his liberty, no created being could rightfully contest. Nor was his right to his property less incontestable. The club that he had snapped from a tree, for a staff or for defense, was his own. His bow and arrow were his own; if by a pebble he had killed a partridge or a squirrel, it was his own. No creature, man or beast, had a right to take it from him. If he had taken an eel, or a smelt, or a sculpion, it was his property. (Somos 2019, 55)

Adams concurred with the empirical claims he summarized, writing that Otis "sported upon this topic with . . . indisputable truth and reason."

The foundation of Samuel Adams's argument against taxation without representation, which played such a crucial role in the U.S. Revolution, was that people exited the state of nature to secure their property (Somos 2019, 55)—the appropriation hypothesis once again.

Hume argued that the history of property is the history of conflict and theft, but he also saw property rights arising as a solution to that conflict: a social convention arises spontaneously to establish peace by recognizing existing holdings as if they were property. To the extent that that social convention comes first and its endorsement by a sovereign state comes later, Hume also uses a version of the hypothesis (Waldron 2005).

Many eighteenth-century philosophers took positions similar to Grotius and Pufendorf. Although the ultimate source of property rights is a social agreement, people in a state of nature initiate provisional possession of property, usually through Lockean appropriation, in expectation that it will be endorsed by a social agreement. Although this position rejects some of the normative claims in appropriation theory, it endorses most of the hypothetical historical claims that concern us. Writers taking this position differ in the relative emphasis they put on original appropriation or social agreement. To varying extents, it fits Immanuel Kant, Thomas Reid, and even Rousseau, who—though famously critical of economic inequality—also writes, "property is the most sacred of all the rights of citizenship, and even more important in some respects than liberty itself" (Horne 1990: 99–100; Rauscher 2012; Rousseau 1984: 25; Waldron 2005).

Antoine Louis Claude Destutt de Tracy (1970: vi, xxxv–xxxvi) used a Lockean story in his justification of property in 1817. Frédéric Bastiat (1996: 204–208) in 1850 told a very Lockean story, in which natural resources are originally both unowned and worthless, becoming valuable only when someone takes pains to improve and appropriate them.

Hastings Rashdall (1915: 39) rejected some and accepted other claims in the Lockean account, writing, "it was a simple matter of historical fact that one at least of the ways in which private property began was by some person or persons 'occupying' or appropriating to his or their own use something which previously was unappropriated." Some "primitive communities" recognized little in the way of private ownership by labor, and "the more careful study of primitive history has taught us that as a rule the first appropriation and cultivation of land was the work of groups rather than of individuals." Despite this skepticism, he gave the Lockean story historical credence, writing, "Still, on the whole, private ownership in things actually and obviously created by labour is a fairly primitive and fairly universal human institution."

4. APPROPRIATION THEORY AS PROPAGANDA FOR THE ENCLOSURE AND COLONIAL MOVEMENTS?

It is striking—and a bit ironic—that appropriation theory appeared and became dominant when it did, because as Chapter 14 shows, the private property system was only then being established through the enclosure movement in Europe and the colonial movement elsewhere. These movements transformed complex traditional systems of overlapping land rights into individual estates held by European elites. Lockean appropriation stories don't suggest anything like enclosure or conquest as the method of privatizing the commons. The story, therefore, has little direct relevance to the way in which most of the world's land was rapidly being privatized at the time

In recent years, some scholars have argued that early propertarian theory functioned (perhaps self-consciously) as propaganda for these movements. By these accounts, the modern Western conception of property is an outcome both of the forcible establishment over the objections of the people (Rossi and Argenton forthcoming) and of the conscious effort by early modern property theorists "to establish presumptively exclusive private ownership of material things by individuals as the essential nature of property" (Olsen 2019: 1–2). According to Olsen (2019: 1–2) "Thinkers like Grotius, Pufendorf, Locke, Hume, and Blackstone were not simply claiming that classical liberal property is better than other types; . . . they were claiming that it is the truest form of property." They were aware that traditional land-tenure systems had been nonexclusive throughout most of recorded European history but they sought to marginalize those forms of ownership, and, over the course of centuries, they succeeded.

Many scholars argue that Locke self-consciously designed at least two of his principles to justify both colonialism and enclosure (see Widerquist 2010a for review).

First, Locke (1960 [1689]: §30–§32) specifically states that the labor-mixing criterion implies farmers appropriate both the crops and the land on which they grow it, while hunters appropriate the animal they kill but not the land on which they kill it, because, supposedly, farming significantly transforms land and hunting does not. Unfortunately for foragers, no matter how long they and their ancestors hunted and gathered on a specific territory, they never gained the right to keep foraging on it when someone wanted to farm it. This principle is important not only for full-time hunter-gatherer societies, but also, as Chapter 14 shows, for many pre-colonial or pre-enclosure farming communities that were partly dependent on large foraging territories in between farms. The labor-mixing criterion gives colonial settlers and European lords the right to take all of that land, i.e. most of the world's land.

Second, Locke's (1960 [1689]: §31) no-waste proviso offered another rationalization for redistribution from peasants to lords and from indigenous peoples to colonists. The apparent argument is that peasants and indigenous peoples with their traditional techniques violate a moral proviso incumbent on property owners to avoid wasting any resources they remove from the commons. Industrious British lords who would use the latest European technology were, according to this logic, justified in seizing land from inefficient peasants and natives (Glausser 1990; Widerquist 2010a: 8).

Locke could hardly have been unaware that his theory provided a justification for an ongoing process disappropriating European commoners and indigenous peoples alike, or that that process amounted to redistribution without compensation from poor to rich. This observation raises serious doubts that the principles contemporary propertarians have inherited from him reflect some deeper commitment to nonaggression or noninterference.

Lockeanism eventually revolutionized the world's conception of what property was by portraying full liberal ownership as if it were something natural that had always existed, even though it was only then being established by enclosure and colonialization. Lockean and propertarian *stories* might have been more important than their *theories* in that effort. The "original appropriator" in Locke's (1960 [1689]) story resembles European colonialists rather than prehistoric indigenous North Americans who first farmed the continent. Locke's appropriator establishes the fee-simple rights that colonial governments (building a global cash economy) tend to establish rather than the complex, overlapping rights indigenous farmers in stateless societies tend to establish (see Chapters 10–14).

That starting point communicates the presumed naturalness of full liberal, individual ownership. Titles can be divided in any way, but only if the original owner chooses to do so (Olsen 2019; Rossi and Argenton forthcoming). Propertarians present little argument and even less evidence to support the presumption that property begins so united, but the appropriation story implies it could not be otherwise. Writers taking this perspective eventually taught the world to think of the person who holds the "title" not as a government-appointed "lord," who rules over the group who mixed their labor with the land to appropriate it jointly but as the natural owner of all eleven incidents, and that this set of incidents is the natural grouping that anyone mixing their labor with the land would always choose to bundle.

According to Olsen (2019: 4–6), Blackstone was "thoroughly aware" that he "was at odds with the complexity of the common law regime of property in the eighteenth century" when he portrayed property as if its essential nature was sole and despotic dominion over the external things of the world.

"Sole and despotic dominion" certainly "struck the imagination" of wealthy men petitioning parliament for acts of enclosure, but Blackstone (2016 [1753]: 2) was factually wrong to proclaim these men's feelings as representative of the "affections of mankind." As Chapter 14 shows, fee-simple ownership did not "engage the affections" of the European peasant majority nor the mass of the world's indigenous people. Both of these groups resisted being dispossessed of their nonexclusive rights.

The intent of Blackstone, Locke, Grotius, and other early modern property theorists was not to describe what property actually was or even what kind of institutions most people wanted at the time (Olsen 2019; Pateman and Mills 2007). Instead, it was "a common strategy of claiming the ground of property so as to preempt serious consideration of alternatives like common property" (Olsen 2019: 30). In that way, private property theory furnished propaganda for the enclosure and colonial movements that forcibly established that institution around the world (Olsen 2019; Pateman and Mills 2007).

And it was effective propaganda. Once property is culturally understood as sole and despotic dominion, it becomes easy to believe that peasants held mere "traditions" or the temporary right of a "tenant." It's easy to think that the peasants' incidents of ownership were not real "property" or real "rights" or anything very important at all. The lord was the real owner all along—or that's what the appropriation story makes you think.

5. THE INDIVIDUAL APPROPRIATION HYPOTHESIS
IN RECENT POLITICAL THEORY

Contemporary propertarians continue to rely on the appropriation hypothesis, usually tacitly. Unfortunately, even those who state it more or less explicitly offer little if any empirical support.

Although Hayek (1973: 108) is not committed to a natural rights justification of private property, he explicitly asserts the appropriation hypothesis and cites sources to support it (see Chapter 10): "There can be no question now that the recognition of property preceded the rise of even the most primitive cultures. . . . [I]t is as well demonstrated a scientific truth as any we have attained in this field."

Epstein (1978–1979: 1241) attempts to justify first possession on the following grounds:

[W]eight should be attached to the rules under which a society in the past has organized its property institutions. . . . Within this viewpoint it is possible to show the unique place of first possession. It enjoyed in all past times the status of a legal rule. . . . In essence the first possession rule has been the organizing principle of most social institutions.

This passage includes no citation supporting the empirical assertion that private first possession actually was enjoyed in *all past times* not to mention *places*. Empirical citations in other parts of the article are to law cases from the Anglo-American tradition and to textbooks on Roman law as if these were the only past times and places that mattered. Epstein cites no evidence showing that private claims precede community claims or that full liberal ownership was more common in all past times than nonexclusive ownership.

Narveson (1988: 83–92) self-consciously incorporates the appropriation hypothesis as an empirical premise in his appropriation theory. He bases the appropriation principle on a principle of noninterference: "The first-comer gets it. Why? Because second-comers would then be interfering with the courses of action initiated and being continued by those first-comers." Narveson's (1988: 83–85) first-comer is a "pioneer," who establishes full liberal ownership because that is,

[W]hat the agent saw herself to be in the way of enabling herself to do. . . . When the first Asian crossed the land bridge to Alaska . . . did she then get title to the whole of North America?

> Certainly not . . . it cannot plausibly be argued that her activity,
> what she saw herself to be doing, was using a whole continent
> or anything like it.

The theory so described requires deep knowledge not only about *who* appropriated every piece of land in the world but also about *what they were thinking.* Yet Narveson (1988: 83–92) presents no evidence about the intentions of all the world's original appropriators. It is unsafe to assume the prehistoric Olmecs, Egyptians, Mesopotamians, Xia Chinese, Polynesians, and the many other peoples who might have established the first fixed land claims in various places around the world, all saw themselves as propertarian pioneers. First-comers could establish full liberal, individual ownership, but they may also establish split, mixed, common, or collective ownership. A theory that requires knowledge of the intentions of people who lived thousands of years ago requires strong empirical evidence. Narveson's argument also requires knowledge of the intentions of every titleholder between appropriation and today. If any buyers and sellers agreed to exchange less exclusive rights, that particular title was weakened forever, regardless of the preferences of later-coming titleholders.

Rothbard (1978: 35) also unambiguously rests his conclusions on the individual appropriation hypothesis. He justifies appropriation with the following statement:

> [T]he pioneer, the homesteader, the first user and transformer of this land, is the man who first brings this simple valueless thing into production and social use. . . . It's difficult to see the morality of depriving him in favor of people who have nothing to do with the land.

This statement says nothing about private versus collective rights without the assumption that collectives had "nothing to do" with first use anywhere on Earth. How could he know this?

Rothbard's (1982: 49, 54, 56–58, 66–67, 183) original appropriator is a "homesteader" or "pioneer", who "clears and uses previously unused virgin land and brings it into this private ownership." His examples of abusive governments all begin when a state entity takes power over land on which homesteaders have already established full liberal ownership—i.e. they all involve the time-based version of the individual appropriation hypothesis.

His response to the possibility of a property-owning government is dismissive:

> If the State may be said to properly own its territory, then it is proper for it to make rules for anyone who presumes to live in that area. It can legitimately seize or control private property because there is no private property in its area, because it really owns the entire land surface. So long as the State permits its subjects to leave its territory, then, it can be said to act as does any other owner who sets down rules for people living on his property. . . . But our homesteading theory, outlined above, suffices to demolish any such pretensions by the State. (Rothbard 1982: 172)

Rothbard doesn't explain how a hypothetical history can "demolish" anything, but he writes, "There is really only one reason for libertarians to oppose the formation of governmental property or to call for its divestment: the realization that the rulers of government are unjust and criminal owners of such property" (Rothbard 1982: 56). Under his theory, this statement implies that governments take things previously appropriated by private individuals. Therefore, if his assertion about homesteading (i.e. the appropriation hypothesis) is false, "libertarians" have *no reason at all* to call for the divestment of governmental property. Yet he provides no evidence that his statements about who appropriated what have any connection to actual history.

Hoppe (1995: 94–95, 100, 117–121, 2001) actually uses empirical citations to support what he calls "the endogenous origin of a monarchy." A landowning aristocracy arises through appropriation and trade. This group of "natural elites" is voluntarily acknowledged by their inferiors as judges. Monarchy's "original sin" is the act of one member of the aristocracy monopolizing the power to judge all disputes in a given territory. If so, although monarchical power has some roots in appropriation and trade, it still involves violations of propertarian theory along the way. For Hoppe then, any argument in favor of the landownership rights of the aristocracy over monarchy (or democracy) rests on the literal truth of the history he recounts.

Machan (1989, 1990, 1997, 2006a) endorses "the natural right to private property," but in several works on the issue he does not explain how a natural resource becomes private property, and, thus, his theory does not indicate whether private titleholders, governments, or other human-created institutions have better ownership claims. The closest he comes seems to be an endorsement of Kirzner's appropriation theory (Machan 2006a: 91–93).

Kirzner tries to avoid reference to prehistory by stressing *present* rather than *past* discovery. An entrepreneur discovers a market opportunity, and, in a sense, creates something new. This argument appears to be a metaphorical interpretation of the appropriation story, but it is incapable of eliminating the need for the appropriation hypothesis, because, as Kirzner (1989: 154–155) admits, a discoverer-creator is entitled to the creation "only insofar as he was entitled to deploy the inputs." And he admits that the issue of how inputs originally became property is of "primordial importance."

Kirzner's (1989: 16–19) entrepreneur takes appropriation-like actions in markets where full liberal ownership rights over resources are for sale. By his logic, if discovery occurs on land where the first discoverer chose to set up a property-owning government, the entrepreneur's latecoming discovery of a marketing opportunity is no reason to dispossess government any more than a renter's discovery that they can sell cookies from their apartment is a reason to dispossess their landlord. To show that government power infringes on private property rights, Kirzner would need to follow the title in a regression back to that "primordial" discovery. Therefore, Kirzner tacitly endorses the appropriation hypothesis that primordial discovery was made by private individuals seeking to establish full liberal ownership.

Schmidtz (who is not committed to a strictly private system of ownership) has an appropriation theory in which property rights appear spontaneously in response to scarcity and conflict, making it a new version of an argument with roots in Hayek, Hume, Grotius, and Pufendorf. In this theory, it doesn't matter how owners establish their claims; it matters that property appears spontaneously and solves problems (Schmidtz 1990, 1994). This theory is less complicated than the Lockean version, but the appropriation hypothesis remains in it: individuals acting as individuals create property; government gets involved only later. Collectives never get together to create limited private titles to solve the problems in his stories. The spontaneous private title makers are not encroaching on land where people had already established a (large or small) collective to be the final problem solver. Therefore, the individual appropriation hypothesis is a tacit background assumption of Schmidtz's entire analysis.

The most important question is not whether propertarians explicitly address the issue or even whether they have thought much about it. The question is whether their theories are capable of ruling out collective ownership on an a priori basis or whether they require empirical historical claims.

6. CRITICISM AND/OR THE LACK THEREOF

The individual appropriation hypothesis is now widely accepted as obvious, even by many critics of propertarianism. Consider four examples.

First, Leif Wenar (1998: 799) writes, "Suppose libertarians could prove that durable, unqualified private property rights could be created through 'original acquisition' of unowned resources in a state of nature. Such a proof would cast serious doubt on the legitimacy of the modern state." Wenar follows with a worthwhile attack on normative "libertarian" theory, but his statement concedes the extensive empirical premises that connect those normative principle to doubts about state legitimacy. Wenar assumes that if private property *could be created* through appropriation, it *was created* through *private* appropriation. Like the "libertarians" he criticizes, Wenar tacitly accepts those empirical premises as if they were obvious.

Second, Cara Nine (2008) uses "a collectivist Lockean theory of territorial rights," but she assumes a dichotomy between the territorial rights held by governments and the property rights held by private entities, each of which are created by different kinds of appropriative acts. She does not consider the possibility of collectives holding property rights in their territory.

Third, both Otsuka's and Hillel Steiner's "left-libertarian" reconstructions of property theory take the existing mythos as representing something real. Like some other left-libertarians, they write as if private property rights stem from some kind of appropriation and government from some kind of contract (Vallentyne and Steiner 2000a, 2000b).

Fourth, Clare Chambers and Philip Parvin (2010) seek to justify "coercive redistributive taxation" of presumably natural private property.

Chambers and Parvin—and perhaps some of the others—merely concede this point for the sake of argument while they focus on other criticism, and there is nothing inherently wrong with doing so. But when the possibility that it could be otherwise often goes unmentioned or unnoticed, even concessions for the sake of argument can feed the perception that the claim is somehow obvious.

The truth or falsity of the hypothesis cannot be obvious because it deals with events that took place long ago and with people who lived in very different circumstances. Perhaps the credibility of the hypothesis comes merely from repetition. So many people have asserted it for so long that one might assume that someone must have verified it at some point.

Yet, the claim's credibility by repetition results more from ignoring skepticism than from any genuine consensus. Criticism exists, and conflicting hypotheses, some older than the appropriation hypothesis, still circulate in philosophy.

Before Locke, Hobbes (1962 [1651]: 186) wrote, "All private estates of land proceed originally from the arbitrary distribution of the sovereign." He presented this claim as an obvious truth as much as propertarians present the appropriation hypothesis as an obvious truth. Although both views remain in use in political theory, few philosophers seem interested in settling the empirical disagreement by empirical investigation.

Jefferson (1905) shared Hobbes's outlook, writing, "Stable ownership is the gift of social law, and is given late in the progress of society." He backed up his assertion with some casual observations of Native American property institutions (Skidmore 1829: 73). Paine (2012) and followers such as Henry George (1976) went even further along these lines, also backing up their claims with casual empirical observations.

Marx and Engels (1994) based a lot of their relevant work on early anthropological accounts of stateless peoples. They shared Lewis Henry Morgan's (1877) view that the earliest property was held in the form of "primitive communism." Similarly, L. T. Hobhouse (1913: 12–17) referred to a significant amount of anthropological evidence to argue that landownership in foraging societies and small-scale agricultural societies tends to rest in the community rather than in the individual.

Peter Kropotkin (2011: chapter IV), who was both an anthropologist and a political theorist, presented a great deal of evidence that various forms of common or collective property systems long preceded private property systems in most of the world.

Unfortunately, although these arguments clearly conflict with the appropriation hypothesis, few of these authors specifically addressed it. Fortunately, contemporary criticism has begun to focus on the narrative accounts of appropriation (Olsen 2019; Pateman and Mills 2007; Rossi and Argenton forthcoming; Widerquist 2009a).

One trend in this literature is that the people who have looked most closely at the empirical evidence for the appropriation hypothesis have found it least plausible. Yet, the mere coexistence of conflicting, conceptually plausible claims implies that none of them is obvious. If (as Chapter 9 argues) the need for empirical claims can't be eliminated, an empirical investigation (such as the one in Chapters 10–15) is necessary.

Chapter 9

THE IMPOSSIBILITY OF A PURELY A PRIORI JUSTIFICATION OF PRIVATE PROPERTY

This chapter assesses attempts to justify specifically private property rights on an a priori basis. It shows how such attempts either resort to special pleading or fall back on one or another version of the individual appropriation hypothesis. It begins by showing that some propertarians have partially recognized the probability of at least some group-based appropriation leading to justified public ownership of some (presumably atypical) spaces, but these propertarians stop short of asking whether collectives might justly own the whole of their territory. It goes on to show that arguments based on negative freedom, opportunity, inequality, market power, self-ownership, and the Lockean proviso all fail to rule out a property-owning government. Even Lomasky's explicit attempt to remove empirical claims from the theory involves both special pleading and the appropriation hypothesis.

1. PARTIAL RECOGNITION

At least some propertarians recognize that some collective and/or government ownership of property follows from appropriation theory. That is, these authors have recognized not only that an empirical claim is necessary to connect the appropriation principle to individualistic private property rights but also that, in some cases, the empirical application of the appropriation principle points toward collective property rights. However, none of these authors seems to recognize that this possibility extends beyond unusual spaces such as thoroughfares and parks. They all seem to presume most territory is naturally private.

Randall G. Holcombe (2005) writes,

> Speculation on the nature of anarcho-capitalism has typically
> proceeded under the assumption that all property in anarcho-
> capitalism would be privately owned. . . . The assumption . . .
> is not justified because property can come to be owned in
> common . . . and libertarian ethics would not allow the private
> appropriation of such common property.

That statement recognizes common appropriation and, therefore, implies agreement with the central point of this chapter.

Roderick Long (1996, 1998) reaches similar conclusions, arguing that at least some forms of property could become collectively owned (either locally or by the people of the world) if people jointly appropriate them or if individual owners give them to the people as a whole. He explicitly rejects property ownership by "the *organized* public" (i.e. the state or the government) in favor of "property owned by the unorganized public," apparently on the grounds that something about government is inherently illegitimate. He seems to consider government as an entity that *must* be justified by some "social contract," rather than as a very large private landowner as we are imagining.

Although Holcombe and Long might be more open-minded than they imply in these three articles, the perspective they take assumes individual appropriation is the norm and collective appropriation is confined to rather exceptional pieces of property such as roads, parks, and libraries. None of these articles considers the possibility that collective appropriation might extend to large pieces of collectively owned territory, nor do they make any effort to look empirically at the kind of property rights the earliest inhabitants in most territories tended to establish.

Long (1996) writes, "I envision a world of many individual private spaces, linked by a framework of public spaces," apparently assuming a Lockean individual appropriator of the individual private spaces. Holcombe (2005: 7, 8) considers what he declares to be a "plausible hypothetical scenario" with a community "springing up on previously unowned land," where people establish "farms," "a bank," "a general store," "a barber shop, a hotel, and a stable."

Is a scenario envisioning businesses opening up in uninhabited territory a plausible representation of the behavior of original inhabitants over much of the earth? Chapters 11–14 reveal that such a story better represents colonial aggressors than original inhabitants. Long and Holcombe have begun to ask the right empirical question, but the answers have much broader implications than these three articles consider.

At least one writer from the propertarian tradition, Carson (2011: 3), takes this observation farther considering not only the theoretical possibility of collective appropriation but also the empirical reality of it, writing:

> The dominant market anarchist view of property takes for granted individual, fee-simple ownership through individual appropriation as the only natural form of property. Although common or collective ownership is grudgingly accepted as a legitimate—if inefficient—form of "voluntary socialism," it's taken for granted that such forms of ownership can only come about through some sort of special contract between preexisting owners of fee-simple individual property.

Carson (2011: 4) examines the issue empirically and finds results very different from the usual propertarian assumption. He writes, "Communal ownership of land was the norm in the stateless village societies of the Neolithic period, from the Agricultural Revolution until the rise of the first states." And he goes much further, showing that in rural areas, communal property was the norm for thousands of years *after* the rise of the first states as well. He shows how it remained common until the enclosure and colonial movements made full liberal ownership the norm (Carson 2011). This observation shows agreement not only with the main point of our theoretical discussion but also with much of our empirical discussion below, but he rejects the idea that foraging territory could be appropriated and therefore leaves much if not most of the world open for purely private appropriation.

If even those propertarians who recognize the possibility of collective appropriation presume private appropriation is the norm, do they have some a priori basis to rule out a property-owning government or collective from owning the whole of a territory?

2. INTERFERENCE

Perhaps the foremost propertarian argument against government taxation and regulation is that it supposedly constitutes interference, coercion, or aggression against individual property owners. Nozick (1974: 169) writes, "Taxation of earnings from labor is on par with forced labor." Rothbard (1978: 25) declares, "Taxation is robbery."

These assertions have no force at all against a government that owns the right to tax and regulate titles within its territory (Widerquist 2009a). Except for the draft and the archaic institution of corvée labor, taxes do not fall on people but on the accumulation of property in assets external to the human body (Otsuka 2003: 21). All property is made partly out of resources, and humans have to live on land to enjoy even incorporeal property. Only the mythological original appropriator is free from payments to the people own the land.

If a property-owning government justly holds rights over its territory, taxpaying titleholders have the same freedom from interference as renters under capitalism: whatever property rights they own are free from interference. They simply do not happen to own the right to hold property free of payments and conditions set by another rights-holding body.

Narveson (1988: 34) unknowingly defends property-owning governments: "coercion is a matter of bringing it about that the coerced person's alternatives are considerably worse than in the status quo ante." Titleholders were born into a world where all territory was government controlled. They accumulated titles knowing that, in the status quo ante, all titles were subject to taxation, regulation, and redistribution. The property-owning government prevents titleholders from assuming greater rights, but according to Narveson (1988: 76–78, original emphasis), "the fact that having [property] entails having the right to prevent others from using it does not show that there is *now* a restriction on others' liberty which there wasn't previously." By that standard, governments' pre-existing powers to tax and regulate coerces no one.

The many emphatic statements in propertarian literature condemning taxation, regulation, and redistribution as "interference," "coercion," or "aggression" amount to question begging. We don't know whether government actions qualify as interference (under propertarian principles) unless we answer the question, "Who owns this part of the earth?" Propertarians assume the answer is private titleholders, beg readers to agree, and only then do judgments about coercive aggression follow.

Some propertarians acknowledge the existence of question begging and circular reasoning on this issue. Billy Christmas (2019: 1), for example, writes, "Lockean theory often exhibits a bias in favour of private property: assuming that only private property can protect one's interest in autonomy." Christmas, however, leaves the propertarian mainstream in his attempt to rid it of this problem.

Most propertarians believe their theory shows that government action is everywhere and always coercive. We need to look further to see whether propertarian theory can do so with purely a priori analytical reasoning.

3. OPPORTUNITY, INEQUALITY, AND MARKET POWER

Propertarians often assert that people only leave the state of nature to secure their property rights. This premise is an empirical claim subject to the analysis presented in Chapters 10–14. The presumption that it *must* happen is inconsistent with propertarian arguments that justice in holdings is unpatterned. To accept unlimited inequality, one has to accept that the following conditions may occur when state society is created. Some people have property; some do not; justice has nothing to do with the size of each group or the level of inequality between them. If propertarian theory does not allow non-wealthy people in a propertarian society to complain that they can only afford short-term leases, it cannot allow titleholders under a property-owning government to complain that they can only afford the limited titles the governments of the world are willing to sell them (Widerquist 2009a).

Propertarians might respond by arguing that only a libertarian state provides the opportunity for individuals to become full property owners. For example, Machan (1990: 80) makes an opportunity-based argument for propertarian capitalism.

Reliance on the opportunity to become property owners is a difficult way to defend a system in which many people will never own a home or a business. The argument forces them to define opportunity extremely broadly: people have the opportunity to buy something even if they can never afford it. In that sense people have the opportunity to trade their human capital for a piece of the territory of one of the world's governments. They might not be able to afford the price any government would name, but they have the opportunity in the sense that propertarianism offers most workers. In a monarchy, for example, they can marry the Queen's daughter and perhaps one day become monarch. That there are few of these opportunities is merely the result of the level of inequality that happens to exist, but the pattern of inequality is not a propertarian concern. In propertarian theory, any effort to increase equality by redistributing property from those who have to those who have not (in this case from the property-owning government to private titleholders) necessarily comes at the expense of liberty.

The acceptance of unlimited inequality also rules out any concern with the property-owning government's market power. A property-owning government has much greater market power than a group of private titleholders, but propertarians have not responded to such criticism by arguing that market power with capitalism is within acceptable limits. They have responded by declaring *categorically* that *all* pattern-based arguments are unacceptable. For example, Mack (2002a: 93) responds to market-power-based objections with a rhetorical question, "Why should this (allegedly) negative externality be thought to render the resulting situation *unjust?*"

Most propertarians argue that opportunity is not an important propertarian value (Kershnar 2004: 159–172). One of propertarianism's central ideas is the denial that any form of economic equality is a matter of justice. Nozick (1974: 157) writes, "The principle of entitlement we have sketched is *not* patterned" (original emphasis). He writes, "Holdings to which [property owners] are entitled may not be seized, even to provide equality of opportunity for others. In the absence of magic wands, the remaining means toward equality of opportunity is convincing persons each to choose to devote some of their holdings to achieving it" (Nozick 1974: 235). That is, under Nozick's theory, titleholders can ask the property-owning government to allow them to buy stronger titles, and the property-owning government can say no. Narveson (1988: 85) expresses the same sentiment, "Acquisition limits opportunity, to be sure. But nobody had a duty to provide you with that opportunity, nor even to maintain it for you."

4. SELF-OWNERSHIP

Propertarians often portray certain government policies, such as income taxes, not as violations of property rights but as violations of the widely appealing principle of self-ownership (Feser 2000; Nozick

1974; Rothbard 1978). Nozick (1974: 172, see also 169–172) argues that redistributive taxation is "a notion of (partial) property rights in *other* people." Samual Wheeler (2000) goes further, "No significant moral difference in kind exists between eliminating my ability to play softball by taking my knees away and eliminating my ability to play the market by taking my money away."

Otsuka (2003: 21) counters this argument with the following.

> [T]he state's forcing each of us to share our harvest with others would be no more an infringement of a libertarian right of self-ownership than in the case in which one purchased a plot of land from someone else on the condition that one share a part of one's harvest with the needy.

Income taxes paid by people with high human capital are no exception to this argument. Income taxes aren't levied on time, effort, skills, or human capital but on the attainment of property—the accumulation of external assets by trade. If the property-owning government has a partial or full property right in all external assets, it can set the conditions of access to them. Therefore, the propertarian objection to income taxation is not a dispute over self-ownership; it is a dispute over the ownership of external assets (Otsuka 2003: 19).

Formal self-ownership is simply too weak a concept to offer individuals much protection from a property-owning government. Such a government may not commit arbitrary executions, but self-ownership in combination with the four principles of distribution in holdings do not provide the tools to block it from depriving people of food and shelter until they agree to do work that directly or indirectly serves the government, just as they do not block a market system depriving people of food and shelter until they agree to accept a job that involves serving the interests of titleholders. Greater protection for individuals requires the endorsement of *effective* self-ownership, which might or might not be protected by any proviso attached to appropriation theory (Widerquist 2013).

5. THE LOCKEAN PROVISO

Locke's enough-and-as-good proviso, which Nozick (1974: 178–182) calls "the" Lockean proviso, supposedly ensures that the property system works for everyone, including nonowners. Nozick tentatively endorses a "weak" version, under which individuals must have some opportunity to reach at least the living standard they could expect in technologically primitive society in which all assets are held in common. Nozick's (1974: 178–179 n*) proviso is not a guarantee, but the right to "strive" to achieve the baseline by taking jobs for people who own the earth's resources. He seems unconcerned that the property-less are effectively forced to work for people with property as long as, once they do, the entire effect of the economic system raises their level of well-being over that of a Stone Age hunter-gatherer.

Nozick (1974: 182) mentions a few benefits of a market economy and dubiously declares, "I believe that the free operation of a market system will not actually run afoul of the Lockean proviso." Our earlier book argued extensively that that claim is false (Widerquist and McCall 2017). Although many, perhaps most, people are better-off today, the least advantaged among us are worse-off than any reasonable baseline. However, whether the proviso is fulfilled at this particular time is not important for the argument here. What's important is that Nozick's proviso, like all or most propertarian provisos, allows for no concern for *effective* self-ownership: no concern that normal people's only effective option is to serve the property-owning group as long as by doing so they can reach the baseline living standard. And the property-owning group could be one person because the principles are unpatterned. Special pleading would be necessary to say that the proviso is violated if one is effectively forced to work for a public institution but not if one is effectively forced to work for at least one private institution. Individuals might have equally reasonable objections to either.

Nozick's position implies that propertarians are wrong to complain that titleholders are not as well-off as they would be in the absence of taxation and regulation. The proviso doesn't give them the right to make that complaint. As long as they have the opportunity to strive for baseline living standards, this proviso implies no reason to strengthen their position at the expense of the rights of people who have chosen to hold their property rights in resources through the institution of a property-owning government. It would be difficult to define a proviso strong enough to justify redistribution from a property-owning government to private titleholders without also justifying massive redistribution from private titleholders to propertyless individuals (Widerquist 2009a).

Mack (1995, 2002a, 2002b) offers a "new and improved" version called "the self-ownership proviso" (SOP), which sounds like a significant limit on the power of property holders, but one important feature of it is immediately favorable to a property-owning government. The SOP is a constraint not on the ownership of property but on how it is used: the SOP does not restrict people from owning a horsewhip, but it does restrict them from whipping other people without their consent. Therefore, the SOP doesn't prohibit the existence of a property-owning government. It can at most put some limits on the government's use of those rights, and those limits aren't very substantial.

The SOP is violated if an individual's ability to exercise "her world-interactive powers is damagingly diminished" relative to a pre-property situation (Mack 1995: 216). Mack (2002b: 248) establishes a very low baseline, writing, "if the whole process of privatization leaves Sally with 'enough and as good' to use as she would have enjoyed (at a comparable cost) had all extra-personal resources remained in common, Sally will have no complaint under the SOP."

Many propertarians recognize that a starving person has a moral right to take what they need, if there is no other way, but this stipulation usually applies only to someone who can't find a job (Machan 2006a: 296). It does not apply to people who refuse to work for whoever happens to own property. Property owners may provide charity to people in this position, but they are not obliged to (Machan 1997: 146).

Mack (2002b: 243, 249–251, 271 n13) seems to believe that indirectly forced labor is unproblematic at least as long as the forced individual has a choice of what work to do. He argues that competition among employers is good for workers, but he focuses on the cost of obtaining goods rather than the forced labor involved in paying that cost, implying that effectively forced labor is inherently unproblematic. Mack (2002b: 244, 249) admits, "Sally would have a just complaint if Harry were to preclude all access to the only waterhole in the desert . . . even if she were to pay some non-monopoly price for the water," but "The claim is not, of course, that when Sally encounters competing waterhole owners she will receive water costlessly . . . costless access is never a reasonable baseline" (2002b: 273, n25).

That is, a property-owning government—like a waterhole owner—has the responsibility of offering people *some* choice of means by which they might gain access to the resources they need to reach the baseline without paying monopoly prices. But the property-owning government can deny access to food and water to individuals who refuse to take the jobs it makes available. Therefore, the property-owning government (like the property-owning class in a market economy) can force everyone else to serve its interests as long as everyone who agrees receives baseline wages (Widerquist 2013). Titleholders pay your taxes: to refuse would be to demand "costless access to the means of production," which is "never a reasonable baseline" (Mack 2002b: 273 n25).

Mack (2002b: 245) admits the SOP is easily satisfied, such that "All sorts of regimes, even well-administered social-democratic regimes, will not run afoul of this constraint." Nozick (1974: 182) and Machan (1997) agree that modern industrialized economies meet whatever standard is necessary to protect the poor. If they're right, the Lockean proviso does not significantly limit government's ability to have full or partial ownership of all property (Widerquist 2009a).

More radical propertarians, such as Boaz, Kirzner, and Narveson, rule out any concern for the proviso or for effective self-ownership, and Boaz (1997: 65) explicitly argues against a right to necessities. Narveson (1988: 101, 1998: 10, 23) argues that no one has a right to resources, that therefore no one has a right to life, and that property owners may take advantage of that situation by offering jobs at whatever terms they choose. Kirzner (1981: 405–406, 1989: 155–160) would allow the owner of the only waterhole in the desert to deny water to people who would otherwise die of thirst. These propertarians offer no protection from a property-owning government that might wish to deny food and water to anyone for any reason.

6. LOMASKY'S ATTEMPT TO REFORMULATE PROPERTARIANISM ON A PURELY A PRIORI BASIS

Lomasky (1987) makes a thorough attempt to rid propertarianism of dubious empirical claims. He recognizes that the "classically liberal theory of property rights" involves at least two dubious claims about prehistory: "natural relations obtain between persons and objects in the world. These relations precede civil society and thereby establish claims to property that are prior to social determination." The first sentence is the appropriation principle. The second sentence is an empirical claim, which he does not name. In our terms, it is the time-based version of the individual appropriation hypothesis.

Lomasky (1987: 113–120) discusses several observations that conflict with classically liberal theory, focusing mostly on its normative aspects rather than with the empirical hypothesis he finds in it. He contends that any claims about the origin of property rights are irrelevant and attempts to reconstruct natural property rights theory without them, promising a purely normative argument based only on respect for contemporary individuals as project pursuers. He lays out a theory of contemporary appropriation without specific reference to the distant past:

- If A comes to possess *I*, to use *I* in the service of his projects, and thereby values the having of *I*, then A has *appropriated I*. . . . A has reason to acknowledge and respect B's having *I** conditional upon B recognizing and respecting A's special interest in *I*. . . . A has reason to reject the imposition of a system of collective control over all goods that will determine whether A is entitled to have *I*. (Lomasky 1987: 130–131)

This argument isn't obviously empirical, but look closely at the order of events: when the first appropriator, A, comes along, there is no system of collective control over goods; and the *reason* that A's rights limit the rights of this system of collective control (i.e. government or collective property rights) to determine whether A is entitled to *I* is that A *already* came to possess *I* before this system was "imposed." What's the role of that empirical claim? Consider how Lomasky would have to revise his story to allow private and public ownership to appear the other way around (square brackets denote revisions):

- If A comes to possess *I* [a share in "a system of collective control over all goods"], to use *I* in the service of his projects, and thereby values the having of it, then A has *appropriated I*. . . . A only has a reason to acknowledge and respect B's having *I** [a private title] conditional upon B recognizing and respecting A's special interest in *I* ["a system of collective control"]. Therefore, A has reason to reject the imposition of a system of [privatized] control over all goods that will determine whether A is entitled to have *I* [a share in "a system of collective control over all goods"].

Certain projects one might pursue are best aided by private individual ownership, others by private institutional ownership, and others by collective or government ownership. Lomasky (1987: 151) claims to be neutral in his respect for even the most unusual preferences. He, therefore, needs to explain why he assumes "*I*" is a share in land held by a marriage, a partnership, or a corporation but not a share in land held by a corporate entity called a government. If his answer relies purely on individuals standing as project pursuers, he might have a fully a priori argument capable of supporting his conclusions.

Unfortunately, Lomasky's (1987: 131) only statement capable of explaining the privileged place of private property begins with an empirical claim:

- [P]ersons come to civil society with things that are theirs. A socially defined system of property rights must be responsive to what persons have. In no respect does a civil order entail the collectivization of property.

Lomasky's (1987: 131) claim, "persons come to civil society with things that are theirs," is not merely similar to the individual appropriation hypothesis. It *is* the appropriation hypothesis in its simplest time-based form. It is an empirical hypothesis about the existence of private claims to land and resources prior to the establishment of collective claims over land and resources. Compare head-to-head:

- *Lomasky's (1987: 131) statement of the appropriation hypothesis:* "natural [property] relations obtain between persons and objects in the world. These relations precede civil society and thereby establish claims to property that are prior to social determination."
- *Lomasky's (1987: 119–120) reason why the civil order must respect private property:* "persons come to civil society with things that are theirs."

He admits the first statement is dubious, voices skepticism about it, and claims it is irrelevant. But then he relies on the second statement, which is very much (or entirely) the same empirical claim in different words. Therefore, his argument explicitly falls back on the appropriation hypothesis.

On an a priori basis, propertarian theory can say people come to civil society with only one "thing that is theirs"—self-ownership. Whether an individual comes into civil society owning anything else is an empirical question. Consider how Lomasky would have to revise this statement to remove its empirical content:

- [P]ersons [might] come to civil society with things that are theirs. A socially defined system of property rights must be responsive to what persons [might or might not] have. In no respect does a civil order entail [either] the collectivization of private property [or the privatization of collective property].

In other words, without his empirical claim, Lomasky's argument says *nothing* about whether governments should have powers of taxation, regulation, and redistribution or whether there is anything natural about private property. To justify that limit he would have to assume that many different individuals held property rights over all resources when civil society was created. In other words, he would have to endorse the same appropriation hypothesis he promises to eliminate from propertarian theory.

Lomasky has three more arguments based on the characteristics of government.

First, Lomasky (1987: 134) writes, "individuals are project pursuers who incorporate the utilization of objects into their pursuits, thereby manifesting a recognizable interest in the having of things; social entities as such pursue no projects and have no interests." It is true that social entities have no interest, but marriages, partnerships, and corporations are also social entities, and as such have no interests. Many project pursuers have interests in creating social entities and owning property through them, whether the entities they create are marriages, partnerships, corporations, peoples, or governments. If governments should be dispossessed merely because they are social entities, the institutions through which most people hold most of their wealth should also be dispossessed. This argument against government ownership of property is mere special pleading.

Second, Lomasky dismissively addresses the possibility of a property-owning monarchy:

[S]uppose that title to all property was conferred to one person, the king, and no one else owned anything. It would follow that should anyone make use of any item except with the sufferance of the king that person would be guilty of interference. By way of contrast, the king would enjoy rightful use of whatsoever he pleased, no matter how inimical that use should prove to be to the interests of anyone else. It would not be interference because the king would only be using that which is *his*. True, this one-sided distribution of property has little to recommend it and needs not be given serious consideration as a potentially *just* arrangement. (Lomasky 1987: 113–114)

The passage has little actual argumentation, and what it has is patterned—the sort propertarians usually rule out offhand. For example, many people believe a distribution in which the wealthiest 10 percent of the population owns 75 percent of the wealth is "one-sided" and "has little to recommend it." Both observations indicate that some *pattern* of holdings is unacceptable. Lomasky (1987: 125) normally gives such arguments no political standing because "any sets of property holdings that emerge from rightful activity are, by definition, distributively just." Categorically dismissing pattern-based objections to the distribution he wishes to defend while relying on a pattern-based objection to attack another distribution of property is simple special pleading. Without special pleading, the property-owning monarch's holdings are "by definition, distributively just."

Third, Lomasky (1987: 134–135) runs into similar problems attempting to rule out community ownership of property:

If there were only one collective entity and if each person had volunteered antecedent consent to be enrolled in whatever enterprise the collectivity undertook and to adhere to whatever standard of value the collectivity should erect for itself, and if such consent were continually renewed, *then* there would be some basis for judging that rights inhere primarily in the group and not in individuals.

Lomasky seems to be distracted by mythology surrounding the social contract story. Rather than recognizing the government as a large land-holding corporation, he's thinking of it as described in social contract theory, which does involve dubious claims about everyone continually renewing their consent. But this argument has no force at all against a property-owning democracy as in Hypothetical History 3.

His argument expects a property-owning government to meet standards that no one expects private landholding institutions to meet. The idea that appropriators need everyone's antecedent consent is anathema to propertarian theory. At no point does an institution holding appropriation-based territorial rights need the consent of "everyone." Neither do institutional owners need the continually renewed consent of all their owners. All that is needed to establish joint ownership is a group of people who agree to perform an act of joint appropriation. Once ownership is established, everyone (shareholders and non-shareholders alike) is ethically obliged to recognize and respect that ownership. If non-shareholders don't consent to a landowner's rules, they must keep off the land. If some individual shareholders don't like the corporation's decisions or don't want the shares they inherit, they can renounce their shares (i.e. their citizenship), but they still have to obey the corporation's (i.e. the property-owning government's) rules as long as they remain on its land.

Consider citizenship as a form of inherited corporate property (Shachar and Hirschl 2007): corporations could not exist if they had to be prepared, at any moment, to give a minority shareholder the power to dissolve the corporation or withdraw their share's worth of the corporation's hard assets. It does not matter whether the shareholder inherited a share of corporate ownership at birth. It doesn't matter whether the shareholder was born on corporate property. Corporate property rights adhere to corporate entities against individual shareholders as much as against non-shareholders. Individual shareholders have to respect corporate property rights until shareholders agree as a group—under whatever procedure the corporation has established—to change the corporation's policy.

With Lomasky's a priori arguments falling into special pleading, his argument cannot do without the appropriation hypothesis. Thus, the most thorough attempt we know of to build a purely a priori justification for a propertarian economy ends up relying on the same empirical premises that have been passed down since 1689.

7. CONCLUSION

This chapter has examined the work of some of the most influential propertarian theorists to show that none provides a workable, purely normative argument that property must necessarily be private. All of them either sink into special pleading or rely (explicitly or tacitly) on the appropriation hypothesis. Propertarian use of hypothetical historical claims is so sloppy that we suspect many propertarians are not clear in their own minds about the extent to which their beliefs rest on empirical premises, exactly what those premises are, and whether those premises have been verified.

We are ready to conclude that if there were a way to construct a purely a priori argument against government ownership of property, someone would have invented it by now. We cannot rule out the possibility that some propertarian theorist somewhere has formulated one, but we have surveyed a substantial portion of the most influential propertarian literature from Locke to the present day, and if there is a purely a priori version out there, it has escaped the notice of all the propertarians we've surveyed (Widerquist 2009a, 2009b, 2010a; Widerquist and McCall 2017).

No one should be surprised that *historical* theories require *historical* premises. The surprising result is the absence of scrutiny those claims have received. Propertarians have not been held to account either to clarify their use of historical claims or to provide support for them. Chapter 10 addresses what little evidence propertarians have provided.

Chapter 10

EVIDENCE PROVIDED BY PROPERTARIANS TO SUPPORT THE APPROPRIATION HYPOTHESIS

Chapters 7–9 have shown that propertarianism requires some version of the empirical claim(s) we call the individual appropriation hypothesis. A few propertarians have provided evidence in favor of it. This chapter reviews that evidence, showing that it is cursory and inconclusive. Therefore, a more thorough investigation is needed.

1. TYPICALLY SHORT TREATMENT

It's hard to find propertarians who consider the possibility of collective or government appropriation seriously. Propertarian literature is filled with bold, explicitly empirical claims about it with little or no evidence in support. This lack of concern is problematic in a theory supposedly based on the idea that "Justice . . . depends on what actually has happened" (Nozick 1974: 152) or that "What is in fact the case carries moral weight" (Lomasky 1987: 130).

Nozick (1974: 152) cites no evidence at all to support the connection his hypothetical histories make between the appropriation principle and specifically private, individual ownership. Narveson (1988: 83–92) cites no evidence to support his claims that virtually all "first-comers" think of themselves as establishing private property. Kirzner (1989: 154) dodges the question entirely despite recognizing its importance. Bruno Leoni (1972: 10, 52–53) disparages the beliefs that land was originally held in common or that the origin of private property is violence but cites no evidence to the contrary.

Epstein (1978–1979: 1241) cites no evidence to support his extremely far-reaching claim, "first possession . . . enjoyed in all past times the status of a legal rule," and the evidence he cites for related claims seldom if ever goes back further or more widely than British

common law and Roman law. Even this extremely narrow historical view does not always fulfill is expectations of specifically private
appropriation. For example, "The Romans . . . began their discussion
of property with the assertion that by the natural law, the air, running
water, the sea, and consequently the seashore were things that were
'common to all'" (Epstein 1995: 67).

Hoppe (2006) presumes owners have some tie to appropriation
and propertyless people and collectives are latecomers. Hoppe (1995:
24–26) cites several sources to support the claim that the first monarchies were preceded by a group of private landowners, but he badly
misinterprets the only one we have been able to locate, Harris (1977).
Hoppe fails to note that the "big men" Harris identifies as existing
before chiefs were not landowners. They were—at best—administrators of communal land and mediators of disputes. Harris (1977: 69)
writes, "Earth, water, plants, and game were communally owned.
Every man and woman held title to an equal share of nature. Neither
rent, taxes, nor tribute kept people from doing what they wanted to
do." Hoppe is probably right that the first monarchies usurped *power*
from village big men and smaller-scale chiefs, but if so, they usurped
common land from collectives.

Rothbard (1978: 51) appears interested in empirical investigation:
"We can only find the answer [to who owns property] through investigating the concrete data of the particular case, i.e. through 'historical'
inquiry." But he neglects the empirical content of his assertion that it's
difficult to see the morality of depriving "the pioneer, the homesteader,
the first user and transformer of this land . . . in favor of people who
have nothing to do with the land" (1978: 35).

How do we know collectives had nothing to do with first use? It's
far from obvious that collectives had nothing to do with the enormous
irrigation projects that made farming possible in Neolithic Egypt and
Mesopotamia (as in Hypothetical History 3). Even if individuals led
such projects, it is not obvious that they would set themselves up as
mere *owners* rather than *monarchs* of appropriated land (as in Hypothetical History 2), a position they would be at liberty to establish
under Rothbard's anarcho-capitalism.

Rothbard (1982: 178, 178 n3–n4) seems to have confused the
appropriation myth for an obvious empirical truth. Although he cites
empirical support for other claims, he cites little or no evidence for
his hypotheses that property actually comes into existence through

individual homesteading and that it actually precedes collective claims over territory. One source Rothbard cites for related empirical issues does provides some support for these claims. It is not an empirical work, but a property rights treatise by Hayek.

2. FRIEDRICH HAYEK AND HIS ANTHROPOLOGICAL SOURCES

Hayek (1973: 108) offers a clear, empirical assertion of the appropriation hypothesis:

> [T]he erroneous idea that property had at some late stage been "invented" and that before that there had existed an early state of primitive communism ... has been completely refuted by anthropological research. There can be no question now that the recognition of property preceded the rise of even the most primitive cultures. ... [I]t is as well demonstrated a scientific truth as any we have attained in this field.

Most propertarians who offer citations to support the appropriation hypothesis cite this passage, but few examine Hayek's support for it.

Hayek (1973) cites only three sources to support this claim: A. I. Hallowell (1943), H. I. Hogbin (1934), and Bronisław Malinowski (1934, 1947), all of which were already becoming outdated when Hayek wrote in 1973. More importantly, a closer look at these sources shows that they neither individually nor collectively support Hayek's sweeping claim nor any other version of the appropriation hypothesis.

Hallowell, Hogbin, and Malinowski were interested in dispelling the idea of a "primitive communism" but largely for reasons having to do with Morgan's (1877) unlinear evolutionary theoretical framework, which was actually highly problematic. Instead, Hayek's inference seems to be: not primitive communism, therefore primitive capitalism with full liberal ownership rights. None of his anthropological sources makes that inference. In fact, they all argue against the validity of any such dichotomy.

Hallowell (1943: 135, emphasis added) writes that "property rights *of some kind* are ... universal," but he also warns that there is a "false antithesis" between "simple alternatives as individual versus communistic ownership" (p. 125). He cites one study showing that individual hunters or nuclear families of the Labrador Peninsula held property rights in hunting grounds. This observation was a bit of an anomaly because hunter-gatherer territorial ownership is usually collective with rights relating to group, clan, extended family, and so on.

Subsequent studies of the beaver hunters of the Labrador Peninsula have explained this anomaly showing that these unusual property rights were established during the early colonial period by a group decision rather than by individual appropriation. Before European demand threatened the beaver population, these groups had treated all the hunting territory as common. When people in the area realized that the beaver population was being depleted, they decided to divide the right to hunt beaver for sale. Rather than establishing individual landownership, individuals retained the common right to hunt for food anywhere. They could even kill a beaver for food in someone else's designated area as long as they left the pelt for the person granted the right to it by the group (Leacock 1954). Although partly private, these property rights were complex, overlapping, partially common, and subject to group regulation.

Therefore, Hayek treats an anomalous observation as the general case and reads far more into the observation than it is capable of demonstrating. It is hard to see how such overlapping rights could have developed into full liberal ownership without the subsequent interference of European colonialists.

Hayek's second source, Hogbin (1934: 94–97, 239), finds extended families owning land and property jointly in the smallest-scale societies. In a slightly larger-scale chiefdom in Tonga, he finds, "The whole of the archipelago was theoretically conceived as belonging to the Tui Tonga [the paramount chief] who reserved certain districts for his own use and allotted the rest among the great chiefs. They in return paid tribute twice a year."

This combination makes the Tui Tonga both owner and monarch of the territory—the very combination that propertarian theory supposedly rules out. It is difficult to use the principles of propertarian theory to determine the extent to which the Tui Tonga was a private owner or a public monarch, because he inherited a very old title in a society without written records in a very different cultural context than the one propertarians claim to be "natural." To try to force an interpretation that makes the Tui Tonga one or the other is to assume the validity of the dichotomy that Hayek's sources warned against. Similarly, it's impossible to portray the lesser chiefs as original appropriators because their claim to land came from service to the paramount chief.

Whether propertarian principles classify the tribute commanded by the Tui Tonga as legitimate "rent" or as illegitimate "taxes" depends on the origin of the chief's claim. Chiefs might have appropriated the land, usurped it from earlier private smallholders, or usurped it from earlier collectivists. Evidence for that usurpation and/or a legitimate assumption of power is what Hayek's citation of these sources was meant to show. If Hayek does not intend readers to take chiefs to represent early landowners, he seems to have little reason cite these sources at all. If he does intend them to represent early landowners, he has to accept the merger of ownership rights and governmental authority.

Hayek's third and principle source, Malinowski, (1934, 1947), is also an important source for both Hallowell and Hogbin. Although Malinowski is interested in refuting the idea of primitive communism, he puts greater stress on the complexity of native property rights than Hayek (1973: 108) admits. According to Malinowski (1956: 318), "Land tenure cannot be defined or described without an exhaustive knowledge of the economic life of the natives." He warns, "any description of a savage institution in terms such as 'communism', 'capitalism' . . . borrowed from present-day economic conditions or political controversy, cannot but be misleading" (Malinowski 1966: 19), and "It is especially a grave error to use the word ownership with the very definite connotation given to it in our own society" (Malinowski 1972 [1922]: 116–117).

By writing, "the recognition of property preceded the rise of even the most primitive cultures," Hayek (1973: 108) makes the very error his principal source warns against.

Malinowski (1934: xlii) writes, "In the Trobriands . . . the chief claims all the soil of his district as his." Although this claim does not amount to full ownership, Malinowski shows "The claim is not idle." The chief receives tribute, some of which he employs for defense and "for the benefit of the community." Malinowski (1972 [1922]: 65) describes Trobriand chiefs in ways that in Western cultural terms make them both owners and governors of their land.

Chiefly ownership creates difficulties for the appropriation hypothesis because chiefs are not the proto-businessmen the hypothesis assumes. Of course, they are not proto anything. They are people with a position well known to their society with no necessary equivalent in other societies. Even taking Hayek's use of chiefs to represent people relatively close to original appropriation, they don't back his case very well. If Hayek takes Trobriand chiefs as appropriators, he must accept that ownership is quickly combined with sovereignty. Such an observation seems to support Hypothetical History 2 above rather than Hypothetical History 1 (the Lockean story illustrating the individual appropriation hypothesis).

Malinowski (1972 [1922]: 94) does describe inter-community markets, but he finds something very different from the type of ownership we would expect if the appropriation hypothesis were true. The markets were regulated by chiefs and contained a major ritual element having to do with the prescribed circulation of prestige goods rather than representing some kind of free market economy. Participation in them was strictly limited. And buyers brought home something, "of which he enjoys a temporary possession, and which he keeps in trust for a time."

Malinowski deserves some blame for Hayek's misreading. Chris Hann (1998b: 26) observes that, although Malinowski exposed the false antithesis of the individual-versus-communal dichotomy, he was "so preoccupied with the need to emphasize the individualistic character of Trobriand life that the very dualism he condemned intruded continuously into this analysis." In a passage cited by Hayek, Malinowski (1947: 132–133) writes, "private property appears very definitely on primitive levels," but Malinowski was trying to dispel the myth of primitive communism, in which people erroneously supposed no one owned anything at all in small-scale societies.

Furthermore, this passage is not from any of Malinowski's primary research but from a political treatise he wrote near the end of his life. This passage contains no citations to primary research. It makes only an a priori argument that people must have established individual property on the supposition that they need secure possession. This passage does not make clear the complex property ownership that Malinowski (1934: xvii–lxxii, 1947: 128–133) stresses in his empirical works on the Trobriand Islanders and other small-scale societies, and neither does it provide the empirical evidence for the "demonstrated scientific truth" Hayek (1973: 108) claims to have found in Malinowski, Hogbin, or Hallowell.

3. HISTORICAL INVESTIGATIONS OF ANARCHO-CAPITALIST INSTITUTIONS

Many propertarians, especially of the anarcho-capitalist tradition, have done excellent empirical-historical work on the question of whether private property *can* exist without government (Stringham 2007). Unfortunately, most of this work does not bear on the questions of whether private property existed *before* government or whether private property is more likely to develop without rights violations than collective or government-owned property, and so it has limited value as an inquiry into the truth or falsity of the appropriation hypothesis.

However, work along these lines by Bruce L. Benson (1989: 8) is relevant to our question. He writes, "private property rights are a common characteristic of primitive societies." Here, he cites only the passage from Hayek discussed above, but making similar claims, he cites four relevant primary sources: Leopold Pospíšil, Walter Goldschmidt, Robert Redfield, and E. A. Hoebel (Benson 1989, 1990, 2007).

Benson's sources do not support the appropriation hypothesis. Pospíšil and Goldschmidt do find evidence of individualistic land ownership among the Kapauku Papuans and native groups of northwestern California, respectively. But neither of them views it as a common characteristic among small-scale societies. Pospíšil (1971: 296–297) writes that ownership is a bundle of rights, that the rights in the bundle differ from society to society, and that "Among the Kapauku the owner's rights to land and water differ from one terrain to another." Goldschmidt (1951: 507) writes that private land rights in northwestern California are so atypical that the natives of that area are, "Like no other hunting-gathering people of which I have knowledge (and very few primitive peoples generally)."

Benson's focus on these two atypical groups seems to be an example of cherry-picking. And even viewed in isolation, they are not as convincing as Benson suggests. Many Native Americans of the Pacific Northwest held much of their land as a commons and had powerful elites (or "chiefs") who both "owned" and "governed" land in ways similar to the Trobriand chiefs discussed above (see Chapter 11).

Redfield (1967: 23–24) makes generalizations about "primitive law," writing, "The materials cited here have included many instances where the wrongs righted are wrongs against kinship groups, the claims are pressed by kinship groups, and the liability of the individual is to his kinship group." He concludes that "primitive society" should be regarded as "an aggregation of families rather than of individuals." The families in question are large clans rather than nuclear families, and they are often the closest thing stateless societies have to governing bodies (see Chapters 11–12).

Such kinship groups resemble Hypothetical History 3 much more than the Lockean story. If property begins as the possession of a kinship collective, one should reject the appropriation hypothesis in the absence of evidence that privatization occurs before the first collectives appear. Propertarians might suppose these kinship groups usurped their claims from earlier individual holders, but that would assume the truth of the hypothesis for which Benson's citations were meant to provide evidence.

Hoebel examines law-like norms in pre-state societies and archaic states at varying scales, finding very different property rights than Benson suggests. According to Hoebel (1954: 143), individual ownership, as we understand it, is only one of many different kinds. In a nomadic society in the American Great Plains, he finds, "All land is public property." In a nomadic society in the North American Arctic he finds, "All natural resources are free or common good," and, "Private property is subject to use claims by others than its owners" (Hoebel 1954: 69–70).

Hoebel (1954: 104) finds the following laws in a small-scale settled community in the Philippines:

> The bilateral kinship group is the primary social and legal unit, consisting of the dead, the living, and the yet unborn. . . . An individual's responsibility to his kinship group takes precedence over any self-interest. . . . The kinship group shall control all basic capital goods. . . . Individual possession of rice lands and ritual heirlooms is limited to trust administration on behalf of the kin group.

Hoebel (1954: 192) draws from Malinowski's observations of Trobriand chiefdoms, writing, "The village belongs to a matrilineal subclan. Surrounding the village are the lands belonging to the subclan." In an archaic state in West Africa, Hoebel (1954: 253) finds, "Basic property belongs to the ancestors. . . . Basic property is only administered in trust by its temporary possessors. . . . A headman or chief is the carnal viceroy of the ancestors of the kinship group he governs." Again, these elites are managers of a system of collective ownership with land access rights guaranteed through membership in a moiety or sodality. This system is not primitive communism, but it is very far from the sole proprietorship that Benson reads into it.

Hoebel (1954: 286–287) summarizes his findings:

> All legal systems give cognizance to the existence of rights to private property in some goods; but among primitives land is legally treated as belonging directly or ultimately to the tribe or the kinship group; it is rarely sustained legally as an object of private property.

That is, Benson's (1989: 8) principle source contradicts his central claim that "private property rights are a common characteristic of primitive societies."

4. EMPIRICAL NATURAL PROPERTY RIGHTS

One propertarian theorist, Hasnas (2005), calls for "a theory of empirical natural rights" based on an investigation of what kinds of property rights actually develop in the absence of obviously aggressive behavior. Hasnas poses the question somewhat differently than we do. He asks whether people recognize rights of appropriation and property. We use the propertarian assumption that a right of appropriation exists (regardless of whether people think it exists), and ask what kinds of property right systems people who meet appropriation criteria establish. There is enough overlap that investigation of either question informs the other.

Several propertarians, using a mix of approaches, do research along these lines without using his terminology.

Hasnas's (2005) article is primarily a theoretical discussion of how such empirical research could be approached. It is oriented toward explaining and justifying the methodology with only a cursory empirical analysis. Hence, he gives it the modest title, "*Toward* a Theory of Empirical Natural Rights" (emphasis added) and does not claim to have developed a full-blown theory.

Hasnas (2005) does not investigate original appropriation, but looks for historical situations that might approximate the state of nature or provide opportunities for appropriation. Unfortunately, he assumes his examples are representative of worldwide tendencies in the development of property rights, even though most of them involve people who are already acculturated to the Western property system, and therefore, are significantly out of the ordinary from a worldwide historical perspective (see Chapters 11–14).

Even with this preliminary investigation, Hasnas (2005: 136–137) finds significant differences between "empirical natural rights" and the institutions that appear obvious to propertarians. Although he claims that his empirical natural rights tend to be a "good approximation" of propertarian rights, he finds that they are not nearly as strong, writing,

> [I]n contrast to the more philosophically pleasing conception of the traditional right to property, the empirical right is a highly flexible, exception-laden one that invests individuals with the exclusive use and control of objects only to the extent that doing so facilitates a more peaceful life in society. Individual empirical natural rights, then, are . . . fuzzy-edged entities.

Mayor (2012: 485), who conducts a similar empirical investigation, dubs hunter-gatherers "The Original Libertarians," writing:

> What version of political economy—collectivist or individualistic— is more consistent with man's basic nature? Does man naturally respect an individual's right to the products of his own efforts, or does he believe that others have a higher claim on those products? . . . [P]hilosophers and political theorists have given different answers to these questions, but almost always without significant supporting evidence. I argue here that such evidence does exist and may in fact be obtained by applying basic principles of evolutionary biology to the voluminous ethnographic literature available in the field of anthropology.

So much is wrong with Mayor's statement that we only scratch the surface here. His search for "man's basic nature'" and his presumption that people in small-scale societies somehow represent this nature or any notion of a "primitive condition" (Mayor 2012: 485) are erroneous ideas that were discarded by anthropologists in the mid-twentieth century. His effort uses evidence about stateless peoples very differently than ours. We're not looking for basic human nature. We're examining whether the people who perform the appropriative acts (as propertarians define them) tend to establish the types of property institutions propertarians claim they do, or whether it is common for people performing such acts to establish other kinds of property institutions.

Mayor (2012: 491) does a reasonably good survey of anthropological evidence despite the discredited presumptions he imposes on it. Focusing on hunter-gatherer bands, he recognizes that "no property rights typically exist in the natural resources the band uses" and that those who have more tools or food are often pressured to share their surplus with others. He fails to draw any inference from this observation for his question, "Does man naturally respect an individual's right to the products of his own efforts?" He views the reciprocal nature of this sharing more individualistically than most anthropologists (see below). He does not look at the establishment of the primary institution that propertarianism defends—permanent elite private ownership of land, natural resources, and all the things humans make out of them, and he admits that the establishment of that institution was not consistent with the exercise of freedom (Mayor 2012: 493–494).

Schmidtz (1994) makes a slightly more theoretical effort, building on Harold Demsetz's theoretical attempt to explain why property rights develop. Schmidtz connects this positive theory both with ethics and with the argument that private property can and does develop to solve coordination problems and regulate access to resources. However, Schmidtz readily admits that many historic examples involve communal and overlapping rights, which are very different from the institutions propertarian theory is meant to justify. He also admits that the most desirable mix of private and public property depends on the particulars of changing social and technological circumstances. This inference seems to imply the abandonment of any natural rights argument for private property.

This empirical natural rights approach is an interesting avenue that should be pushed farther, but the evidence propertarians—such as Hasnas, Mayer, and Schmidtz—have found so far tends to undercut rather than bolster the natural rights justification of private property.

5. ANIMAL TERRITORIALITY AS PRIVATE PROPERTY

Jeffrey Evans Stake (2004: 1764) empirically searches for, "The Property 'Instinct'" in animal and human examples, but this section argues that Stake's observations fall far short of demonstrating an instinct for any particular property institution.

Stake's human examples all involve people acculturated to an established Western property right system. He makes no effort to discuss humans who live with very different property rights conventions, and still his examples don't support his claims. Consider two of them. First, Stake (2004: 1764) writes, "Historically, first discovery gave nations rights in foreign lands." If this example implies anything about an instinct, it implies one for government-owned property, the convention that propertarian theory supposedly rules out.

Second, Stake (2004: 1764) writes, "The common law of property in England and the US has, as one of its cornerstones, the notion that the first person to possess a thing owns it." This example ignores that the people proclaimed by these legal systems to be "first" possessors were not so original. They usually dispossessed peoples with common or collectivist landholding institutions (see Chapters 13–14).

If there is evidence of an instinct in Stake's review of human history, it is an instinct for some kind of territoriality or at most for some kind of land-tenure convention, but certainly not one that implies a propertarian instinct for significant moral limits on government powers to tax, regulate, and redistribute property.

Stake's (2004: 1764–1767) animal examples come almost entirely from distant evolutionary relatives such as birds, spiders, and butterflies. Above all, these putative examples have to do with territoriality, which as we explain below is very different from the human legal concept of private property. His observations mostly involve a greater willingness to fight on the part of the defense than on the part of the invader. This inference has obvious difficulties. This preference might be an example of status quo bias rather than an instinct for proprietorship. And the existence of regularly observable physical fights between rival claimants implies that any "right" to territory is not well recognized in butterfly society.

Although animal territoriality has some superficial similarities with landownership, it is a major exaggeration to say that property and territoriality are the same thing or even that one is evolutionarily ancestral to the other. Territoriality and land ownership are different phenomena, especially when considering the modern individualistic formulation of private property. Animal territoriality is characterized by the defense of resources from (usually) conspecific competitors; generally either in the form of a concentration of food resources or an aggregation of potential mates or often a combination of the two. In cases in which resource concentrations are spatially bounded, animal territoriality amounts to the defense of a recognizable unit of land.

Consider five of the many ways animal territoriality is incongruous with full liberal ownership.

First, there is tremendous variability in terms of how aggressively animals patrol and enforce territorial boundaries. Many animals actually employ a "home range" territorial strategy in which their mobility is concentrated around important resources, although they make no effort to defend their territories from outsiders (Burt 1943; Mitani and Rodman 1979). Stake (2004) ignores examples of this form of territoriality.

Second, there is tremendous flexibility in the sizes and locations of animal territories based on seasonality, social structure, migration patterns, and so on. Even animals belonging to the same species may often exhibit radically different forms of territoriality based on the contingencies of a particular time and place (Burt 1943; Mitani and Rodman 1979).

Third, most territorial animal species are gregarious and defend territories through cooperative behavior while using its resources collectively as a group (Burt 1943; Mitani and Rodman 1979). Stake (2004) ignores examples of this kind as well.

Fourth, nonhuman animals respect no moral right to hold a particular piece of land or to respect the inheritance of that land by its holders' descendants. Animal territoriality beyond a merely familiar home range is generally maintained through aggression (Burt 1943; Mitani and Rodman 1979).

Fifth, although human groups—especially nomadic hunter-gatherers—have concepts of territory that, in some respects, accord with patterns inherent to some other animal species, the inheritance of private property, the transfer of property, and the concepts of moral or legal recognition of property "rights" are unique to humanity but not ubiquitous among humans. No species recognizes some individuals as a "criminal" for "stealing" territory from a "rightful owner." Attackers and defenders of territory would do the same if their positions were reversed (Burt 1943; Dyson-Hudson and Smith 1978; Mitani and Rodman 1979). In fact, it's likely that humans developed cultural systems of land tenure to avoid conflict with one another.

Stake's animal examples seem cherry-picked. None of them comes from herding animals or our closest evolutionary relatives, most of whom live in foraging groups.

Consider one of our closest living animal relatives, chimpanzees, who are often employed as an analog, or at least as a point of reference, for our earliest hominin ancestors. Under most conditions, chimpanzees live in foraging groups with well-defined, well-defended territories that are clearly understood by their neighbors. In many cases, they define and defend their territories more rigidly than most modern human hunter-gatherers (Boehm 2001: 29). Chimpanzees patrol and defend their territories cooperatively, either as a unit of the whole or as a coalition of prime-aged adults. They also exploit the resources within their territories collectively with the order of access to resources determined by a social ranking corresponding to a dominance hierarchy.

Dominant individuals (or pairs) come and go. Members of the group defend the territory no matter who is dominant. Territorial boundaries shift as the result of conflict between neighboring groups and as groups fission and fuse. The importance of these observations can hardly be overstated. Together they show the chimpanzee territory has no owner.

The dominant individual does not own the land either from the perspective of individuals within the group or from the perspective of neighboring groups. The dominant male does not provide services for the previous dominant individual in exchange for receiving the title of dominant male as a gift or an inheritance. They fight their way to dominance, and they remain dominant only as long as they are able to fight to protect it. No one "respects" the dominant male's "ownership rights;" they try to fight their way up the dominance hierarchy just like he did. The collective defends the territory in the same way regardless of who is dominant. They do not act as employees of the dominant male.

But the group doesn't own the land either. The group can't make any collective decisions over it or restrain the dominant male within it other than by ganging up and clearing the way for a new dominant male. Mutual lack of respect for any group rights to territory applies between groups just as the lack of respect for dominance applies between individuals. That is, each group controls whatever territory it successfully defends.

There is also great variability in chimpanzee territoriality between major research sites, between observers, and over time. For example, the warlike tendencies and hyper-aggressive territorial boundary defense observed by Jane Goodall (1990) in the Gombe forest of Tanzania contrast sharply with the toleration of overlapping group ranges in the Taï forest of the Ivory Coast (Herbinger et al. 2001). In general, all animal species, including humans, exhibit variability in their patterns of territoriality in relation to the spatial and temporal distribution of resources and the demographic characteristics of the species.

Chimpanzees have not been observed to command "sole and despotic dominion" (Blackstone 2016 [1753]) over almost anything, perhaps the only exception being alpha males' sexual dominance over females. Similar behavior is found in many species including, sadly, sometimes in humans. We doubt Stake (2004) would want to claim the tendency of males to treat females like property as an example of "The Property 'Instinct.'" We doubt he would want to infer that sexual slavery is therefore a "good" institution for humans to enforce. But to reject this inference without cherry-picking, we have to reject all such naturalistic, animal-instinct-based inferences.

6. CONCLUSION

This chapter examines evidence provided by several propertarians in support of the appropriation hypothesis, finding the following pattern:

- Most propertarians who cite evidence don't cite very much of it.
- If a more thorough historical-empirical investigation supporting the appropriation hypothesis exists, it has escaped the notice of the prominent propertarian theorists cited throughout this book.
- In many cases, the anthropological sources propertarians cite undercut rather than support the appropriation hypothesis. They tend to show that flexible, exception-laden, overlapping, and partly collectivist property rights are more common among indigenous peoples than the full liberal ownership rights that propertarians present as natural.
- Propertarians tend to play up the aspects of the empirical sources that support their expectations and play down the aspects that contradict their expectations.

The evidence provided in this chapter demonstrates that propertarians rely on poorly elaborated and poorly supported empirical claims. Without better evidence for their empirical premises, propertarians have so far failed to provide reason to accept their conclusions. A more thorough historical-empirical investigation is needed to confirm or reject the hypothesis. If nothing else, we are confident that Chapters 11–14 present a more thorough investigation of this hypothesis than any we can find in propertarian literature.

Chapter 11

PROPERTY SYSTEMS IN
HUNTER-GATHERER SOCIETIES

This is the first of four chapters examining the origin and development of property rights (private, public, collective, common, and other) in order to investigate the individual appropriation hypothesis and related claims outlined in Chapter 7, section 3. Although propertarians often present these claims as self-evident or beyond investigation, standard anthropological approaches are very useful in investigating their truth-value. The overconfident repetition of the appropriation hypothesis can't be attributed entirely to the absence of evidence. Although bad evidence has circulated widely on this issue, good evidence has been available for a long time in the fields of anthropology and history.

These chapters argue that there is a general consensus in the field of anthropology about how and when property commonly became understood as sole proprietorship and about what kinds of land-tenure systems preceded it. These chapters argue that the individual appropriation hypothesis is not merely unproven: it is disproven in all its permutations.

This chapter begins our investigation with a search for the first people to fulfill propertarian appropriation criteria. Section 1 considers whether appropriation theory applies to animals and how that might affect our view of human property claims. Section 2 explores the broad variation of systems of territoriality among modern human hunter-gatherers and uses the results to think about territoriality among the earliest human occupants of most of the globe. Section 3 considers three questions about hunter-gatherer territoriality and propertarian appropriation theory: do hunter-gatherers have private landownership; do they have private property rights in other goods; and do they qualify as original appropriators under propertarian criteria? This chapter shows that hunter-gatherers were the first people to appropriate most land around the world according to all or most appropriation criteria and that they chose not to establish individual private property—neither in land nor in other goods.

1. ANIMAL APPROPRIATION AND HUMAN INHERITANCE AS THE ORIGIN OF PROPERTY

Chapter 10 ruled out the claim that animal territoriality is equivalent in any meaningful way to individual private property, but this observation does not rule out the possibility that the appropriation principle might apply to animals. Propertarians should explain whether it does, and if not, why not?

Many nonhuman animal species—such as fire ants and beavers—fulfill the appropriation criteria including labor-mixing. Does this observation imply that nonhuman animals are the original appropriators of a significant amount of the earth's land? Without at least some qualification, appropriation theory would imply a duty to respect a great deal of animal property rights around the world. We know of no propertarians who have considered the possibility. Perhaps they believe it goes without saying that appropriation requires sentience. Even so, it might be difficult to define sentience in a way that excludes all animal property rights and includes all human property rights.

Relying on sentience creates another problem for propertarians. It implies that property does not begin with a person performing an appropriative act on a previously unused resource. The first being to pass the relevant standard of sentience probably lived in a group with a delineated territory, perhaps as modern chimpanzees have today. It is unlikely that this being would *also* have established a new territory for the group upon the attainment of human-like sentience. Perhaps then, the first property began with inheritance from non-sentient ancestors rather than with an act of appropriation. The idea that all property is ultimately an inheritance is at odds with the stories of bold individualist entrepreneur-appropriators that propertarians like to tell.

We set these issues aside, and examine appropriation theory on its own terms, which seems to assume (for whatever reason) that only humans can appropriate property.

2. LAND-TENURE SYSTEMS AMONG HUNTER-GATHERERS

Hunter-gatherers play a particularly important role in propertarian theory because the only areas on Earth not originally occupied by hunter-gatherers are remote locations, such as Antarctica, a few islands, mountain tops, glaciers, and so on. They should, therefore, be taken seriously as potential "original appropriators."

As frequent stand-ins for the "state of nature," historically and ethnographically observed hunter-gatherers have often been used as an analog for our early hominin ancestors, because we humans have been hunter-gatherers for more than 99.5 percent of our time on Earth. Early anthropological views of hunter-gatherer land-tenure systems were based on a limited range of modern case studies, such as the Ju/'hoansi of the Kalahari (Marshall 1960). Mid-twentieth century anthropologists such as Service (1962) argued that modern hunter-gatherers living in remote places, such as the Ju/'hoansi, represented an undisturbed manifestation of an ancient hunting and gathering lifeway, which descended directly from our early hominin ancestors. As such, they concluded that our Stone Age ancestors normally held territories collectively with each group member having more or less equal rights to the resources within that territory, and that, in general, they had weak ethics of individual property ownership. Many anthropologists still hold this basic position today despite some problems with it.

Among both nonhuman foraging primates and nomadic foraging humans, no individual can claim exclusive use of any piece of land, and no individual can be excluded from the resources she needs to maintain her existence (Bird-David 1990; Ingold 1986: 148–150; Isakson and Sproles 2008: 6; Johnson and Earle 2000: 63; Lee 1979: 456, 1990: 231–232; Woodburn 1998: 53). At this point, it might be enough for us to say that there is an overwhelming consensus that basically all hunter-gatherer societies have some form of collective landownership; that our early ancestors also had at least partially collective land-tenure systems; and to be done with the issue of hunter-gatherer land rights.

But there is no single hunter-gatherer lifeway. A deeper look at the spectrum of modern hunter-gatherer territoriality sheds light on the eventual move away from collectively held territories and the origins of more restrictive systems of rights to land and resources. Service's (1962) view of hunter-gatherers as a monolithic cultural type has been rejected by anthropologists who began to recognize extreme variability among both modern and past forager societies. In the aftermath of the *Man the Hunter* conference (Lee and DeVore 1968a), it became apparent that no single generalization about forager land-tenure systems was adequate to the diversity inherent within the ethnographic and archaeological records.

Among this new way of thinking about foraging societies, there were several influential examinations of variability in foraging territorial systems. The first of these was that of Rada Dyson-Hudson and Eric Smith (1978), who explored territorial system variability according to the density and predictability of food resources in the environment. At one end of the spectrum, when food resources are scarce, sparsely distributed, and unpredictable, forager groups exhibit large territory sizes, very high mobility, and open, "home range," territorial systems. In these systems, territories are large and unbounded, with open access to members of other groups. In the terminology of property rights theory, the land is an "open commons."

In more recent syntheses of modern hunter-gatherer variability, Kelly (1995) and Binford (2001) add several important dimensions to Dyson-Hudson and Smith's (1978) model. Among the most important of these is population density—an issue with which Dyson-Hudson and Smith are clearly concerned but which does not feature much in their formal modeling. Kelly points out that there is a clear relationship between population density and territoriality, with home range systems being characterized by very low population densities and territorial defense systems being characterized by much higher population densities. The connections here are fairly simple: environments with scarce food resources are capable of supporting fewer people; territories with abundant food resources tend to have more packed populations. Higher population density usually requires clearer boundaries.

Dyson-Hudson and Smith (1978) argue that home range territorial systems emerge because territories are too large to patrol effectively and too sparse in useful resources to be worth defending (see also Cashdan 1983 and Kelly 1995). For example, the Inuit of Arctic North America and the Hadza of tropical Africa have no exclusive territoriality at all. Woodburn writes "The Eastern Hadza assert no rights over land and its ungarnered resources . . . they do not even seek to restrict the use of the land they occupy to members of their own tribe" (Woodburn 1968a: 50).

Slightly more restrictive territorial systems tend to develop where food resources are scarce but predictably concentrated in space and time. Here, territorial boundaries are established between neighboring groups, though these boundaries are seldom actively patrolled or defended and neighbors are frequently granted access to territories for occasional foraging activities. In the terminology of property theory, the land is a "closed" or "partially closed" commons.

For example, the Ju/'hoansi of the Kalahari maintain fixed territorial boundaries between groups, with territories including seasonally abundant food resources such as mangetti nuts, also called mongongo nuts (Lee 1979). Predictable resources like mangetti groves are collectively owned in the sense of being resources included within group territories and accessible to all members. The "closed" nature of the Ju/'hoansi commons and therefore the exclusive nature of their "ownership" should not be over-interpreted given the frequent circumstances under which members of neighboring groups are granted access to food resources within a group's territory. Such access to key foraging resources for members of neighboring groups is one of many features of the Ju/'hoansi's sharing and reciprocity systems.

In Dyson-Hudson and Smith's (1978) model, a low density of predictable resources or a high density of unpredictable resources seem to foster societies with a high frequency of mobility and information sharing, as forager groups seek to overcome the inherent unpredictability of their environment. Here, territories are not structured according to the need for defense but rather the dispersal of a network of small groups capable of sharing information about the environment and moving people to the location of unpredictable food sources. For example, the Pumé of Venezuela seasonally disperse into a network of small settlements to take advantage of unpredictable food resources on the relatively featureless alluvial plains of the Venezuelan *llanos* (Greaves 1997). Here, too, there is collective ownership and common use of land and resources at the scales of families and villages, with the territorial system serving as a mechanism of information sharing and coordination.

Groups as different as the Ju/'hoansi, the Hadza, and the Pumé are all typically lumped together as "hunter-gatherer bands," because they share the attributes of being nomadic, exclusively foraging societies that do not store food. Indeed, all do have some form of collective territoriality with each individual having more or less equal access rights to the resources within that territory. None of them conforms to the norms propertarians portray as "natural," but neither do the many diverse foraging groups conform to any one view of territoriality.

Martin Bailey (1992: 185) examined anthropological observations of more than fifty hunter-gatherer bands and autonomous villages, finding that they all had at least partially collective claims to territory. Many foragers have systems of collective land "ownership" in which rights to land access are guaranteed by complex systems of memberships in groups, clans, moieties, sodalities, and through networks of individual reciprocity, such as the Ju/'hoansi (Hitchcock 2005). Richard Lee and Richard Daly (1999: 4) observe that one characteristic "common to almost all band societies (and hundreds of village-based societies as well) is a land-tenure system based on a common property regime. . . . These regimes were, until recently, far more common world-wide than regimes based on private property."

As diverse as these band societies are, they do not capture the full range of hunter-gatherer land use. At the other end of the spectrum are complex hunter-gatherers who live in environments where food resources are densely and predictably packed at particular points in space and time. Such localized and predictable occurrences of food are capable of monitoring and defense and, in such cases, territorial defense is very much worthwhile. In such circumstances people often give up nomadism and settle into large-scale permanent or semi-permanent communities with more complex social, political, and economic structures with differentiation in social prestige and economic and political stratification (Arnold 1996: 78–79).

For example, the foraging societies of the Northwest Coast of North America, such as the Kwakiutl and Tlingit, are heavily dependent on the exploitation of seasonal salmon runs, which are highly concentrated in space and time. Therefore, salmon fishing spots on major rivers and other territorial features are firmly owned by familial clans, are heavily defended from other clans, and are passed down through generations in a fixed system of land and/or resource tenure. Their societies, often labeled as chiefdoms, were highly stratified with wealthy and powerful chiefs at the top and sometimes slaves at the bottom (Flannery and Marcus 2012: 83–84; Kelly 1995: 293–294).

These territorial systems do feature more cultural regulation in terms of access and rights over particular pieces of land and the resources within them, but they are not individual private property in the modern sense; they are instead the collective ownership of land at the scale of familial clans. Chiefs were less like private property holders and more like clan representatives with a combination of what contemporary political theorists think of as separate economic, political, and religious powers.

The discussion so far has involved observed hunter-gatherers, whose practices, we have said, cannot be presumed to be the same as hunter-gatherers of the deep past. What can we say about deep past foragers from the available evidence?

Most likely, early humans and our hominin ancestors lived in population densities that were *much* lower than virtually all modern hunter-gatherer societies (Kelly 1995) and occupied environments in which food resources were not densely aggregated—neither in space nor in time (i.e. the semi-arid regions of sub-Saharan Africa during the Pleistocene).

It is always difficult to draw firm conclusions about social practices in the deep past, but the available evidence points against the existence of a private ownership system in prehistory. What we know about modern hunter-gatherer variability suggests that early hominins did not have strongly defended territories but instead had loosely defended or undefended home ranges. In this sense, all or most land would probably have been a commons with very weak collective ownership or no ownership at all of land and resources—as is the case for modern hunter-gatherers living in very low population densities and in similar environments today.

The evolution of more restrictive land-tenure systems is likely the outcome of increasing human population densities in concert with more specialized foraging techniques. More restrictive territorial claims (such as closed-commons hunting and gathering territories) were aimed at buffering risk, protecting against over-exploitation, and/or discouraging conflict. As we have elsewhere argued, reciprocal territorial systems, like those employed by the Ju/'hoansi, actually came about in the context of the major human population increases that occurred in the terminal Pleistocene, beginning perhaps 10,000–20,000 years ago and continuing through the Holocene (McCall and Widerquist 2015; Widerquist and McCall 2017). Therefore, even the "classic" features of reciprocal land-tenure systems among modern hunter-gatherers, such as the Ju/'hoansi, are not timeless and universal features but rather relatively recent developments in the grand sweep of hunter-gatherer history.

The complex hunter-gatherer societies that are somewhat closer to the liberal private property model are also recent developments. Some evidence suggests that sedentary and relatively large-scale hunting and gathering societies might have appeared occasionally as early as 15,000 years ago or perhaps somewhat before in isolated instances, but the evidence that these communities persisted for any length of time remains inconclusive at best, and these societies do not show the signs of persistent inequality present in later complex hunter-gatherers (Flannery and Marcus 2012: 83–84; Kelly 1995: 293–294; Wengrow and Graeber 2015).

The earliest clear archaeological evidence of persistent complex hunting and gathering societies includes the various Mesolithic societies of Eurasia and the Jōmon of Japan, all of which emerge no earlier than the terminal Pleistocene (10,000–15,000 years ago). The bulk of complex hunter-gatherer societies with boundary defense territorial systems likely came into existence contemporaneously with early farming societies within the last 10,000 years. In later-settled areas, such as the Americas, early inhabitants might have adopted complex hunting and gathering practices shortly after arriving in the territory but, for the most part, complex hunting and gathering developed thousands of years after the first human occupation.

3. HUNTER-GATHERERS AS APPROPRIATORS

Three questions for our property-rights discussion follow from this review of hunter-gatherer territorial systems.

A. *Assuming Hunter-Gatherers are the Original Appropriators, Have Any of Them Established Full Liberal Ownership Systems as Propertarians Assume Appropriators Naturally Would?*

Clearly the answer is no: even though hunter-gatherer territorial systems are extremely diverse, no foraging societies have been observed to establish the supposedly "natural" system of individualistic private ownership. The vast majority of modern hunter-gatherer land use systems are not only dominated by collective land ownership but also by common access rights. Most hunter-gatherers assertively oppose all individual claims of special rights to the use of particular units of land. Any such attempt by a Ju/'hoansi person would be anathema to the community, which would apply forceful social sanctioning (Lee 1979).

Common access rights to land have been noted in nomadic hunter-gatherer societies in southern Africa, eastern Africa, South America, Australia, India, the North American plains, the Great Basin, Labrador, the Arctic and many other places (Bird-David 1990: 190–192; Cashdan 1989: 40–42; Hamilton 1982; Hoebel 1954: 59; Ingold 1986: 148–150; Isakson and Sproles: 6; Johnson and Earle 2000: 63; Leacock 1954: 2; Leacock and Lee 1982: 8; Lee and Daly 1999: 4; Woodburn 1998: 53).

Exceptional cases of hunter-gatherer land tenure tend to be the complex hunter-gatherers like the Kwakiutl and Tlingit, which have clan elites who strictly control particular foraging resources, but even these are forms of collective land ownership in relation to clan hierarchies (Arnold 1996; Binford 2001; Kelly 1995). The origins of these forms of territoriality with more rigid political control of land and food resources potentially offer some insights about the evolution of human land-tenure systems.

The stricter hierarchical control of resources among the complex hunter-gatherers almost certainly relates to a tragedy-of-the-commons problem inherent to more open territorial systems under similar circumstances. That is, given the dense and predictable occurrence of food resources, there would be massive conflict over access to or dangerous depletion of those resources in the absence of a political system capable of controlling resource access and settling potential disputes. Such a system, in turn, fosters ethical norms and moral obligations having to do with the rights over specific resources. This combination of political and ideological constructs mitigates potential conflicts over the richest food resources and assures social order in maximizing the productivity of such food resources.

Importantly, only the dense concentrations of food resources, such as the locations of salmon fishing access on rivers, are so strictly controlled by elites even in the largest-scale hunter-gatherer societies. Vast territories for terrestrial foraging activities are basically open or collectively owned by the village or chiefdom as a whole rather than specific clans (Arnold 1996; Binford 2001; Kelly 1995). In this sense, the political control of particular dense concentrations of food resources nowhere near implies a pervasive system of individual landownership. The existence of a commons remains hugely important in the most complex hunting and gathering societies.

From an analytical perspective, at least three lessons can be learned from the evolution of stricter systems of land control and resource access found among complex hunter-gatherers.

First, the emergence of such systems depended on a particular combination of highly specialized economic practices to take advantage of food resources that are highly concentrated in space and time in the effort to support dense human populations. The balance of the costs and benefits of defending foraging territories in these cases tilted to strongly favor territorial patrol and defense; and, thus, people did so assertively and aggressively.

Second, human hunter-gatherers have tended to develop land-tenure systems and concomitant norms about land and resource rights in order to head off potential conflicts and to coordinate foraging activities. Neither modern humans, nor our hominin ancestors, were evolutionarily programmed with only one way of dealing with property rights and land-tenure systems as propertarian theory has had it since the 1600s. Instead, land-tenure systems have been tremendously variable over space and time, with the land-tenure systems of the last 10,000–15,000 years being quite exceptional relative to deeper prehistory and with the modern concept of private property of the last 400 years being the most recent and exceptional of all.

Third, the progression in response to the possibility of a tragedy of the commons runs from open commons, through closed commons, to collective control and management—i.e. essentially from nonownership to clan appropriation and public ownership. The individual appropriation and private ownership that we are led to believe are the only natural kinds play no role in hunter-gatherer responses to the tragedy of the commons.

The supposedly natural right of private property contravenes a principle that anthropologists have found to be far older: that wild places could not be appropriated by any individual (Katz 1997: 284). Hasnas's (2005) portrayal of individual private property as an "empirical natural right" requires ignoring the entire hunter-gatherer period, as if all humans exercised their free will by choosing to live *unnaturally* for most of our existence as a species. A more reasonable conclusion is that the people who discovered, made the first use of, and established the first claim to the vast majority of the earth's land treated it as (either an open or closed) commons.

B. Do Hunter-Gatherers have Private Property Rights in Moveable Goods such as Food and Tools?

The nature of hunter-gatherer claims to moveable goods is important because Locke's (1960 [1689]) labor-mixing criterion applies more clearly to food and tools than to foraging territory. If hunter-gatherers without property claims in land had strict private property rights in those goods, they might be interpreted as conforming to a specifically Lockean conception of property. But it is not so.

Although complex hunter-gathers might have full liberal ownership of some movable goods, egalitarian band societies clearly recognize far fewer incidents of ownership at the individual level. "Ownership" is seldom exclusive and not usually appropriated by individualistic labor-mixing. Gathered food and small game are usually consumed by the person who obtained it or by her immediate family—though they may be subject to demand sharing or any number of other anti-accumulation norms. Big game is more universally shared with everyone present regardless of who was involved in the hunt and whether individuals have contributed meat in the past. Possession of tools is also subject to demand sharing, meaning that members have a strong obligation to share when they have more than they can use or when something is particularly needed by another group member (Bird-David 1990; Dowling 1968; Hawkes 2001; Hawkes et al. 2001; Ingold 1986: 223–228; Leacock 1998: 145). Furthermore, although individuals do have some sense of ownership over particular objects, all individuals have equal access to the raw materials necessary to make anything that anyone else might have. Therefore, individuals seldom need something that someone else has usually because either they have one of their own already or they are free to make one of their own from resources freely available on common land.

Interestingly, band members who receive shared meat have little reciprocal obligation to produce meat to share at another time. The most common rule seems to be, if you have found or produced more than you can use, you must share, but you are not obliged to find or produce anything. Some anthropologists find limited evidence for reciprocity in responsibility to provide for the group (Gurven 2006). Others find almost no evidence of it (Bird-David 1990, 1992; Hawkes et al. 2001). According to Kristen Hawkes (2001: 219), "Among modern tropical foragers . . . [a] hunter cannot exclude other claimants, nor can he exchange portions of meat with other hunters (or anyone else) for obligations to return meat (or anything else)."

Kim Hill and A. Magdalena Hurtado (1996: xii), referring to the Ache of South America, write, "Property was never really private, and sharing was the most important aspect of the behavioral code." Fried (1967: 75) observes, "the taking of something before it is offered is more akin to rudeness than stealing."

Simply put, a massive amount of evidence supports the observation that "individual ownership" in band societies is far weaker than the form propertarians portray as "natural."

A propertarian clinging to the individual appropriation hypothesis might suppose bands' treatment of tools and big game was an early example of collectivist aggression against duly appropriated individual private property rights. Such a claim would be, at best, wishful thinking, derived not from observed events but from imagining events prior to those observed.

A closer look at the evidence disproves this wishful thinking. Nomadic hunter-gatherers almost invariably exercise individual choice to create and to live under largely collectivist property rights structures. All band members are free to leave. They can join another band nearby; a skilled nomadic hunter-gatherer could live on their own for some time; and any like-minded group can start their own band (Johnson and Earle 2000: 75). Six to ten adults are enough to start a band in most niches. In propertarian terms, these observations make virtually all obligations within bands "contractual obligations," which propertarians consider to be fully consistent with freedom and reflective of human will.

If six to ten foragers wanted to start a band that recognized the eat-what-you-kill rule, no one from their previous bands would interfere with them. Yet, although bands have been observed to split for many reasons, none has been observed to split because someone wanted to start a private property rights system. Band societies have been observed on all inhabited continents, but none practices elitists ownership institutions—even those made up of outcasts from other bands (Boehm 2001: 72–73).

Therefore, we must conclude that *individuals* in band societies *choose* to establish weak-to-non-existent private property rights. As original appropriators, it is their right to do so. The group's informal contract seems to be those who camp with us accept that many centrally important incidents of ownership are held at the band level. The exact terms of informal contracts are seldom if ever explicit, but the general terms of these informal agreements are obvious to the people involved, clearly enforced, and demonstrably voluntary in propertarian terms.

The extent to which band members assent to these rules is further demonstrated by most hunters' preference for big game, which unlike small game is treated as common property. Anthropologists disagree about why hunters have this preference, but some combination of social approval, prestige, competition for mates, and the feeling of accomplishment seems to be an adequate incentive to get individuals to provide large game for the whole band (Hawkes 2001; Hawkes et al. 2001: 695; Leacock 1998: 145; Woodburn 1998). That is, band members are allowed to choose whether to hunt under more or less individualistic rules, and they tend to prefer the less individualistic rules.

To the extent that studying any particular lifeway can answer Mayor's (2012: 485) question of whether people "naturally respect an individual's right to the products of his own efforts," the answer is emphatically no. Epstein (1978–1979: 1241) was entirely wrong to say first possession held a unique position in all past times as the organizing principle of most social institutions. If the wide sample of observed bands are predictive of what a reasonable person would do in those circumstances, we can conclude that all or most people (including ourselves and our distant ancestors) would reject private appropriation in similar circumstances.

C. Do Hunter-Gatherers Qualify as Original Appropriators under Propertarian Criteria?

The issue of whether foragers appropriate land might seem esoteric in a world so remote from full-time foraging, but it is in fact central to the private property debate, because although the vast majority of people around the world were agriculturalists by the time the worldwide privatization trend got underway around 1500 CE, the great majority of the world's land was still used for hunting and gathering, mostly by farmers who were part-time foragers.

Under most appropriation criteria—first use, first claim, first occupancy, discovery, etc.—hunter-gatherers certainly qualify as appropriators. Only the labor-mixing/first-labor criterion might put some limits on their territorial claims. Arguably, Locke (1960 [1689]: §30–32) chose his labor-mixing criterion in hopes of excluding foraging territory from the realm of property. He asserted specifically that hunters appropriate their kill, but not the land on which they killed it, apparently to justify both the enclosure movement in Britain and colonial settlement in the British empire (Widerquist 2010a).

Therefore, supposedly, no matter how many generations a group might have labored by hunting and gathering on a particular piece of land they never obtain the right to keep hunting and gathering on it. Later-arriving agriculturalists are free to dispossess them without disappropriating them under the theory (Narveson 1998: 14 n28). This principle is popular even today with propertarians despite its obvious conflict with the other appropriation criteria and with the notion that propertarianism is motivated by an underlying ethic of nonaggression. Colonial invaders might look like they're aggressively interfering with indigenous peoples as they seize foraging grounds, but the native resistors are the "aggressive," even "warlike" violators of the "noninterference" principle. Sounds disingenuous, doesn't it?

Unfortunately, many philosophers have dealt with the difficult empirical fact of hunter-gatherer dispossession as they have with many other difficult facts—by ignoring it in favor of mythmaking (Widerquist and McCall 2017). The mere assertion of the first-labor criterion is not mythmaking; it's a first-best a priori moral principle. But it's possible to accuse adherents of the first-labor criterion of principle shopping: choosing the moral principle that gives the result they want instead of demanding the result moral principles imply. But the kind of mythmaking we're focusing on involves the assertion of dubious *empirical* claims, at least two of which typically appear in propertarians' treatment of this issue.

First, propertarians since Locke (1960 [1689]: §37) have claimed that farmers do not actually take land from hunter-gatherers but give it to them. This giving of land is a *theoretical* possibility. In most geographical circumstances, more people can live on the same amount of land as farmers than as hunter-gatherers. It helps explain why the transformation of resources is included in the first-labor criteria and supports the claim that the Lockean proviso is fulfilled.

Unfortunately, the *theoretical possibility* that agriculturalists could effectively give land to hunter-gatherers is irrelevant in a world where the *empirical reality* is that the transition from hunting, gathering, and small-scale swidden agriculture to large-scale agriculture and commerce in most of the world was an aggressive process of dispossession, oppression, and murder. This tendency has been observed throughout history, apparently because large-scale agricultural and commercial societies tend to increase in population, desire more land, and then seize territory from smaller-scale societies with more stable populations. Supposedly, propertarian justice "depends on what actually has happened" (Nozick 1974: 152).

Second, the claim that hunter-gatherers do not transform their land also requires empirical investigation. Just because hunter-gatherers refrain from clearing, planting, digging, and drilling does not mean that they leave the land as they found it. Earth was very different in 10,000 BCE, after human foragers covered it, than it was in 100,000 BCE, when humans were confined to a small part of Africa. Perhaps the most significant difference being the disappearance of most of the earth's megafauna (larger than human-sized animals), some of which were dangerous predators. Human action—such as hunting, competition for game, and competition for habitat space—was probably a contributing factor to the extinction of all these species (Martin and Klein 1984).

Permanently ridding the land of a predator or a competitor species seriously transforms land and greatly alters the environment— perhaps a greater transformation than opening a mine and probably more so than the usual labor-mixing example of clearing the land of trees, which eventually grow back. The human-caused extinction of megafauna might have been unwise from an environmental standpoint, but many of the ways private property holders transform land are also environmentally unwise.

This discussion implies that the application of the labor-mixing criterion doesn't clearly exclude foraging territory from appropriated property. Yet, propertarians unanimously (as far as we can tell) presume that it does, forcing the discussion to move on to agricultural societies.

4. CONCLUSION

The analysis above supports two conclusions. First, no innate human (or animal) private property instinct exists. Second, our early hunter-gatherer ancestors, who have the best claim to original appropriation under all or most propertarian criteria, treated the land as an open or closed commons in the sense of ensuring each group member had access to foraging resources according to a range of environmental and social variables. No natural inclination to establish individual property rights in land or other goods exists among observed hunter-gatherers, nor is it likely to have existed among hunter-gatherers of the deep past.

Chapter 12

PROPERTY SYSTEMS IN STATELESS FARMING COMMUNITIES

To avoid recognizing forager land claims, propertarians tend to fall back on Locke's labor-mixing appropriation criterion and use it in tandem with the claim that farming provided the impetus for the first privatized land ownership systems. Many property theorists and legal scholars have made this speculation, but is it true? Does this tandem strategy succeed?

The evidence below shows that the origin of private property is long after the origins of agriculture and even the origins of the first states. Ethnographic research on modern small-scale farming societies has provided key insights into this set of issues. We argue that land-tenure systems in the first farming societies in places like the Fertile Crescent probably involved the defense of resource concentrations within larger territories and in keeping with our characterizations of "complex" hunter-gatherer territoriality in Chapter 11.

The first farmers originated around 10,000–12,000 years ago in the Fertile Crescent region of the Near East and farming was subsequently developed independently in numerous other centers of plant and animal domestication in both the Old and New Worlds over the next several millennia (Harlan 1971). What, then, do we know about the land-tenure systems of early farming societies? And how does the prehistory of the first farmers in various places around the globe match up with the act of private appropriation imagined by Locke and other propertarians?

By virtue of the inherent limitations of the archaeological record, direct evidence concerning the exact nature of land-tenure rules and the political systems that governed them is limited. Once again, our best opportunity is to link archaeological features of past societies with observed variability among modern small-scale farmers. The ethnographic record of the nineteenth and twentieth centuries is rich with descriptions of the land-tenure systems of small-scale farming societies; with many of these descriptions considered "classic" texts in cultural anthropology (Barth 1953; Evans-Pritchard 1951; Geertz 1956; Malinowski 1921; Mead 1930; Rappaport 1968; Sahlins 1957; and innumerable others). This ethnographic record provides a framework for thinking about how and why different kinds of land-tenure systems emerged among early agricultural societies and, at a minimum, to the kinds of land-tenure systems that existed prior to the colonial movement and that to some extent continue to exist among contemporary non-Western cultures.

Usually, societies that practice any farming at all are considered "agricultural," even if a majority of their diet comes from foraging. This definition establishes a sharp dichotomy between farming and foraging societies but it also obscures the varying role foraging plays in small-scale farming economies and the varying extent to which livestock or plant food replace foraging in farming societies depending on the availability of foraging opportunities.

Stateless farmers are good candidates as original appropriators both because they transform land in the very way most propertarians describe and because the smallest-scale farming techniques seem to have spread more by imitation than by conquest. There are some ethnographic observations of tensions between farmers and hunter-gatherers in neighboring areas and some archaeological indications of this phenomenon in prehistory, but the overall pattern seems to be that violence drops as hunter-gatherers initially make the transition to farming. Relatively low levels of violence might continue for hundreds or thousands of years until population density catches up to the capacity of the new techniques (Moore 1985). Therefore, although no direct observations of independent groups making a permanent transition from foraging to farming exist, it is reasonable to suppose the transition often happened voluntarily.

Non-state agricultural societies exist on as broad a spectrum as foraging societies. Important dimensions of variation include the type of farming techniques, the size of the polity, and the centralization of authority. Early non-state agricultural societies used at least three different farming and land-tenure strategies before states appeared in most areas.

First, many of the earliest farmers probably practiced swidden, or slash-and-burn, agriculture—as farmers continue to do in many places today. Though slash-and-burn farming has something of bad reputation today, it usually sounds more environmentally damaging than it actually is. Cultivators periodically relocate gardens as a strategy for dealing with soil fertility problems, which occur at the scale of years or sometimes decades (Scott 2009). Once they move on, natural vegetation gradually returns. Swidden farming requires a fairly large wilderness surrounding each village. Virtually all swidden farmers supplement their diets by foraging, and the rearing of livestock is also a common strategy. Swidden villagers normally share in the act of clearing the land and burning the vegetation with the expectation of a guarantee of individual (or family) access to an agreed-upon amount of land to farm and access to the commons for foraging or grazing, if they have domesticated livestock (Conklin 1961; Spencer 1966). Swidden agriculture and transhumance (seasonal movement of livestock between summer and winter pastures) were prevalent across both the Old and New Worlds from the time of the origin of agriculture (Conklin 1961)—and they are still common in the twenty-first century in places like the rainforests of South America, Africa, Southeast Asia, and New Guinea (Nye and Greenland 1960).

Later, farmers living in larger and more permanently settled communities developed alternative strategies for maintaining soil fertility, such as field fallowing. Rather than moving to an entirely new settlement as soil fertility declines, cultivators maintain fertility by rotating crops and by letting some fields lie fallow while using it as pasturage. The rotation of crops slowed the loss of soil fertility and droppings from livestock grazing among the fallow fields acted to recharge soil fertility.

In fallowing strategies, some land within the village at any given time is designated for individual farming and some for shared pasturage, while surrounding "wastes" or "commons" (if any exist) are usually open for foraging. Using fields for pasturage as they lie fallow for a period of years restores soil fertility partly from the nutrients in the animals' excrement. In contrast, using the swidden method people usually don't return to the same spot in living memory. The result of fallowing is a system of permanent communal land ownership in which individuals in the community have hereditary rights to land access for farming and common rights of pasturage, but rarely more than temporary rights over particular plots. Small-scale elites play an important role in assuring individual claims to parcels of communal land for farming and in managing the complex rotation of farmed and fallow fields. In such fallowing systems, communal land tenure shields individuals from declining soil fertility, distributes the immediate costs of leaving land fallow, assures people adequate space to graze their livestock, allows farmers to focus their efforts on the most productive land, and maintains soil fertility across the village's land as a whole (Benneh 1973; Bogaard et al. 2017; Smith 2000; Trigger 2003: 316).

The efficacy of the fallowing system is demonstrated by the diversity of places in which it has been employed and the length of time it has lasted. For example, some early Neolithic farmers, who for centuries or millennia continuously occupied large, permanent villages—such as the famous sites of Çatalhöyük in Turkey and Jericho in the Levant—likely employed some variant of the field fallowing strategy. But it also appears that they suffered significantly from declining soil fertility over time (Bogaard et al. 2017). Fallowing was used by pre-Columbian Peruvian highlanders (Trigger 2003: 316) and likely numerous other regions of Central and South America. Fallowing was still an important feature of the open field systems in Western Europe at least as late as the nineteenth century (Smith 2000) and it is still a prevalent strategy today wherever non-industrial farming is practiced (Benneh 1973).

Later still, farmers began to move into regions with great agricultural productivity but which required the development of new technologies, such as the plow and irrigation, in order to farm successfully. These regions included above all the alluvial lowlands of major river systems like the Nile, the Tigris and Euphrates, the Indus, the Yellow, and so on. On the one hand, the increased agricultural productivity in these regions was ultimately an impetus for increasing political complexity, including eventually state development, through the production of an agricultural surplus (Childe 1950, 1957). On the other hand, these agricultural systems required great political coordination in doing things like building irrigation systems and transportation networks for moving surplus crops from the fields to consumers in distant towns and cities (Wittfogel 1957). This last set of dynamics is therefore typical of highly complex political systems, including paramount chiefdoms and early states, and it also witnessed new approaches to land tenure.

1. LAND-TENURE SYSTEMS IN SMALL-SCALE STATELESS FARMING COMMUNITIES

Political variation among swidden and fallowing agricultural societies depends largely on the ability of individuals within communities to split off and start autonomous communities of their own, on whether they have a single leader or group of leaders, and on the extent of the leaders' power over individuals. Kin groups tend to be important among stateless farmers at all scales of social organization. They are large extended families including many sets of in-laws and fictive kin making them more of a community. Big men emerged within kin groups to ensure individual common rights of access to collective farmland, to coordinate labor in clearing and maintaining collectively held farmland, and to settle any resulting disputes.

Villages that practice swidden agriculture and retain the ability to split up and form new communities are what we mean by autonomous villages. These tend to exist in places where swiddening is possible by virtue of the availability of suitable land and population density is low. Autonomous villages' tendency to habitually under-exploit resources gives them the opportunity to settle disputes by splitting. Many have been observed doing so (Bandy 2004; Boehm 2001: 93; Carneiro 1970: 735, 738 n19; Kirch 1984: 31). Autonomous villages tend to have populations of at least 100 people, and because of fission, they tend not to have populations of more than about 600 (Boehm 2001: 3–4; Lee 1990: 236; Renfrew 2007: 142; Wilson 1988: 3). Many autonomous villages survived into the twentieth century; a few survive today and have been extensively studied by ethnographers (Roscoe 2002). Observed autonomous villages tend to have little economic inequality, no explicit fixed rules, and virtually no trade or specialization. Archaeological evidence of peoples of the deep past living at this scale indicates that they were similar in these respects (Boehm 2001; Fried 1967: 129–130). They usually have no fixed property rights in land; all members of the village are entitled to access to land, but not necessarily a particular plot (Bailey 1992: 92; Johnson 1989: 50–53; Sahlins 1974: 93–94).

Observed villages and chiefdoms tend to have a leader or a group of leaders. We use the terms "big man," "headman," and "chief" with our usual caution that these are obviously English terms coined by anthropologists to identify ranges on a spectrum of leadership positions across different societies. It is questionable whether these gender-specific terms reflect the sexism of the observed people or of the observers.

As we use the terms, a big man or a headman is a non-inherited leadership position that might involve arbitrating disputes between members of the village and allocating plots to individuals each growing season. Headman implies greater unity of power than big man, although a fully unified power structure is seldom observed in societies at this scale. Headmen cannot exclude any villager from access to farmland, and they cannot order lower-ranking people to work for them. In autonomous villages, all individuals, including headmen and religious leaders, produce their immediate family's consumption (Fried 1967: 129–132, 177). Headmen do obtain a certain amount of wealth, power, and prestige through their competition, but their wealth is in many ways the group's wealth: land remains the property of the clan or village (Johnson and Earle 2000: 170–172, 180, 191–192). Big men and headmen might appear superficially to resemble businessmen (Sahlins 1963), but their government-like powers over village lands and kin groups make it impossible to put them on one side or another of the public-private dichotomy that doesn't exist in their cultural context.

A headman in an autonomous village is sometimes spoken of as the "owner" of the group's real estate (at least as translated by Western observers), but he more often acts like the administrator of his group's possessions, and he does not have exclusive control over resources (Harris 1977: 69; Johnson and Earle 2000: 126). To the extent any entity can be identified as an "owner" in Western legal terminology, it is the community or kin group as a whole (Ingold 1986: 157–158). The land can most accurately be described as a regulated commons— usually closed or partly closed. The rights holder with the authority to regulate the commons is most often the group as a whole, with headmen making decisions on behalf of the kin group. No individual, not a headman and usually not even a chief, has the power to alienate the group's holdings. No reasonable way of understanding the role of big men and headmen makes them into full liberal owners.

The periodic relocation of swidden agriculture fits the classic Lockean model of an appropriative act, but *individual* appropriation is unheard of. When villages relocate farm plots, they clear land collectively and rely on traditions and the political authority of headmen or chiefs to regulate use of and to ensure individual access to farmland (Bailey 1992: 191–192; Earle 2002: 326–327; Malinowski 1921, 1956; Sahlins 1974: 92–93) among individuals who often require overlapping claims to the use of particular pieces of land with neither having full liberal ownership.

It is wrong to say that people living in autonomous villages have no property rights at all. The group often holds land rights against outsiders. Each family keeps the crops they produce, subject to the responsibility to help people in need (Bailey 1992: 191–192). Often different individuals hold different use rights over the same land. Land rights in small-scale farming communities have been described as "ambiguous and flexible" (Earle 2002: 326–327) and "overlapping and complex" (Sahlins 1974: 92–93).

In Honoré's (1987: 11) terms, the incidents of ownership are dispersed: some incidents held by various members of the community, some incidents held by the community as a whole, and some or all incidents subject to revision by the group. Throughout this book, we describe "traditional" or "customary land-tenure systems" (both in stateless societies and in many villages within state societies) variously as complex, overlapping, flexible, nonspatial, and at least partially collective with a significant commons.

The complexity and ambiguity of indigenous land-tenure systems is perhaps the reason so many outside observers—anthropologists and political philosophers included—have so much difficulty understanding them. Indigenous land rights often do not fit into the narrow range of property rights systems that people in large-scale, contemporary state societies have conceptualized (Banner 1999). This cultural difference is why we struggle so much to talk about stateless indigenous societies using modern Western terms like "ownership," "businessman," "big man," and "chief."

These societies are neither primitive communists nor Lockean individualists. Autonomous villages, bands, and many small chiefdoms around the world are simultaneously collectivist and individualist in the extremely important sense that the community recognizes that all individuals are entitled to direct access to the resources they need for subsistence without having to work for someone else. Independent access to common land is far more important to them than the right to exclude others from private land. The right of access to the commons is probably the most important tool to maintain individual freedom in stateless farming communities (Anderson 1998: 65; Bailey 1992: 92; Hann 1998a: 11–12; Hann 2005: 113; Macfarlane 1998: 106; Sahlins 1974: 93).

Land in most swidden and fallowing villages is a commons in at least three senses. First, individuals have access rights to cultivate a portion of the village's farmland though not to any particular spot each year. Second, individual members usually have shared access to farmland for other uses, such as grazing, outside of the growing season. Third, individual members have access rights to forage on or make other uses of uncultivated lands or wastes.

A propertarian might once again be tempted to interpret the land-tenure institutions of swidden and fallowing farming communities as examples of original individual appropriators being victims of group interference. But again, such wishful thinking is contradicted by evidence. In propertarian terms, villagers' independent access to resources and their ability to split makes each village a voluntary association. Individuals are free to leave and set up a society with a private property regime. None has been observed doing so, although many autonomous villages have been observed splitting for other reasons. All of the thousands of village societies known to ethnographers, archeologists, and historians exercised collective control over land and recognized a common right of access to land, even though individuals were free to do otherwise (Bandy 2004; Boehm 2001: 93; Carneiro 1970: 735, 738 n19; Kirch 1984: 31).

The reasonable conclusion is that the first farmers almost everywhere in the world voluntarily chose to work together to appropriate land rights that were complex, overlapping, flexible, nonspatial, and partly collective, and they chose to retain significant common rights to the land. As original appropriators, it was their right to set up property however they wanted it.

Individuals choose to live in groups that established traditional land-tenure systems, because that rights structure met their needs. Bailey (1992: 191–195) argues that private plots of land simply aren't very valuable to the farmers with the simplest, swidden techniques. What they needed at any given moment was access to some land, not permanent exclusive control over any particular piece of land. Stronger individual claims to land come when they make sense economically, perhaps in the context of more fertile lands requiring more intensive farming techniques, irrigation, substantial scarcity, larger scale, or a cash economy.

With the replacement of swiddening with fallowing systems, higher levels of population density become possible, "Access to land is tightly controlled through kin groups" (Johnson 1989: 53), fission becomes more difficult or impossible, violence increases, and headmen gain power. Leaders of villages or kin groups become more chief-like as they obtain powers to exact tribute, to conscript labor, to regulate trade, and perhaps to demand to be treated like royalty (Johnson and Earle 2000: 203–244). If the position becomes heritable, if leaders and warriors are freed from the need to produce their own food, and if they have the power to exclude individuals from access to resources (thereby effectively forcing them to work for the leadership), the leader is more clearly a "chief" rather than a "headman" (Drennan and Peterson 2006; Earle 1997, 2000, 2002; Renfrew 2007: 152, 164, 173–176; Thomas 1999: 229; Yoffee 2004: 5–6, 23–41).

None of these characteristics is found in all societies that have been labeled as "chiefdoms." Indeed, few characteristics are. No clear dividing line exists between "autonomous villages" and "chiefdoms," nor should we expect one when the two names merely identify ranges on a spectrum.

The chief(s) and the elite group can have varying levels of authority usually depending on the size and economic complexity of the chiefdom. Some chiefdoms are extremely inegalitarian with powerful rulers, rigid class distinctions, and sometimes even slavery. In larger societies, chiefs might command powers of life and death over their subjects (Bellwood 1987: 31–33; Boehm 2001: 98, 255; Kirch 1984: 3–4; Lee 1990: 239; Trigger 1990a). But individuals might retain traditional rights of access to the land along with an obligation to pay tribute to a now fixed class of elites. Some chiefdoms, such as the Iroquois Confederation, manage to retain significant elements of egalitarianism at much larger scales (Trigger 1990a).

The earliest chiefdoms in the Near East likely employed boundary defense territorial systems that were similar to those used by their complex hunter-gatherer ancestors discussed in the previous chapter. Several lines of archaeological evidence point to this conclusion, including the construction of fortifications and walled enclosures. For example, the ancient town of Jericho in the modern-day West Bank of Palestine has large masonry walls dating to around 11,000 years ago, making it one of the world's first fortified farming settlements (Bar-Yosef 1986; Barkai and Liran 2008; Kenyon 1957). The exact function of the wall at Jericho is debated. Even if it was not defensive, other fortified settlements become common over the course of the next several millennia.

Similarly, Neolithic farming in the Near East is marked by a high frequency of violence and the oldest known examples of inter-village warfare, evidenced by skeletal trauma and the first mass graves (McCall

2009; McCall and Shields 2008; Widerquist and McCall 2017). Osteo-
logical evidence from this period shows that catastrophic food resource
failures, likely resulting from droughts or pest plagues, were common
and often led to periods of starvation (Hershkovitz et al. 1986). This
combination of conditions was a perfect recipe for violent conflict
between communities.

Yet, as discussed above, it is unwise to conflate boundary defense
territoriality with private landownership. In fact, in a certain sense, it
may actually imply the opposite: boundary defense territoriality and
inter-village warfare is more likely to imply collective ownership of
land at the scale of the village, because farmland was defended collectively at the scale of the village.

Land rights remain complex, flexible, and overlapping despite the
greater political unity of chiefdoms. Malinowski (1921) provides a
famous early description of the land-tenure system of the horticulturalists of the Trobriand Islanders, as well as its relationship with
political hierarchy and its mythological basis. He describes a system
in which chiefs have "over-rights" to horticultural land and enforce
social norms regarding the distribution of land and resulting agricultural produce. This system is backed in ideological terms by an elaborate complex of magical associations. Trobriand chiefs do not have
unlimited rights over garden plots, and their control is effectively
checked by ritual specialists who deal with magical associations
of gardens and the social rules surrounding their use (Malinowski
1921, 1956).

None of the land-tenure systems discussed so far involves anything
like the modern private property concept. Furthermore, in such systems, the closest thing to the "individual owner" of the land is usually a chief, but (though highly variable) the chief's claims to land
rights are never exclusive or unlimited. Chiefs are both owners and
governors (Earle 1997, 2002). In fact, the chief is as much or more
like a monarch than the Lockean proprietor now presumed to be fundamental to human resource use. In an important sense, most chiefs
are not owners at all but act as representatives of the people's claims
to the land: coordinating agricultural activities to maintain farmland,
enforcing individual access claims to both farmland and foraging land,
and settling disputes having to do with those claims. The more chiefs
exceed the limits the people might expect of a representative, the more
they resemble monarchs.

Contemporary Western readers probably want to ask why the chiefs combined economic, political, and religious powers. The answer probably lies in the scale of the society: the separation of different areas of power (economic, religious, political, etc.) only seems to become possible in larger-scale forms of socio-political organization with more complex economies (Earle 1997: 210–211). We might better ask why political, economic, and religious powers were eventually separated and how that separation came to seem so natural. But to look at it that way is to reject the propertarian myth in which private property develops outside and even in advance of the political process that is eventually imposed over it.

The development of private property begins through the political power of chiefs. Timothy Earle (1997: 74–75) writes, "In all cases, economic power was in some sense basic to the political strategies to amass [political] power." And, "[T]he evolution of property rights by which chiefs control primary production can be seen as basic to the evolution of many complex stratified societies . . . the significance of economic control through varying systems of land tenure is a constant theme" (Earle 2002: 327–328).

Although observed chiefs had private control of some property, chiefdoms are still far from having anything like the property institutions familiar in state societies today. Chiefs claims of landownership are often tenuous. Little if any trade exists. Common access rights to the land are the norm. What varies most is the level of control chiefs can assert over that community and the tribute they can extract from the people in exchange for their leadership and protection.

Are chiefs necessary leaders or usurpers of political power? They are probably a little of both. Communities with populations in the thousands or tens of thousands almost certainly need some kind of leadership to play a coordination role. But in most cases, chiefs probably abused their position, taking more power than necessary and more than the people would voluntarily have given had they been able to retain a check on the chiefs' power. By amassing power, chiefs are able to increase the benefits for the elite group at the expense of everyone else—making them similar to many leaders in the world today.

The propertarian question is whether chiefs—the first people with something approaching individual private property—were "appropriators" or "usurpers" of earlier appropriators' landownership. Unfortunately, neither answer gives them what they want. If chiefs were appropriators, the original appropriators were also the government of the village, more like monarchs than private owners, as in Hypothetical History 2. If chiefs usurped landownership, their victims were the village collective as in Hypothetical History 3.

Neither interpretation implies that the original appropriator was an individual private property holder. Locke's hypothetical history has little resemblance to the actual history of either the earliest people to transform land with labor or of the earliest private owners. There's a good case that chiefs usurped or abused their powers, but whoever they stole from was not a private landowner. In the whole range of indigenous stateless farming communities observed all around the world, there is no role for the fee-simple, individual proprietor the Lockean myth teaches us to accept as "natural."

The propertarian framing of the question misses the point. The land-tenure and "property" systems that indigenous stateless farmers set up around the world over the last 12,000 years have been extremely diverse, but all, that we know of, are distinct from the modern conception of full liberal ownership. The pattern varies significantly, but the pattern is complex, overlapping, nonspatial, flexible, and at least partly collective property rights with significant common access rights to land—except when chiefs become powerful enough to deny people access to the commons. Private property systems are not inherent to agricultural societies. Quite the opposite; private property systems are extremely unusual and perhaps non-existent among people using agricultural techniques similar to those of early farmers.

2. LAND-TENURE SYSTEMS IN PARAMOUNT CHIEFDOMS

Propertarians might suppose that, although communal land tenure was ubiquitous among small-scale, stateless farmers, the private property system originated before the state and perhaps even enabled state formation as population density increased and land became scarce. Although this claim deviates significantly from the appropriation hypothesis as usually stated, it might suffice to support some propertarian conclusions. We investigate it by examining evidence from societies that are hard to classify as states or stateless. "Paramount chiefdoms," which reach a level of centralization that allows several ranks of chiefs, managed to set aside common access rights almost entirely and created a highly stratified organizational structure.

Paramount chiefdoms are either the largest-scale, most tightly integrated stateless societies or the smallest-scale, most loosely integrated state societies. They are large and centralized enough to fit the political theory definition of a state (the existence of sovereignty) but not generally the archaeological definition (the presence of cities). Individuals might work their own plots of land during some parts of the year and work as corvée laborers on centralized projects (such as maintaining irrigation or public buildings) during other parts of the year, or they might work directly all year for a collective agricultural project controlled by a chief. Such societies tend to have significant stratification and sometimes slavery.

Large-scale irrigation, a farming strategy that is crucial to the expansion of food production in fertile but poorly watered land, is one example of public infrastructure favoring the formation of paramount chiefdoms. Irrigation was once proposed as the primary way in which states could develop (Wittfogel 1957), although the idea that there is any single path to state formation has lost much favor in recent decades (Dubreuil 2010: Kindle position 4250; Maisels 1990: 213). One can imagine irrigation being introduced by a private entrepreneur-appropriator but, in the cases where early farmers introduced such projects, they tended to be community operations (Bailey 1992: 192), providing opportunities for appropriation by the community as a whole or by a paramount chief as owner-governor. No private entrepreneurs are found in the ethnographic record.

Pre-contact and early post-contact Hawaii provides examples of paramount chiefdoms because chiefdoms existed there without contact with larger-scale societies until the late 1700s, and good historical records were taken in the early years of contact. Timothy Earle's (1997: 43, 44, 72, 73, 2002: 61–62) in-depth studies of Hawaiian chiefdoms find that only chiefs could be spoken of as owners: of colonizing canoes, of landholding descent groups, of irrigation projects, of the irrigated land, of particularly productive land. Chiefs did the things a Lockean appropriator is supposed to do. Chiefs financed the construction of irrigation canals and thereby appropriated the most productive lands. They acted as managers of irrigation projects. And their ancestors might have financed and led the expeditions that originally brought people to the islands in about 600 CE (Earle 1997: 43, 68–72, 82). "[T]he environment was transformed into a cultural world owned by a class of ruling chiefs" (Earle 1997: 45). Therefore,

Hawaiian chiefs could claim that their rise to power was consistent with Hypothetical History 2.

The Hawaiian chiefdom is also an interesting case because they were the first human inhabitants of all or most of the islands that their descendants now inhabit, and they brought the institution of the chiefdom with them. Under all propertarian appropriation criteria, as long as individuals voluntarily joined the expedition, the discovery, colonization, and exploitation of uninhabited lands is a clear act of appropriation.

By the time of contact with Europeans, paramount chiefs were well-established as owner-governors who treated their chiefdoms as for-profit businesses. Earle (1997: 79, 82–83) explains that they hired and fired community chiefs, who hired and fired "konohiki" (local managers), who allocated lands to commoners in exchange for labor and maintained the power to rescind land for nonpayment of labor, much as employers today stop paying the money people need to obtain housing if they stop providing labor. Earle (1997: 7) writes:

> In Hawai'i, community chiefs allocated to commoners their sub-sistence plots in the chief's irrigated farmlands in return for corvée work on chiefly lands and special projects. By owning the irriga-tion systems, and thus controlling access to the preferred means of subsistence, chiefs directed a commoner's labor. Where you lived was determined by whose land manager "put you to work".

Earle (1997: 94–95, 102, 2000, 2002: 61–62, 345) finds corroborating evidence that ownership is based on chiefly power in places as diverse as pre-Columbian South America, the pre-Columbian Mississippi basin, Iron Age Denmark, Olmec Mexico, Bronze Age Britain, and pre-Roman Spain. Other researchers find a similar pattern in complex chiefdoms or pre-colonial states in Africa, but where land is plentiful enough political authorities seem to have been obliged to provide all individuals with enough land to meet their subsistence needs (Hann 1998a: 12, 2005: 112–113)—retaining access to a commons.

The closest analogue in Hawaiian chiefdoms to a truly *private* titleholder is the konohiki, but they were managers rather than entre-preneurs. They were appointed by the chief—the owner—to serve his interest. Thus, the relationship between government and smallholders was the opposite of the relationship Nozick (1974: 10–52) or Locke

(1960 [1689]: §24–51) suppose in their hypothetical histories. Instead of smallholders with an appropriation-based claim appointing a government to serve the smallholder's interests (by protecting their claims), we see a government with an appropriation-based claim appointing smallholders to serve its interests.

The example of the konohiki is much more consistent with Hobbes's (1962 [1651]: 186) claim that private property originates with the arbitrary decision of the sovereign. The only connection that the konohiki have to original appropriation is *through* the government. The konohiki's claim to hold some of the incidents of ownership in the land they claim is because the paramount chief, the ultimate landlord, chose to bestow those rights on the konohiki in exchange for services. Even if the chief's ancestors illegitimately usurped power, giving the chief's ownership rights to his appointees would do nothing to rectify that wrong.

Instead of a limit on sovereign power over private titleholders, appropriation theory provides a justification for it once its mythical stories are replaced by real historical inquiry. If the institution of individual private property developed by strengthening the claims of people like the konohiki, the belief that government somehow *infringes* or *interferes* with appropriators is backwards. Taking away the sovereign's power to regulate titles is more likely to interfere with someone who has a connection to original appropriation.

Although this Hawaiian case study appears similar to highly centralized early states, such as those in Egypt and Mesopotamia, it can't be taken as a general model. There is no single evolutionary path from small- to large-scale society. The Hawaiian paramount chiefdoms were between chiefdoms and states in size, the power of sovereignty, and economic diversity, but they were not between them in time. They cannot be presumed to have been on a transition to anything. It is plausible to imagine property systems like those in Hawaii preceding the earliest states in Mesopotamia and Egypt; it might even be the best guess given the available evidence, although it is still an open question. However, our goal is not to establish our best guess as the most reasonable one. It is to assess the hypothesis that individual appropriation plays the most significant role. So far, evidence indicates that that is a very bad guess.

Even if Hawaii were a model of transition for societies dependent on large-scale irrigation, it would not be a model for all state transitions.

Allen Johnson and Earle see a very different path for societies with economies that didn't lend themselves to such centralization. Earle (1991b: 333) writes, rent "began as a reluctant 'gift' from the producer to one or more current big men, hardened into the tribute demanded by a powerful chief, and eventually became the legally sanctioned right of landowners and bureaucrats to a share of peasant production." On a path like that one, many of the sharing practices of autonomous villages could last as they are incorporated into chiefdoms and states. The role of chiefs in controlling land tenure and in managing individual claims to land sets the stage for usufruct systems, which were common among the earliest state-level civilizations and which continued in many places into historic times (see Chapter 13).

3. IMPLICATIONS

In summary, our current understanding of stateless farming societies strongly suggests the following four conclusions:

1. Early farming societies had complex, overlapping, flexible, non-spatial, and at least partly collective land-tenure systems with a significant commons in the sense that individuals retained one or another kind of access rights to land for different purposes, such as farming, grazing, foraging, and other activities.
2. Elites with varying levels of power were usually responsible for coordinating systems of individual land use.
3. Private ownership and individual appropriation played no role in the consolidation of even the largest-scale observed chiefdoms. Group or monarchical appropriation are far better than individual appropriation as descriptions of the acts of the first farmers.
4. A secondary and more complex observation is that the land-tenure systems among small-scale farming societies, such as our earliest agricultural ancestors, tend to vary in relation to the sizes of human populations, the scale and intensity of agricultural activities, and the effects that these variables have on agricultural productivity, especially in terms of declining soil fertility.

These conclusions have two important implications for our investigation of the appropriation hypothesis:

1. The earliest farmers, who have an excellent claim to original landownership under Lockean criteria, have not been observed to establish private property systems. Instead they usually or always choose to establish complex, overlapping, flexible, non-spatial, and largely collective landownership with strong common access rights.
2. The origin of genuinely private individual landownership appears to have had nothing to do with any act of appropriation but rather the amassment and disbursement of centralized political power for the benefit of chiefs and other elites.

These conclusions seem fairly obvious from the history recounted above. We suspect they would achieve general consensus among anthropologists familiar with the land-tenure systems of small-scale societies and with the prehistory of early farmers and the first states. The observations throughout this chapter and Chapter 11 strongly contradict the premise that appropriators tend to be individuals who are intent on establishing private property. In short, the evidence above strongly indicates that the individual appropriation hypothesis is false: there is nothing "natural" about individualistic private property rights.

As original appropriators who worked together to clear land and establish farms, swidden and fallowing communities had the right—under propertarian theory—to set up any property rights system they wanted to. They set up their complex, overlapping system because it met their needs. They had little or no need for sole and despotic dominion over the external things of the world. Swidden farmers needed to work together to clear land. They needed secure access to a given amount of land for farming, but not to any specific plot. They needed shared land access for foraging. Fallowing farmers need to work together and make decisions together to make their fallowing system work. They needed different land access rights for grazing animals than for growing crops. Most of them also needed shared land access for foraging. They needed to ensure that community members used land in ways that maintained the viability of these activities.

These systems of complex, overlapping, collective, and common land rights have far more in common with a property rights system in which individual titles are subject to taxation, regulation, and redistribution by the community than with the institution of full liberal ownership.

So far, it seems that propertarian myths, rather than their principles, make us think there is something natural about their preferred system of ownership. The original appropriators that we examined did not do what propertarian theory supposes, and, possibly worse for propertarianism, the movements toward individualized rights that we've seen so far have been imposed by chiefs using their political power to establish economic privileges for themselves at the expense of people with better connections to original appropriation. Chapter 13 continues to follow the history of land-tenure systems in ancient, medieval, and early modern states to see whether a private property system is likely to develop without rights violations from this unpromising starting point.

Chapter 13

PROPERTY SYSTEMS IN ANCIENT, MEDIEVAL, AND EARLY MODERN STATES

A fuller picture of land-tenure systems is available for early states because archaeological evidence is often buttressed by the first historical documents. This section shows that early states had land-tenure systems in which political elites—kings, pharaohs, lugals, etc.—were considered the owners of all of the land in their kingdoms and subjects had various forms of usufruct rights for farming or other practices. No period of private, individual appropriation is found in the formation of states. The beginnings of individual private property occurred gradually, long after the formation of states, not with individual acts of appropriation but with elites using their political power to name themselves or their underlings as owners of assets. Even then, private landownership did not become the dominant property rights system in ancient or medieval times. Variations on the theme of communal village agriculture, not so different from those described in Chapter 12 remained the most common system in state societies throughout the world until the early modern period.

1. LAND-TENURE SYSTEMS IN EARLY STATES

In the run-up to the formation of the first states in places like the Middle East, Egypt, the Indus Valley, and China, more advanced farming techniques and technology caused a surge in agricultural production, which unsurprisingly affected land-tenure systems. For example, the invention of the plow (Pryor 1985) and irrigation systems (Davies 2009; Wittfogel 1957) allowed farmers to occupy regions with richer but heavier soils, such as the alluvial lowlands of the Nile and Yellow River valleys, and in arid alluvial regions such as Mesopotamia. The first states in these areas arose in the valleys of major rivers where soils were inherently rich and often re-fertilized by annual flooding, obviating the need for extensive fallow periods. Although other forms of ecological degradation eventually ensued (Helbaek 1960), irrigation and other forms of landscape enhancement ensured that farmers could operate sustainably in the most productive portions of the landscape.

While the chiefs of smaller-scale agricultural societies seem to have coordinated collective action in relation to land management and field maintenance, the kings of the earliest states tightly controlled the core regions of agricultural production and coordinated the construction of roads, irrigation systems, and other large-scale public works (Childe 1950; Davies 2009; Flannery 1999; Wittfogel 1957). In this way, early kings tended to exert stronger political control over land than did their chiefly ancestors, with commoners being granted access to land through a system of usufruct. Rights of usufruct had many sources: in many cases, they were hereditary and, in others, they were a form of political patronage, such as rewards for military service or material support. While there is some variability in how strongly claims to usufruct rights could be enforced, the king ultimately owned the land and had the final say over who was allowed to make use of it.

For example, as Herodotus (1998) describes, the ancient Egyptians believed all land on Earth was inherently the property of the gods and that political control of that land was invested in the pharaoh as the living manifestation of the gods on Earth. In general, the same could apparently be said of the Early Dynastic kings of Mesopotamia based on a wealth of cuneiform administrative texts. Johannes Renger (1995: 279) describes:

> The underlying concept was that the supreme god of the central urban settlement of a territorial entity or state was the ruler of its territory. The human ruler of the state was considered the god's deputy (*vicarius*) on earth. In this capacity he headed the household of the god, i.e., the temple household. The arable land in a given state was part of the divine *patrimonium* and as such was administered by the god's deputy.

In Dynastic Egypt, the pharaoh managed the system of usufruct rights for his subjects and assigned titles to particular plots of land for particular purposes to particular people. In this sense, pharaohs awarded usufruct rights (which were generally lifelong) to elite subjects as rewards for loyalty and service to the state. In Mesopotamia, core agricultural land was administered through "institutional houses," which were headed by palace elites and which administered royal control over the land. Mesopotamian kings were thought of as the heads of the gods' institutional house and thus administered divine affairs on Earth (Renger 1995: 279).

Most scholars of the land-tenure systems of early civilizations draw correlations between the consolidation of royal authority over land, the institutionalization of usufruct systems, and the necessity of a centralized political authority in coordinating agricultural production by means of large-scale public building projects (Adams Jr. 2017; Childe 1950; Trigger 1990b; Wittfogel 1957; Wright 1977). Indeed, one perspective on the origins of states is that early kings emerged from their less powerful chiefly ancestors by means of the consolidation of land through military conquest, alliance, trade, or some combination of the above.

Early kings, in a sense, exaggerated the existing authority of chiefs to administer individual land claims and they did so in relation to the dramatically increasing productive capacity of core regions of farmland through the construction of irrigation systems, roads, and other such public works. Ideological justifications, such as the tendency to regard the king as a living god on Earth, and usufruct land-tenure systems both followed from this process of royal power consolidation.

Trigger (2003: 71, 79, 91, 147, 153–155) studied seven widely separated early civilizations: the Aztecs, the Maya, the Yoruba-Benin of sub-Saharan Africa, the Inca, Egypt, Southern Mesopotamia, and the Shang of China. He found that they all had kings who united religious, economic, and political power. Even the highest-ranking commoners were most often state employees, such as scribes, soldiers, and administrators who received land or other privileges as a revocable reward for service to the monarch.

Trigger (2003: 332) argues that although private land cannot always be *ruled out*, there is "no evidence that such land existed in most early civilizations." He does in fact rule out private ownership in five of the seven (the Aztecs, the Maya, the Yoruba, the Inca, and the Shang): "That leaves Mesopotamia and Egypt as early civilizations in which some land might have been privately owned." In Mesopotamia, private land was a late development. Charles Keith Maisels (1990: 219) finds that land in prehistoric and early historic Mesopotamia was owned by temples, clans, or collectives. Nearly all of it was held collectively prior to 3000 BCE, after which "increasing amounts of land fell under the control of temples or palaces, but some of it appears to have become the property of individual creditors. . . . It is less certain that private land existed in the Old Kingdom of Egypt" (Trigger 2003: 332–334).

Kings often claimed ownership of all lands (perhaps an idea carried over from chiefdoms?), but in practice their hold over land was weaker than full liberal ownership (Earle 2000: 47; Trigger 2003: 314–315).

In the Americas, institutions owned land and assigned it to individuals in return for service. Revenue from these assignments "constituted a major source of revenue for the nobility, all of whose active male members were involved in some sort of state service" (Trigger 2003: 323). Michael E. Smith (2004: 79) finds considerable variation in the level of commercialization in ancient state economics, including more complex economies, such as those of Greece and Rome, but the earliest states in his study (including Inca and Egyptian societies) had strong central control in all sectors of the economy. There is a case to be made that such usufruct rights may be considered the ancestor of modern individual property rights. Indeed, similar systems are found among virtually all early civilizations for which we have adequate historical evidence, including the Greece and Rome (Pugliese 1965) where property systems in urban cores eventually began to show some resemblance to modern property rights systems.

In all early states for which adequate documentation exists, the legal system protected government property and upper-class privileges (Trigger 2003: 265). "A defining feature of all early civilizations was the institutionalized appropriation by a small ruling group of most of the wealth produced by the lower classes. . . . Farmers and artisans did not accumulate large amounts of wealth, although they created virtually all the wealth that existed in these societies" (Trigger 2003: 375).

Outside of urban cores, land-tenure systems often resembled the traditional systems of stateless agriculturalists. In some cases, local kin groups continued to hold land collectively and, though expected to pay taxes and tributes to the state, they were otherwise afforded relative independence in their operation. Earle (2000: 48) suggests this practice was probably a hold-over from earlier forms of social organization.

In many cases, governments appointed or recognized local lords who took on the role of chiefs as well as acting as the state's liaison to rural villagers. Lords oversaw a usufruct system in which peasant farmers had rights of access to estate farmland for the production of food and other goods. In this sense, peasant farmers and elites had complex, overlapping land rights with an obvious resemblance to smaller-scale systems. Although the individuals who make up the community as a whole might owe a tributary duty to the lord and the state, villagers or peasants usually retained a right of direct access to common land and sometimes power to make decisions about it as a group. The elites had ultimate authority over the land in the estates that they controlled, often resembling the strongest chiefs. How much autonomy and decision-making power they conceded to peasants varied greatly over time and place.

Traditional peasant communities seem to have been a nearly ubiquitous feature of the rural peripheries of states around the world from the earliest times. Although they gradually became less frequent, they were still common all over the world until the colonial period (Scott 2009, 2017).

2. PRIVATIZATION IN EARLY STATES

The complex part of this story is the process through which monarchical power over land within states became limited over time allowing usufruct land-tenure systems to transform into the modern system of private property. Despite the propertarian claim that private property has ancient roots, only the barest beginning of this transaction happened in antiquity.

Most experts in the development of early civilizations seem to agree that private property is a recent invention, which did not exist in the earliest states (Hudson and Levine 1996; Johnson and Earle 2000; Trigger 2003: 332). In urban cores of early states, there were only two classes: governing elites and workers. A third merchant class tends to develop only in later states, and at first it is "often attached in one way or another to the ruling class" (Johnson and Earle 2000: 329). Taxation developed simultaneously with the transfer of land from collective property to private property (Earle 2000: 48), very much the opposite of the propertarian story.

Something truly recognizable as individual private ownership of land emerges only later and only in certain places such as Rome and late medieval Northern Europe (Hudson and Levine 1996: 4). Chinese civilization, for example, never evolved a strong sense of private property (Trigger 2003: 239) except perhaps, ironically, under the late twentieth- and early twenty-first-century communist regime. People who portray private property as an ancient and ubiquitous institution usually begin their analysis in late antiquity with selected examples from Greece and Rome and skip to the British common law tradition (Epstein 1978–1979; Widerquist 2010a). Although the examples they draw on are real and sometimes significant, any conclusion that property is therefore ancient and ubiquitous involves ignoring most of the world including most of the rural areas of Rome and Britain. Hann (1998a: 12) writes, "The popular modern sense of property may be foreshadowed in Roman law ... but in fact the great bulk of land in the ancient world was farmed by peasant smallholders and transmitted within their communities according to custom. Most historians would argue that the same was true under feudalism."

Property in the earliest states looked different, and it appears in a way that seems to support the hypothesis that the earliest private property holders were more like the konohiki than Lockean appropriators. To draw a later example from medieval Europe, consider how similar the following example is to the Hawaiian konohiki from Chapter 12:

> [L]and was ultimately owned by the king, who granted land to lords or "tenants-in-chief" in exchange for services. These in turn granted plots to "mesne'" tenants, who might or might not be the actual cultivators. At each level the tenant acknowledged obligations to provide services in return for the rights devolved to him. (Hann 1998a: 12)

Propertarians have consistently assumed some private freeholder must have been dispossessed to establish that chain of obligation, but no such person appears in our empirical investigation. Only the peasants with their complex, overlapping access rights to common land consistently appear as the dispossessed.

Hudson and Levine's (1996: 8–14, 26–27, 33–37, 43, 47, 55, 148, 177–178, 197, 228–230, 253, 255, 266, 270, 298–301) coedited volume examines the process of privatization in the ancient Near East. Hudson and most of the other authors find a consistent trend in which individual private property begins from the top (with the most connected government insiders) and works its way down. The first people to assert private property rights are kings; then the royal family, temples, high government officials, and so down the hierarchy. The first large-scale businesses were not entrepreneurial initiatives but public enterprises such as temples, which often obtained property by lending money to peasant collectives who could not pay their taxes or were facing emergency and then foreclosed on them. One common source of private property was the use of it to reward soldiers after a successful military conquest or reconquest after rebellion. Rome created private property in this way throughout its history. Sometimes ancient royal managers or warlords seized the royal lands when palace power collapsed, very much the way Russian "oligarchs" appointed themselves capitalist owners as the Soviet Union collapsed. Many private entrepreneurs in Rome were people who bid for the right to collect taxes in exchange for a commission.

Although limited private property rights existed in ancient Israel, none of the three terms for property in the Hebrew Bible translates into fee-simple private property (Levine 1996: 236, 243). Hudson and Levine (1996: 46, 51) argue that the private property system emerged most strongly in the centralized temple-royal, family-government sphere rather than "in the subsistence sphere, which long remained communally based," and which had the most reasonable claim of appropriation rights. Even craft labor began not on the free market but with slaves and servants of temples and well-place officials. Giorgio Byccellati (1996: 131) writes, "the dichotomy between public and private is coterminous with the origin of the city ... the very distinction between 'public' and 'private' was inoperative in pre-urban times."

A commercial sector and market did exist in the ancient Near East and Mediterranean in very early times. Authors of Hudson and Levine's (1996) volume disagree about how large the private sector was in the region, but they have little disagreement about the pattern of how privatization came about. None of the authors found evidence for a private ownership class of freeholding individual appropriators. Hudson (1996b: 301) summarizes, "Each region examined at this colloquium exhibits a common economic phenomenon, although not all members thought that it should be called privatization."

Once again, the findings of this investigation have important consequences for natural property rights theory. Little or no evidence supports the supposition that property begins with individual private acts of appropriation. Early states certainly interfered with someone, but individual landholders tended to be beneficiaries rather than victims of that interference. The institution of private, individual landholding owes its very existence to these acts of aggression, which provide the opportunity for elites to establish new powers.

Any connection that private landholders have to original appropriation seems to have come *through* the state, and the legitimacy of their ownership is, therefore, directly or indirectly dependent on the legitimacy of the state's ownership of its territory. As Hudson (1996: 52) summarizes the implications of his findings, "If John Locke's natural-law views were universally valid, Sumer's archaeological sites would reveal private rather than temple and palace estates and workshops."

We have much further to go to find economies dominated by the private property system. For now, we can safely say that the private property land-tenure system did not predate the origins of states nor did it emerge particularly soon after the origins of the first states; and to the extent it did emerge, it was from the top down by exercise of government power rather than by appropriation. The private property system was somewhat unusual against the backdrop of a much more common pattern of elite control of land and the granting of various land access rights to subjects through a system of usufruct. While the power and authority of elites over land rights has varied considerably over space and time, this pattern seems nearly universal.

In short, the actual creation of private property resembles the Hobbesian story of arbitrary distribution by the sovereign rather than the Lockean story of individual appropriation.

3. LAND-TENURE SYSTEMS IN MEDIEVAL AND EARLY MODERN STATES

Although limited privatization began in ancient states, full liberal ownership was still uncommon throughout the world including throughout most of Europe only a few hundred years ago. Something resembling it was gradually becoming more important in urban areas in late medieval Northern Europe, especially in Britain as trade increased in importance throughout the continent (Hann 1998a), but examples of it were very unusual and did not represent the norm even in Britain (Standing 2019).

Traditional, communal land-tenure systems were the norm throughout Europe during the Middle Ages. They continued through the period of industrialization in some areas and into the twentieth century in isolated communities especially in Eastern Europe. Communal land-tenure systems offered peasant farmers a degree of political autonomy, protected laborers from exploitation, and held certain advantages for agricultural production at the scale of the small communities in which they tended to remain.

Virtually all the small-scale agricultural villages that dominated the world in the 1400s practiced some system of communal land tenure irrespective of the political system in which they were involved (to say nothing of hunter-gatherer societies, which were still plentiful at the time). Scott (1998a: 43–44) describes the pattern,

> Let us imagine a community in which families have usufruct rights to parcels of cropland during the main growing season. Only certain crops, however, may be planted and every seven years the usufruct land is redistributed among families according to family size and the number of able-bodied adults. After the harvest of the main-season crop, all cropland reverts to common land where any family may glean, graze their fowl and livestock, and even plant quickly maturing, dry-season crops. . . . This description is a simplification, but it does convey some of the actual complexity of property relations in contexts where customary local arrangements have tended to prevail.

Many, if not most, communal villages were surrounded by common wastes, which might be used for hunting, gathering, herding, or other purposes, and people with access to common land (both wastes and common agricultural land) tended to have a great deal of independence because they were able to meet some of their needs on their own. Depending how much chiefly or lordly control was exerted over it, the communal nature of the village itself also supported political independence in an important sense. Peasant farmers living in autonomous villages had either no boss at all or a kin relation who served as the head of their household (Carson 2011: 8–10; Katz 1997: 284; Smith 2000: 134). There were also many farming systems within chiefdoms and states that retained the partial character of an autonomous village "with a parasitic layer of kings, priests, bureaucrats and feudal landlords superimposed on it" (Carson 2011: 8).

Most European feudal estates were essentially chiefdoms with a duty to pay tribute to the king. Local lords governed the land and held some incidents of landownership, while peasants retained many of their traditional complex, overlapping land-tenure rights and decision-making powers. The surviving words "landlord" and "title" reflect a time when land ownership was equated with the power of local governing elites—i.e. to individuals, such as dukes, earls, and counts, who held power over the people who worked the land rather than to appropriators who originally worked the land themselves.

The village farming system was not some kind of primitive communism or any archetypal "natural" community. Although the evidence in this book rejects the claim that a private property system is somehow "natural," it does not argue that any other system *is* "natural." People create very different land-tenure systems based on their power relations and on their economic, environmental, geographic, and demographic circumstances.

However, some attributes recur frequently. Communal land tenure in farming villages tended to be collectivist in the sense that certain domains of decision-making, especially those regarding land access rights and farming activities, were done in some corporate fashion involving some segment of the community. In chiefdoms and states, communal land was politically controlled by elites who held a degree of overarching ownership of the commons and who could expect some form of tribute for granting access to land—although the ownership claims of such elites varied significantly in terms of their strength, enforceability, and overlap with those of their tenants and those of their overlords.

The living conditions of people in village communities varied tremendously over time and space. While people often hold idyllic conceptions of agrarian peasant life, feudal villages were often extremely violent, prone to economic disaster, riddled with disease, and subject to the whims of irrational elites. People in village communities were sometimes largely free but other times subject to oppressive control of lords or chiefs. In certain contexts, such as in sixteenth-century Russia and the Levant during the Crusades, peasant villages devolved into serfdom, which was effectively a form of slavery. It was more common, however, including in Russia, for the people to retain significant individual independence and shared economic autonomy, protected partly by access to the commons (Carson 2011: 10).

A major variant of such communal land-tenure systems was the "open field system," which survived across Western Europe from the early medieval period into the nineteenth century. Within the open field system, large communal farms were generally held under the political control of aristocratic elites, who granted land access to tenant farmers in exchange for corvée labor and/or taxation of their produce.

Although Britain led the way in the establishment of sole proprietorship (see Chapter 14), even there many villages retained partially collectivist land claims into the nineteenth century. In England, archaeological evidence for the medieval open field system can be seen in the form of the "ridge and furrow" pattern, which resulted from the plowing of communal farm fields and the division of the land into ploughstrips measured in terms of the number of plowed ridges. Tenant farmers were granted the rights to grow crops on land of various sizes measured according to the number of ploughstrips and, hence, did not have rights to particular plots of land but rather indeterminate parcels of a particular size. In England, land claims were often administered (and disputes adjudicated) by juries of experienced farmers who literally staked claims for the tenants involved in growing crops in a particular common field instead of deferring those decisions to the aristocratic land owner (Ault 2013), who likely had little farming experience and, we imagine, might have been too busy with things like fox hunting to be bothered with trivial issues such as peasant land claims and farming disputes.

The open field system had a number of practical benefits for agricultural production that often go unacknowledged. Above all, it provided a framework for field fallowing and crop rotation in addressing problems of soil fertility, while also ensuring that farmers had access to the amount of land to which they had a claim (Dahlman 2008). In the English system, experienced farmers were given the authority to make decisions in managing land use in the interest of maintaining soil fertility and crop health, while also assuring that individual land claims were honored. In addition, this system also allowed fields to be plowed in non-rectilinear fashion such that plowing could follow natural contours of the landscape, avoid obstacles, etc.

By the late medieval period, many British peasants had an unusual system called a "semicommons," in which individuals would in some way "own" specific plots—specifically several small, scattered fields.

They could lease, sell, or bequeath those fields, but they had no choice but to open them to communal grazing outside of the growing season, and any buyer would have to understand that they were buying into a village with many communal rules made by village juries (Carson 2011: 9; Katz 1997: 284; Smith 2000: 131–135).

The complex, overlapping, nonspatial, and partially collective nature of property systems was not limited to European communal villages. Stuart Banner (2002: S365–S366) summarizes:

> In most of the non-European world, European colonizers found property systems in which resources were allocated on a functional, not a spatial, basis. A person or a family would not own a zone of space but rather the right to use particular resources scattered in a variety of different spaces. . . . A family might own the right to one spot for sleeping, another for cultivating, and a third for catching eels. The Maori, like most of the indigenous people over whom Europeans assumed sovereignty, had a well-developed property system, but it was a system in which property rights were not bundled into a single geographic space. Similar nonspatial property systems also existed throughout much of Europe before enclosure. Participants in common fields did not control all the resources within defined boundaries but rather possessed rights to use different kinds of resources in different places. An individual might possess the right to cultivate several strips of land scattered over several fields during the farming season, the right to graze a certain number of animals of a certain kind in certain pastures at certain times of the year, the right to gather twigs in one place and nuts in another, and so on.

Before suppression by various states and empires, variations on the communal village have been documented by anthropologists and historians around the world, including in India, the Roman Republic, the Roman Empire, Slavonia, the Baltic, England, Wales, Scotland, Ireland, France, Scandinavia, the Nordic countries, Germany, East Africa, central and southern Africa, many Pacific Islands, Italy, Russia, etc. (Carson 2011). Kropotkin (2011: chapter IV) observes, "In short, we do not know one single human race or one single nation which has not had its period of village communities."

Communal land-tenure systems persisted through the period of European colonialism into the modern world in a small but significant number of contexts. For example, one of the authors of this book frequently does anthropological fieldwork in Namibia, where communal land continues to be a fairly common phenomenon and where the concept, as well as the traditional authorities that administer it, are formally enshrined into the country's law (Communal Land Reform Act 5 of 2002[1]). Namibia, of course, is not unique and there are many instances in which communal land-tenure systems that originated among traditional societies prior to European colonization have persisted into the twenty-first century or have been resurrected post-colonially. The Pueblo Indians in the United States, for example, have retained collective landownership to the present day (Edzar 1996: 111).

4. CONCLUSION

Neither individual appropriation nor sole proprietorship were commonly found in the history of state societies from the earliest prehistory to the early modern period. We see instead "original appropriators" setting up various form of complex, flexible, nonspatial, overlapping land-tenure systems with significant collective and communal elements. Elites eventually use governmental powers to take control of the land and resources, but as late as 1500 CE, only a few elites worldwide had yet set up private property systems. To find the true origins of the global private property system, Chapter 14 has to look at modern history.

---

[1] See https://laws.parliament.na/annotated-laws-regulations/law-regulation.php?id=91

Chapter 14

THE PRIVATIZATION OF THE EARTH, 1500–2000 CE

Chapter 13 showed that private landownership emerged only in late antiquity, and even by the early modern period it existed in relatively few places. Traditionally complex communal village land-tenure systems were still the norm a few hundred years ago. The questions for this chapter are: how did the now-ubiquitous system of unitary private ownership spread around the world, and what role did individual appropriation play in that process? The answers to those questions are complex but enlightening.

Once the institution of private property is established, it can spread in at least five ways: (1) people who practice the institution can go into previously uninhabited territory and establish it (as the appropriation story portrays it); (2) people who had not previously practiced the institution could voluntarily take it up; (3) states or looser political entities could force more people within their territories to adopt the institution; (4) conquerors could force a subjugated people to adopt the institution; (5) colonists practicing the institution could largely or entirely replace the original inhabitants.

Only Possibilities 1 and 2 are consistent with the nonaggression and/or noninterference principle that supposedly underlies propertarian respect for property rights. These possibilities might have happened somewhere at some time, but it's hard to find historical evidence of much or any of it, while—as this section shows—there are many historical records of the aggressive Possibilities 3, 4, and 5 happening even as aggressors told themselves the benign Lockean story.

This chapter discusses two parallel trends that made full liberal ownership ubiquitous around the world between about 1500 and 2000 CE: the enclosure movement mostly within Europe (section 1) and the colonial movement mostly outside Europe (section 2). Privatization did not begin in 1500 CE, nor was it complete by 2000 CE, but the bulk of the privatization of the world's resources happened during that period. This chapter demonstrates that the process of enclosure and the waves of colonists who went out from Europe armed with ideas of Hobbes, Locke, Grotius, and More—and with significant military power—established landownership rights that were both outside of historical traditions worldwide and only then being established in Europe itself (Pateman and Mills 2007: 47–51). As Lee (1988: 263) explains, "private property in land . . . is a relatively recent notion. Starting from the Enclosure movements in fifteenth-century England . . . the whole land-tenure system of Europe and the Americas was transformed from communal to private within the space of a few hundred years."

Our discussion focuses on two false empirical claims connected to the appropriation myth. First, in the context of "enclosure," which literally refers to the bounding of individually owned fields by fences, the elimination of commons was supposedly a return to a more natural system of private property for the benefit of all parties involved. In fact, the enclosure movement was legally enacted by a government representing the interest of lords and intended to separate peasant farmers—who had a better claim to landownership in terms of all appropriation criteria—from their land rights for a variety of political and economic reasons. Second, colonial lands—or some significant part of them—were supposed to be essentially empty or unclaimed at the time they were seized by European colonists. In fact, European colonial territories were almost never empty; indigenous peoples often had very good appropriation-based claims to their lands, which were violently seized from them one by one over a period of centuries.

Perhaps the most important claim to be debunked is one that usually lies between the lines: the belief that long-ago seizures don't matter, because the same private property rights system would exist today even if there had been no rights violations. This claim is also false. The enclosure and colonial movements not only stole property; they forced the private property rights system on unwilling people around the world.

1. THE ENCLOSURE MOVEMENT

Within Europe, the process of creating private property in most places was the gradual replacement of individual access rights and group regulation traditions discussed above with top-down ownership of "lords," as they gradually became "landlords" with full liberal ownership of the land. This process is known as the "enclosure movement" in Britain. We also apply this name to the enclosure movement's many parallels across Europe (Hann 1998a; Katz 1997; Neeson 1993: 11–14, 319–330; Smith 2000; Yelling 1977: 232).

Over a period of four or five centuries the British government systematically interfered with and dismantled the traditional (common, collective, and overlapping) property rights of British peasants to strengthen incidents of ownership held by lords, whose titles often traced back to arbitrary assignment by William the Conqueror and other monarchs. Parliament forced enclosure on unwilling peasants with little or no compensation. Similar transitions happened gradually throughout Europe (Hann 1998a; Katz 1997: 284; Neeson 1993: 11–14, 319–330; Smith 2000; Yelling 1977: 232).

There is substantial controversy about the roots of the enclosure movement in England and of its counterparts elsewhere in Europe. Most scholars date the beginning of England's enclosure movement to the fifteenth century, but some elements might have begun as early as the twelfth century (Macfarlane 1998: 108). The movement substantially replaced the open field system by the middle of the eighteenth century (McCloskey 1991), although it was not fully complete for another century or more.

One standard version of the justification of enclosure had to do with inefficiencies in the open field system caused by issues such as the "tragedy of the commons." Enclosure is, after all, the context in which that term was coined (Hardin 1968). According to this justification, enclosure increased farming efficiency by incentivizing individual maintenance of farm fields, such as removing weeds, controlling pests, and that sort of thing, which was argued to have disincentivized somehow the collective nature of open-field farming because of tragedy-of-the-commons issues. Similarly, enclosure was thought to eliminate the travel time between traditionally scattered ploughstrips, which was slow going with ox-drawn plows. Or so the story goes (see Dahlman 2008 for a counter-argument).

Several political and economic factors shifted in favor of private landownership when the movement gained traction in the seventeenth and eighteenth centuries. At this time, the restructuring of the overlapping, complex land rights of peasants into the lords' sole proprietorship was imposed unilaterally by a government that represented only the lords. As trade increased and capitalism began to take shape, a class of wealthy elites began to push for changes that would allow them to maximize the productive value of their land by excluding many of the traditional forms of peasant agriculture and land tenure. According to J. M. Neeson (1993: 329), "enclosure was an institutional or political intervention. . . . No other means could be found to raise rents as far or as fast."

Changes in farming techniques and technologies also had much to do with the roots of the enclosure movement. For one thing, this time period saw a significant shift from subsistence crops intended for direct, local consumption to cash crops intended for trade to distant urban centers. This transition was augmented by the development of elaborate and increasingly efficient trade networks and of new forms of transportation to move cash crops to markets. Consequently, lords found it more profitable to replace traditional peasant agricultural activities, which were minor sources of tributary revenue, with the intensive production of cash crops, which could be sold at market for much greater returns. In addition, the development of new farming techniques, such as the use of commercial manure and eventually chemical fertilizers, dramatically increased agricultural production and eliminated the need for field fallowing and crop rotation. In this sense, the lords of large, rural estates found that there was an ever-increasing opportunity cost involved in allowing the traditional open field systems to persist.

Finally, as the Industrial Revolution commenced in the late eighteenth and early nineteenth centuries, enclosure became part of the systematic effort to undermine peasant agricultural economies in order to provide industrial labor (Black and Thomas 1974; Chambers 1953; Mingay 2016). The Industrial Revolution momentously altered the political-economic balance between labor and capital and between rural agricultural economies and urban industrial centers. As Olsen (2019: 329–330) puts it, "Enclosure, sanctioned by law, propagandized by the Board of Agriculture, and profited in by Members of Parliament, was the final blow to peasants in common-field England." Although enclosure was justified partly as an effort to improve farming efficiency, making things better for everyone, many of the disappropriated and alienated commoners were far worse off for the rest of their lives, if not for generations. For perhaps a century, meat almost disappeared from commoners' diets. "Long after enclosure had created compact farms, and renting more than an allotment had become almost impossible, labourers still felt a longing for land. Well into the second half of the nineteenth century . . . the ground-swell of rural grievance came back always to access to the land" (Neeson 1993: 329).

One of the most important ways enclosure harmed commoners was by assaulting their independence. Before enclosure, peasants with access to land for farming, grazing, and hunting had no need to work for wages. They could work for a boss if they wanted to, but very often potential employers were unwilling to offer wages high enough to make peasants accept employment. Enclosure took away the commoners' power to refuse labor by taking away their ability to work for themselves (Katz 1997: 284; Neeson 1993: 12–14, 297, 320). The importance of this loss to the commoners should not be underestimated, because, "While their lords equated economic freedom with leisure, peasants equated free status with independence, drawing a sharp distinction between working for their own sake and for that of their lords" (Katz 1997: 280).

The importance of independence wasn't lost on the lords, who demanded enclosure not simply because they wanted full landownership for its own sake, but also because control of the land gave them control over the peasants. The enclosure movement in Britain was explicitly designed and justified in part as a way to eliminate the economic independence of peasants to force them to become full-time laborers who would, therefore, sell their labor to elites much more cheaply and work much longer hours than they would as independent peasants.

Contemporary defenders of unequal property rights deny that propertyless individuals are dependent wage laborers, but in doing so they deny the stated intentions of the people who created the institution of private property (Carson 2011: 30). Carson (2011: 15–17) compiles hundreds of years of lords' attestations that increased control over the commoners was a primary reason for enclosure. These include the preamble to the Game Laws passed by Parliament in 1692, an anonymous pamphleteer in 1739, an "Essay on Trade and Commerce" in 1770, J. Arbuthnot in 1773, the "Report on Somerset to the Board of Agriculture" in 1795, John Clark in 1807, and the "Gloucestershire Survey" in 1807. Perhaps, "Report on Shropshire" in 1794 best sums up the attitude of this literature: "[T]he labourers will work every day in the year, their children will be put out to labour early . . . and that subordination of the lower ranks of society which in the present times is so much wanted, would be thereby considerably secured."

All or most of the authors Carson (2011) cites argued that these changes were in the interest of both landlords and laborers on the paternalistic-yet-self-serving grounds that it would make commoners "industrious" rather than "lazy," as if working independently is some-how "lazy" and working in subordination to a privileged person is inherently "industrious."

Enclosure worked as desired: "[C]ommoners became utterly depen-dent on miserable wages [and] to earn them they worked harder" (Neeson 1993: 13–14). "The loss of access to forests, wasteland, and common pasturage undermined the bedrock of [commoners] economic independence" (Katz 1997: 284). The transformation of lords into landlords "dispensed with all paternalistic obligations to safeguard subjects' welfare" and effectively privatized "human interchange with nature" replacing the commoners' economic independence with wage dependency (Katz 1997: 284).

Yet, little or no compensation was offered: "the poorest common-ers often had their use rights valued at zero," ignoring how they, "saw enclosure as the confiscation of their primary means of subsistence," and therefore, as the source of their priceless status of independent individuals (Banner 2002: S368).

The British enclosure movement is only one example of a trend that gradually spread across Europe roughly from the fifteenth to the twentieth centuries. The open field system persisted longer in parts of Eastern Europe, sometimes until the post-Second World War imposi-tion of the Soviet Union's so-called collectivization, which was essen-tially another version of enclosure. It replaced traditional shared access with a top-down structure so that individuals who had enjoyed direct access to the land for centuries became dependent laborers under the direction of a government-sanctioned person who took over (and sometimes extended) the lord's authority but who was no longer officially called a "lord" (Carson 2011: 17–23).

By the twentieth century, and owing greatly to the consolidation of private estates during the Industrial Revolution by wealthy elites, virtually all of the open fields had disappeared. But a few remain. In England, for example, the open field system continues—though in a largely symbolic way—in several locations, such as Laxton, Notting-hamshire, and Braunton in North Devon (Beckett 1989; Finberg 1949).

2. THE COLONIAL MOVEMENT

It might seem obvious that individual appropriation actually hap-pened in some places: Australia, Canada, or the United States? Many historical records show individual homesteaders going into unowned wilderness, clearing land, farming, and making it their own. Locke based his story on real events that were happening in British North America at the time (Widerquist 2010a). Did a substantial portion of the world's private property originate with individual appropriation, even if it developed by other means in previously settled areas?

The question is not whether people have ever performed acts resembling the individual appropriation story. During the colonial period, some people certainly did. The questions are: how did colonized territory become unowned, and who said it was up for grabs? The answer is almost invariably government-sponsored or government-approved aggression.

It is worthwhile considering why the Lockean appropriation story so closely resembles some of the things that actually happened during European colonization and, in particular, the early British colonization of eastern North America. From the start, appropriation theory was more directly tied to colonial dispossession of native peoples than it was to the original establishment of land-tenure institutions anywhere. European settlement of the Americas, Australia, and other places was not so different from the Roman colonial project in the sense that virtually all the land that was appropriated by settlers was already being used by people practicing very non-propertarian land-tenure systems. Rome conquered inhabited lands and only then made it available for "appropriation" by favored insiders, such as retiring members of the military (Pateman and Mills 2007: 36–37, 61–64). Modern colonial aggressors did much the same.

To make individual appropriation possible in ancient and modern times, settlers had to designate land as "terra nullius" (nobody's land) and therefore open for appropriation. Before colonial settlers could perform the appropriation criteria recognized by their culture, some legal authority had to decide that some or all of the rights colonized people held over the land did not count (Maine 1861: 246–247; Pateman and Mills 2007: 36–37, 61–64). The Romans initially declared all land and property held by foreigners to be res nullius (nobody's thing), eventually limiting it to the land of conquered enemies (Leage 1961: 176–178). In more remote areas, many of the societies conquered by the Roman Empire would have been organized as chiefdoms or autonomous villages practicing land-tenure systems that were more complex and collectivist than Rome would establish.

Even after terra nullius was declared, colonial appropriators did not usually resemble Lockean farmers. In many cases, the Roman government created private property in conquered lands by awarding titles to Roman elites, including generals, whose acts of "first possession" would have been little more than assuming control of an existing manner. They *were* first possessors in terms of Roman law but in no other sense.

The more recent colonial period wasn't so different. European colonialists had many rationalizations for declaring terra nullius. The inhabitants were an inferior race; they had an inferior religion; they were nomadic; they failed to farm the land; they were savages (whatever that means); or they were warlike (an ironic yet popular claim coming from mass-murdering imperial invaders). Claims like these sound like self-serving excuses for aggression. Perhaps they are. For example, when indigenous people did farm the land, settlers sometimes declared that it still wasn't property because native farmers failed to put up hedgerows or fences to mark their territory (Watner 1983: 154).

One of the most popular rationalizations was the Hobbesian argument that indigenous peoples could not have had any real rights because they had no sovereign government to enforce them (Pateman and Mills 2007: 36, 54). This justification, as popular as it was among actual homesteaders, directly contradicts the Lockean premise that appropriation is a pre-political right.

Over the course of several centuries, the wave of European colonial disappropriations of indigenous peoples gradually spread to almost every region of the globe: the Americas, Africa, Australia, the Russian possessions in Asia, and even across rich and powerful states Europeans had recognized as having some level of "civilization," such as on the Indian subcontinent, Southeast Asia, and so on. Colonial powers revolutionized the economic systems in conquered territories, dispossessing indigenous peoples and gradually introducing the full liberal ownership system. In the states and regions where colonial powers didn't quite reach, or where the colonial powers left before they completed disappropriation, local elites often carried on the process themselves, sometimes with the aid of and partly for the benefit of Western businesses.

Colonizing nations systematically transformed traditional, complex property systems into unitary private property, and awarded ownership of the newly established "rights" to privileged elites from or working for the conquering nation. Common access rights were virtually eliminated, forcing almost everyone to work for one of the elites who controlled access to resources essential to everyone's survival. At home, philosophers from colonial nations declared the resulting situation "natural." The history of European colonization and its effects on land-tenure practices is well documented (Banner 1999, 2000; Hann 1998a, 1998b; Levmore 2002; Scott 1998b; Wagoner 1998).

There is little doubt who the winners and losers were. According to Banner (2002: S368), "Britain had big landowners and everyone else; the colonies had settlers and indigenous people. The winners in each transition were the rich and powerful." There is also little doubt that the process was government-facilitated aggression rather than uncoordinated appropriation. "The big winners from reorganization were the same people who ran the governments that decided whether reorganization would take place. By skewing the payoffs in favor of the powerful, these programs facilitated the reallocation of property rights" (Banner 2002: S368). Although there was no global plan to privatize the world's land, most of the acts of privatization required government support.

The British occupation of India, for example, created "full owners with rights of inheritance and sale where none had existed earlier. At the same time, literally millions of cultivators, tenants, and laborers lost their customary rights of access to the land and its products," with little or no compensation (Scott 2019: 94). The events in India had parallels throughout the British Empire. For example, in Cyprus the British established a private property rights system by undermining the complex indigenous property relations that existed while it was part of the Ottoman Empire (Hann 1998a: 39; Scott 1998b: 142–159).

As soon as Spain subjugated Mexico, colonists began to establish haciendas, which were much like medieval villages with a settler on top and indigenous commoners understood to be "tenants" at the bottom. The tenants who had been working the land for centuries (and thus "appropriating" it?) often lived in serf-like conditions even as the settlers became sole proprietors. Similar examples abound in both the New and Old Worlds (Hann 1998a: 39; Scott 1998b: 142–159).

France colonized Madagascar relatively late in the colonial period; rather than taking away the natives' direct access to the land, the French colonial government imposed a "moralizing tax"—a head tax designed to force every native into the cash economy. It worked well, often also forcing natives into debt, default, and landlessness (Graeber 2011: 50–52).

The areas where colonialists did things that at all resembled the mythical original appropriator were relatively rare, and in virtually every case these "original appropriators" were dependent on at least three forms of government action.

First, even in the few places that were still uninhabited by the time Europeans arrived, any Lockean appropriators were dependent on previous government-financed acts of discovery, which would seem to give the governments some right in those lands by all of the appropriation principles discussed in Chapters 7–9.

Second, probably the greatest help the colonial governments provided for settler-appropriators was the defeat and removal of indigenous peoples: acts of violence, acts of displacement, and sometimes acts of genocide. Indigenous peoples—whether they were agriculturalists or hunter-gatherers—were seldom happy to see newcomers occupy lands in ways that would make traditional native lifestyles impossible. Therefore, indigenous peoples often had to be violently subdued before uncultivated, foraging territories could be occupied. As our earlier book argues, the expansion of states into formerly stateless environments is often associated with a demographic collapse of the indigenous peoples. The indigenous population of the Americas declined by at least 90 percent and perhaps as much as 98 percent following European conquest, and many indigenous peoples disappeared entirely (Widerquist and McCall 2017: 140). Not all of the demographic collapse was intentional, but much of it was, and whatever the cause, it was a necessary precursor to Lockean acts in most land that was proclaimed terra nullius.

Third, individual settler-appropriators needed colonial legal systems to declare the land open to appropriation. Even as colonialist governments replaced indigenous governments and/or non-state social systems, they could have respected and defended indigenous property rights. Had colonial governments done so, both the distribution of property and the type of property regime prevailing in most of the world today would be very different. Instead, colonial governments legally recognized land claims of settlers who resembled the Lockean "original appropriators" only as long as one ignores that these settlers were not really original.

Not-really-original appropriations with all these forms of government aid occurred on an ad hoc basis in much of British North America
(which is clearly the place Locke had in mind when attempting to
justify settler property rights), and on a more systematic basis in
the later independent United States with the Homestead Act, which
Rothbard (1982: 34–35, 47–49, 56, 172) takes as a model for his
"homesteading principle" justifying "original" appropriation. The
British colonial administration in Australia declared the whole continent to be terra nullius and, therefore, open to not-really-original
appropriation—aboriginals notwithstanding (Pateman and Mills
2007: 61–64).

3. POST-COLONIAL ASSIGNMENT OF PROPERTY RIGHTS

Once colonial governments set up full liberal ownership rights, they
retained the rights to tax, regulate, and redistribute titles. To limit
those rights now would not restore anything. It would create a stronger form of ownership rights than has ever existed.

Even ignoring the unoriginality of colonial appropriation, the settlers did not spontaneously establish systems based on full liberal
ownership. North America, for example, quietly went through its
own enclosure movement long after European settlers arrived. Until
the mid- to late nineteenth century, Americans in most places had a
presumptive legal right to use any unfenced, uncultivated land for
foraging and grazing regardless of whether the land was privately
owned—and very little private land was fenced. This right made it
possible for people who owned little or no land to maintain their
independence outside the monetary economy by grazing livestock on
the open range. This legal right was gradually eroded largely because
railroads wanted to keep people and livestock off their land without going through the expense of building fences, and because in the
post-Civil War era, white-dominated governments did not want freed
blacks to have the independence that direct access to grazing land
would give them (Freyfogle 2007: 29–60). Even where colonial and
post-colonial governments set up full liberal ownership rights, they
retained the rights to tax, regulate, and redistribute titles.

Right through to the present day, government assignment rather
than private appropriation continues to be the main source of new
property rights. William H. Riker and Itai Sened's (1991) examination
of recent history finds that individual appropriation followed by legal

recognition seldom happens. Although private property is capable of performing functions such as regulating the commons, it seldom arises spontaneously to do so. Instead, private corporations usually wait passively for governments to grant property rights. Riker and Sened (1991: 967) conclude, "Locke's description is, in fact, exactly backward. He argued that possessors create government to protect their assets. Conversely, our theory, supported by our evidence . . . holds that governments create rights." Even the corporation—the status through which most of the world's productive capacity is owned—owes its existence to legal fiat.

Even in the rare instances of individual appropriation without government aid, actors often set up something other than liberal private property rights. For example, in 1965, a man named Paddy Roy Bates occupied an abandoned military platform just outside what was then British territorial waters. He declared it, "the Principality of Sealand," and "bestowed upon himself the title of Prince . . . of the Principality of Sealand" (Dennis 2002: 264). Bates passed on the title of prince to his son on his death in 2012. This modern-day appropriator followed Hypothetical History 2.

The wealthy resource-exporting monarchies of the Persian Gulf are essentially large, family-owned estates. Bahrain, for example, comprises only 184,000 acres, which would not be enough to make the ruling Al Khalifa family one of the fifty largest landowners in the United States. The fiftieth holds 260,000 acres. The largest holds nearly twelve times as much land as the nation of Bahrain—more than 2.2 million acres (Stebbins 2019). Were the largest U.S. landlords suddenly freed from all higher governmental authority—as the "anarcho-capitalist" version of propertarianism demands—one should expect most of them to act the way families in that situation have tended to act. That is, we should expect most of them to appoint themselves monarchs. Anarcho-capitalism simply is monarchy.

4. ATTEMPTS TO DIVORCE PROPERTARIAN THEORY FROM THE EXCESSES OF THE COLONIAL AND ENCLOSURE MOVEMENTS

Although propertarianism was invented and used for hundreds of years as a justification for the dispossession of peasants and indigenous peoples (see Chapter 8), some propertarians today argue that their theory, properly applied, would actually protect those very groups from dispossession. What was wrong, supposedly, in the colonial movement (and perhaps the enclosure movement as well) was that powerful European individuals stole land and other property from indigenous individuals. Had the Europeans confined themselves to settling truly unowned land, colonialism and enclosure could have happened without conflict.

Although most Native Americans—like many indigenous peoples worldwide—were farmers, many of them were part-time foragers on the "wastes" surrounding their farming villages. Most of the earth's land area, including Europe's land area, was foraging territory at the outset of the colonial and enclosure movements. Combining this observation with the labor-mixing criterion (ignoring the other criteria, such as discovery, first use, etc.) makes it possible to believe that most of the world was unowned and up for grabs in the fifteenth century and that many aspects of the colonial and enclosure movements were justified, even as one intellectually distances oneself from the worst colonial atrocities.

Many propertarians, even some who are skeptical of elite confiscations of communal peasant property, have endorsed this idea. Carson (2011) clearly believes propertarian theory often supports traditional communal villages, but yet he also criticizes "the village commune's illegitimate and unlibertarian power to control access to uncultivated waste." He writes, "[L]and can only be homesteaded collectively by actual development in common—not simply by making claims to unused land. Having not homesteaded the uncultivated waste, the village has no right to restrict either landless outsiders, or its own comparatively subordinate members, from colonizing a new village on the waste land" (Carson 2011: 24).

Carson implies without argument that "landless" or "subordinate" people tend to do most appropriations. But propertarian theory allows appropriation by anyone including people who are already wealthy. We should expect landlords, with all their advantages, to be in position to appropriate far more land than subordinates who needed the commons to maintain their independence.

Carl Watner's (1983: 151) "Libertarians and Indians: Proprietary Justice and Aboriginal Land Rights," argues more thoroughly along these lines. He initially states what appear to be very indigenous-friendly appropriation criteria, "The American Indians, by virtue of being first users and occupiers of parts of the continent, were its rightful owner," but he quickly drops these two criterions in favor of first labor, "If cultivation and enclosure are deemed to be the hallmarks of establishing occupancy and use, then that large portion of the Indian claimed land which was never 'homesteaded' must be viewed as actually ownerless (and thus open to settlement by the actual first user)" (p. 152). He clarifies, "At most, they could claim the wild animals they killed and the trails that they cleared" (p. 153). He blames natives for a significant portion of the ensuing conflicts by writing, "The actual settler—the first transformer of the land—whether white or Indian—had to fight his way past a nest of arbitrary land claims" (Watner 1983: 151).

Watner (1983: 153–154) concludes "[I]t is conceptually possible that the bulk of Indian landholdings could have passed legitimately into non-Indian control. . . . Thus the historical picture clearly demonstrates that libertarians and Indians could have lived peacefully together under a regime of proprietary justice." With this kind of reasoning, one can imagine America being dotted with Indian towns that survived and even thrived as white people settled the vast majority of the continent's land area. But it is nothing but fantasy.

This strategy involves ignoring four important issues we've discussed above. First, almost all appropriation criteria including first use, first occupancy, first claim, discovery, and so on, indicate that foraging territory is owned. This line of reasoning is forced to employ a strict interpretation of Locke's labor-mixing criterion as if it were the only possible one even though it clashes with the others and was concocted as an excuse to disappropriate indigenous peoples (Widerquist 2010a).

Second, even this criterion fails to give propertarians the result they want if one takes seriously the ways foraging transforms land (see Chapter 11).

Third, full liberal ownership of "the trails that they cleared" (p. 153) would give indigenous people effective control over the whole continent, because even crossing perpendicularly over a trail would be trespassing—allowing Native Americans to prevent Europeans from entering the vast majority of the continent. Colonization would have to wait for the invention of aircraft or until settlers invented an excuse to limit the incidents of ownership established by trailblazers.

Fourth, common foraging lands were essential to the lifestyle of many or most communal farming villages. Swidden agriculturists need to move every few years. Even people practicing fallowing or irrigation systems are often dependent on supplementing their farming diet by foraging. Interfering with these activities often forces people to enter the cash economy as dependent laborers.

Watner (1983: 153) takes an inconsistent position on indigenous peoples' ownership of hunting territory. He writes, "The fact that the tribes each had their own hunting areas . . . indicates that they only wished to live in peace with one another." But he favorably quotes Benjamin Tucker, "The English who colonized this country had no right to drive the Indians from their homes; but on the other hand, there being here an abundance of unoccupied land, the colonists had a right to come and settle on it, and the Indians had no right to prevent them from doing so." These statements create a double standard. It is morally acceptable for one native group to forcibly keep other natives from temporarily foraging on their grounds, but it's morally unacceptable for them to use force when white settlers permanently take over those same grounds.

Watner's position is not significantly more favorable to indigenous land claims than the actual colonial movement was at the time. Colonialists seldom moved into native villages. They more often took over foraging lands in between villages until natives saw it as a threat to their lifestyle and conflict developed. Even if settlers had stuck strictly to Watner's rules, violence would have occurred and it would have ended with the destruction of indigenous communities.

Watner's rules would not have prevented the demographic collapse of indigenous peoples or even some acts of genocide. By Watner's reasoning, almost all of the Great Plains would have been "unowned." Every live buffalo was available for appropriation by whoever killed it. The whites were free to kill all the buffalo, thereby using starvation to force survivors to abandon their lifestyle and become dependent laborers.

This logic would even justify aggression against the northwest Pacific Coast and Labrador natives who propertarians praise for having something approaching private property rights (see Chapter 9). The northwestern nations were hunter-gatherers making their living mostly by fishing salmon during seasonal runs, and storing the fish for use all year. They mixed their labor with the fish, but not the river. Thus, a strict application of the labor-mixing principle would give them no special right to the salmon run. Settlers could build houses and businesses near the river, dump their waste into the river, and fish the salmon to extinction if they wanted to. Settler interference would force these groups to give up the lifestyle they had led and the territory they had occupied for thousands of years.

In Europe, Watner's logic would not have significantly slowed enclosure. Instead of petitioning parliament for an act of enclosure, the lords could have simply hired workers to clear and plant the common "wastes," giving the lords most of the land and all the dependent laborers they wanted.

In the Amazon today, Watner's logic would not slow ongoing aggression against native peoples. Companies can clear-cut and plant a monoculture on any size territory that doesn't have a dwelling or cultivated crops on it, and the Amazonians should peacefully accept that they have "no right to prevent them from doing so" (Watner 1983: 153).

This sort of reasoning suspiciously resembles principle-shopping—rationalizing whatever ethical standard gives the theorist the result they want. It disconnects "libertarianism" from its claims to respect an underlying principle of *noninterference* or *nonaggression*. Propertarians might like to restore the theory's appeal by disavowing all disappropriations of peasants, farmers, and foragers around the world, but doing so requires giving up the elite ownership system propertarianism was created to justify.

5. CONCLUSION

For many centuries, and into surprisingly recent times, the open field system and other related forms of communal agricultural land tenure persisted alongside privately owned farm land all over the world. Two related observations are important. First, even in the recent history of Western Europe, vestigial instances of communal land tenure descended from the feudal past directly contradicting conventional stories about appropriation and the origins of private property. Indeed, the enclosure movement itself contradicted the appropriation principle. Second, the modern concept of private property solidified during a period in which there was still considerable variability in land-tenure and landownership systems around Europe and the world. The private property system took hold as landowners and ruling elites secured stronger land rights during the seventeenth and eighteenth centuries through a period of major civil unrest, force, and, in certain cases, violence. In this way, land claims that had started off in the medieval past as lordly rights of usufruct transitioned to the modern rights of private property ownership recognized today.

The implications of these findings for propertarian theory are significant.

The actual origin of the private property system had no resemblance to the individualistic appropriation stories often proffered by political philosophers to justify the institution. Instead, in Western Europe, and especially in England, the private property system took shape as wealthy elites conspired with political authorities to alter the legal framework governing land rights in their own favor.

The Lockean appropriation myth had much more to do with European elite colonial seizure of land in the New World than with "original" appropriation. Even then, colonial appropriators were reliant on government force to eliminate the indigenous peoples who already held land claims that were supported by all or most appropriation criteria in contemporary propertarian theories. The inescapable conclusion, therefore, is that the appropriation mythology misrepresented the ways in which property rights transformations were occurring domestically and around the world to justify not appropriation but the disappropriation of peoples who met the various appropriation criteria propertarians themselves propose.

Because of this transformation, the prospect of "sole and despotic dominion . . . over the external things of the world" "engages the affections" of many more people today than when Blackstone (2016 [1753]: 2) wrote those words, thanks to the campaigns to establish, enforce, and popularize sole proprietorship throughout the centuries in between. As Rossi and Argenton (forthcoming) argue, propertarians rely heavily on the desire for individual private property to justify it, when in fact the need and the desire for private property are the combined product of the process that created the private property system. People today want (or need) full liberal ownership not because it is some "natural" desire but because it is the only game in town. Aggressive governments, with help from some philosophers' sales pitches, have made it the only form of property one could hope to obtain.

The appropriation trope in property rights theory was not just factually wrong: it was blatant in its political motivation as a justification both for the seizure of land from indigenous people and for the alteration of property rules to favor elite European landowners, colonial aggressors, and eventually industrial elites. There may be valid philosophical justifications of the modern private property system, but justification involving any "natural right of private property," which we have seen requires appropriation mythology, is both inaccurate and directly tied to the twin legacies of the dispossession of peasant farmers in Europe and the atrocities of colonial land seizure by European powers in the New World, Africa, Asia, and Australia.

Chapter 15

THE INDIVIDUAL APPROPRIATION
HYPOTHESIS ASSESSED

The history recounted in Chapters 10–14 shows that private property does not arise spontaneously by appropriation or any other method. In historical terms, full liberal ownership is a very recent phenomenon. If modern humans originated 200,000 years ago, the "natural right" to individual private property was apparently rejected by most people exercising individual choice for the first 97.5 percent of our existence, and it remained uncommon for more than 99.75 percent of our existence. The first people to discover, claim, use, occupy, or mix labor with resources over most of the earth established complex, overlapping, flexible, nonspatial, partly collective land-tenure systems with significant common elements. Attempts to maintain traditional systems like this have been thwarted all over the world by people aggressively seizing and privatizing resources.

The individual appropriation hypothesis is not merely unproven: it is disproven. The first individual property holders were not homesteaders or businesspeople but chiefs and kings who were both owners and governors of their territory. The first *private* property holders were elite individuals and institutions who were assigned rights by higher authorities or who used government power to take control of resources. In this way, private property began to emerge in antiquity in some places, but it was still rare only a few centuries ago.

The origins of the first private property systems were well after the origins of the first states. They appeared in ancient times in a few places but became dominant only after the enclosure and colonial movements—gradual processes that took most of the last 500 years to complete. The international private property system did not develop or become dominant spontaneously: state-sponsored campaigns of aggression and violence imposed it on peasants and indigenous peoples who tended to have customary complex land-tenure systems.

The pervasive pattern of aggression supports Stefan Andreasson's (2006: 4) observation, "an examination of historical and contemporary processes that turn human and natural resources into property suggests that [it] is *necessarily* a violent process."

Every formulation of the individual appropriation hypothesis discussed in Chapter 7 is false:

Speculative claims:

1. Before governments or any other collective institutions appear, individuals acting as private individuals intending to establish private property rights appropriate all or most resources.

2. "Land can only be appropriated, runs the usually tacit assumption, by individuals" (Carson 2011: 3).

3. Even if collective property claims come first, only private individuals acting as private individuals perform appropriative acts (i.e. discover, occupy, use, claim, or mix their labor with unowned resources).

4. People involved in collective entities consistently fail to meet the appropriation criteria necessary to give their claims ethical legitimacy as property rights.

5. Individuals intending to set themselves up as private owners perform appropriative acts.

6. Individuals intending to set themselves up as monarchs don't perform appropriative acts.

7. Groups intending to establish private corporations or partnerships perform appropriative acts.

8. Groups intending to establish collective-, public-, or government-held property rights do not perform appropriative acts.

Empirical findings:

Long before individual private property rights appeared on Earth, individuals acting as collectives appropriated all or most resources (according to propertarian criteria) and created "traditional" complex, overlapping, flexible, nonspatial, partly collective, and partly common land-tenure systems.

Speculative claims: 1. People who are free from aggression almost always establish property rights systems based on full liberal ownership.
2. Collective property-holding institutions do not tend to come into existence or to remain in existence for long without violating the principles of appropriation and transfer.
3. Subsequent transfers of titles are likely to maintain the private character of property rights (e.g. no private trader ever obtains enough land to appoint herself monarch of a viable territory).
4. Even if collectives perform appropriative acts, subsequent transfers of titles (in the absence of rights violations) are only likely to produce private property rights.

Empirical findings: People who are free from aggression have tended to set up "traditional," complex land-tenure systems.

Speculative claim: In a world free from violations of the appropriation and transfer principles, only the private appropriation and accumulation of property rights is plausible.

Empirical findings: The ubiquity of complex traditional property rights systems among indigenous peoples and the violence involved in the establishment of the private property rights system indicate that a world free from violations of the appropriation and transfer principles would have traditionally complex land-tenure systems.

Speculative claim: Private property rights tend to arise spontaneously in response to collective action problems, such as the tragedy of the commons.

Empirical findings: Private property rights tend to be created and distributed intentionally by government authorities. Collectives and governments tend to address the tragedy of the commons either by creating private rights or by regulating the commons.

Speculative claims: 1. Private property rights are natural; collective and common rights are not.
2. Only private property develops naturally; collective or common property does not.

Empirical findings: Given the facts above, it's difficult to imagine any definition by which private property qualifies as "natural" and collective or common rights do not.

The supporting and related claims outlined in Chapter 7 are also false:

Speculative claim: Unappropriated resources are useless or nearly useless.

Empirical findings: People who have been observed to make a significant part of their living from common resources have tended to find it extremely valuable, sometimes essential to the maintenance of their status as independent individuals.

Speculative claim: Farmers are the first to significantly transform land.

Empirical findings: Foragers significantly transformed most of the earth before farming first came into use.

Speculative claim: Private property rights tend to arise without aggression against groups holding land collectively (i.e. their establishment is not usually a method to take power and wealth from indigenous peoples).

Empirical findings: The establishment of the private property rights system virtually everywhere in the world involved systematic acts of aggression designed to redistribute wealth from peasants and indigenous peoples often with the additional motive of forcing disappropriated people to become dependent wage laborers.

Speculative claim: First possession has held a unique position in all past times as the organizing principle of most social institutions (Epstein 1978–1979: 1241).

Empirical findings: The "obligation to share food and the taboo against hoarding is no less strong and no less ubiquitous in the primitive world than the far more famous taboo against incest" (Lee 1988: 267).

Speculative claim: The history of the limited private property rights system that exists today will show continuously thwarted attempts to establish systems based on full liberal ownership without the limits implied by collective rights to tax, regulate, or redistribute titles.

Empirical findings: The history of the limited private property rights system that exists today shows continuously thwarted attempts by peasants and indigenous people to establish and maintain complex, overlapping, flexible, partly collective, and partly common land-tenure systems.

Most simply, the individual appropriation hypothesis is false.

Locke's appropriation story (Hypothetical History 1) is a myth with a very important function: it predisposes people to think of full liberal ownership as the natural form of property, yet it is not a plausible description of the origin of property rights or the kind of rights appropriators tend to establish when free from interference. Individuals acting as monarchs (as in Hypothetical History 2) have a somewhat better claim to have performed appropriative acts in some places such as pre-contact Hawaii, but the best evidence indicates that groups intending to establish at least partly collective or common land-tenure systems (as in Hypothetical History 3) performed the first appropriative acts over most of the earth's land area.

Hobbes's (1996 [1651]: 186) assertion that property traces back to the arbitrary decision of the sovereign is a fairly accurate description of the origin of specifically *private* property. At one time or another, sovereigns around the world used their arbitrary powers to replace nearly all traditional land-tenure systems with private titles: "Locke's description is, in fact, exactly backward" (Riker and Sened 1991: 966, 967).

The rejection of the individual appropriation hypothesis has profound implications for private property theory. Our findings challenge conventional beliefs not only about who owns what but also and more importantly about what ownership is. Propertarians usually admit that there have been many injustices in the history of private property, yet they seldom if ever consider that the private property system owes its existence to this history of injustice. Only by ignoring the relevance of this history can they portray the individual appropriation hypothesis as unchallengeable truth.

Propertarians often argue that injustices were so long ago that they can be forgotten (Rothbard 1982: 63); that the property system makes everyone better-off anyway—a claim our earlier book refuted (Widerquist and McCall 2017)—or that even if large rectifications are in order, once that payment is made we must go on with the presumably natural system of propertarian capitalism (Nozick 1974: 231). All of those solutions rely on the assumption that we have now disproven—that there is something natural about an elitist ownership system. Nozick (1974: 231) argues it would be wrong "to introduce socialism as the punishment for our sins." It would be at least as wrong to introduce propertarian capitalism for our failure to demand rectification before the statute of limitations ran out.

Propertarian myths, rather than their principles, make us think that there is something natural about elite private property rights. Although unpatterned propertarian principles allow property rights to be divided or pooled in any conceivable way the original owners decide, the story of the mythological individual appropriator predisposes people to believe individual appropriators and their successors would not share their incidents of ownership with the rest of the community. If complex rights are held by democracies, then they must have stolen them from propertarian individualists. If complex rights are held by peasants or indigenous people, then they must be merely "customs" or "traditions," not real rights. Peasants are not "owners" of nonspatial rights who have been forced to pay tribute but "tenants" paying "rent" to the real landowner, the lord of the manor. What other plausible way is there to get from individual appropriation to such complex divided ownership? That question only seems relevant to someone who has accepted the Lockean myth as representative of some greater truth. The false assumption of an individual original appropriation is the whole of the theory: the sole claim connecting propertarian principles with propertarian policies.

That's the power of an unrecognized myth—the power of an unspoken empirical claim. The individual appropriation hypothesis has remained largely tacit, unnoticed, and free from scrutiny for 350 years.

The most popular argument for propertarianism heavily involves the twin beliefs that private property rights are natural and that protecting them is essential to freedom. Supposedly, what propertarians really care about are the normative principles underlying their theory: that people be allowed to appropriate; that appropriators and their successors be allowed to decide what happens to the resources they've appropriated, free from interference, violence, or aggression. Supposedly, these principles lead us to respect individual private property (largely or entirely) free from taxation, regulation, and redistribution, only because individuals exercising their natural rights without interference would spontaneously create that institution.

Instead, the facts of history are that original appropriators tend to establish something resembling the very things appropriation theory was invented to rule out: partially collective control over and common access rights to the land. The appeal to the rights of the original appropriators—that propertarians have relied on for hundreds of years—not only fails to support full liberal ownership; it provides good reason to reject it.

Propertarians portray their efforts to free property owners from taxation, regulation, and redistribution as the restoration of a natural right. To establish such a system would not be the restoration of anything. Propertarians are not *defending* the private property system from collective encroachment; they actually favor *strengthening* a private property system that owes its existence to force and aggression. Propertarian reforms would make incidents of ownership stronger and more individualistic than they have been at virtually any time or place in history or prehistory. Only the most powerful monarchs, emperors, and dictators have had so much power over land, resources, and the things we make out of them.

To strengthen elite-held ownership rights—and/or to privatize what is left of the commons—would continue the aggressive disappropriation of the mass of humanity that has been going on since the formation of the first states and chiefdoms. Propertarianism is not a revolt of the people against a grasping monarch. It is a revolt of the lords who would make themselves into petty monarchs and everyone else into subjects.

Propertarianism has nothing to do with anarchy or a minimal state. Enormous political authority is necessary to establish and maintain the rights system propertarians want to see. Propertarianism might move governmental and nongovernmental maintenance mechanisms into the background, but those mechanisms involve great force and give property owners enormous political authority over everyone else (Widerquist 2013). The more closely ownership approximates the strong propertarian version, the more political power private owners have to govern the land. Control over the land and resources is control over the people. That is why so many stateless peoples insist on the common right to resources.

This book neither endorses nor rejects propertarian principles as an ethical guide to justice in holdings. It simply argues that propertarian principles don't support full liberal ownership. This book is not about what kind of system propertarian principles *do* support. People who agree with this book's findings might disagree on how to respond. We briefly consider the question, but a full answer would probably require another book.

One reply is simple: does anyone care about propertarian principles now that we know they fail to support propertarian capitalism? The theory venerating the principles of appropriation, voluntary transfer, rectification, and the statute of limitations was invented to justify an elitist private property system. Now that we know these principles individually and collectively fail to justify that system, maybe we don't need to discuss them anymore?

Not all arguments for propertarian capitalism rely on the natural rights argument discussed here. This book isn't relevant to those arguments, and people who support propertarian capitalism or any other version of the market economy for any of those reasons are unaffected by the arguments here.

But people who have relied on rights-based arguments for propertarian policies would pay an enormous cost for shifting to a non-rights-based approach. They would have to ask themselves whether they really believe in those principles or whether they really believe in the policies they were using those principles to support. Are propertarian principles sincere ethical values or 350-year-old rationalizations for propertarian policies? As Groucho Marx might say, "If you don't like my principles, I have others."

Political theory and philosophy journals are rich with arguments for rejecting propertarian principles on ethical grounds. The anthropological evidence cited here could be used in an "empirical natural rights" argument (Hasnas 2005) against them as well. Epstein (1978–1979: 1241) was entirely wrong to claim, "first possession . . . enjoyed in all past times the status of a legal rule, not only for the stock of examples of wild animals and sea shells, but also for unoccupied land." The earliest peoples applied no such principle, at least not on an individual level, neither for land nor for food and tools. In the view of many stateless peoples, "land is not an object that can be owned but something that people can be closely associated with and related to" (Bird-David 1990: 192). First possession contradicts "one of the core principles of ancient practice: 'the feeling that wild places and water, untouched by human hand, could not be appropriated by any individual'" (Katz 1997: 284). One of the authors of this book has written elsewhere about what principles should be used to make resources into property once these principles are rejected (Widerquist 2013, 2016), but that question is beyond the scope of this book.

Assuming that anyone still cares about propertarian principles once they are shown not to support propertarian capitalism, what kind of system do they support? It's hard to tell. These four basic and rather vague principles are incapable of determining anything very specific without detailed and controversial specification of each principle.

One solution uses a tactic propertarians typically rely on to justify private property despite past injustice: interpret the statute-of-limitations principle strongly enough to eliminate concern with colonialism and enclosure. If so, the answer is simple.

Most of the world has been controlled by one property-owning government or another for an awfully long time. There is nothing special about the public sector. The government is just a big landholding institution. It's just one way that people might choose to hold property. Applying the statute of limitations to property-owning governments implies that anarcho-capitalism exists; property ownership just happens to be dominated by about 200 corporations that call themselves "governments." Propertarian principles imply a non-ideological nationalism; they support whatever property rights regime has been in place for a sufficient amount of time to be legitimized by the statute of limitations: feudalism, socialism, welfare capitalism, and unregulated capitalism are equally "propertarian" (Widerquist 2009a).

One conception of the statute-of-limitations principle, relative title (Epstein 1995: 64–67), has important implications for contemporary titleholders. Assuming the United States government stole its land from Native Americans, under relative title, only the heirs of dispossessed Native Americans have claims against the United States. Relative title blocks any effort to strengthen whatever weak property-holding titles the United States chose to issue to settlers after it seized the land.

If we loosen the statute-of-limitations principle, it's clear that everyone has ancestors among the dispossessed of the world, although the three remaining propertarian principles don't say much about what kind of land-tenure system they might want to create with their rectification. How the people can best share the earth is up to them. They are likely to disagree. That disagreement has no easy solution. The four stated propertarian principles are little help in resolving disputes about what ownership should be. But we'll say what we can within the limits of this theory.

When individuals separately appropriate pieces of property, each individual fully controls all eleven incidents of their piece and therefore has full decision-making power over it. When two or more people appropriate property together without a previously specified agreement, it is not at all clear who holds what incidents, and what the process is for transferring, dividing, combining, or changing the nature of the ownership system they have created. Few if any of the peoples who originally appropriated the earth thousands of years ago specified any contract beforehand. They developed land-tenure customs for the context in which they lived without specifying how to change it in the event that a worldwide industrial economy might develop.

The history of government-sponsored aggression recounted above calls into question the justification of most existing governments, but it does not necessarily call into question the justification of all potential governments. Although there are no records of societies going from small to large scale without violence and injustice, there are many thwarted attempts of people to set up and maintain complex, communal land-tenure systems. If they had been free from rights violations, they might have found ways to organize themselves on a larger scale. At least it is more reasonable to think so than to think that large-scale propertarian capitalism could have developed from appropriation.

The heirs of the dispossessed are most of the citizens of the world. People might choose to take rectification in some form of small-scale mutualism, but they might choose to take rectification in the form of truly democratic control of their governments. The closest contemporary way to express the complexity of overlapping, flexible, nonspatial, partly collective, and partly common land-tenure systems might be to make use of taxation, regulation, and redistribution. The earliest swidden and fallowing farmers chose to regulate farming as a group because the way one farmer used her field affected how everyone else was able to use their fields and graze their animals. People today want to regulate pollution and greenhouse gas emissions because the way one person treats the environment affects whether everyone else can live and be healthy in that environment. The demands of the underprivileged for the power to redistribute property can be understood as redress for lost access to the commons that their ancestors enjoyed for 200,000 years.

Even as the people exercise these powers, they might not want to significantly change what property is. They might wish to retain some of the more attractive aspects of the private property system. And they would be wise to avoid any hugely disruptive sudden change. Rectification does not necessarily imply wholesale dispossession—especially of people who have played by the rules and acted in good faith under what turns out to have been a flawed system. But the privatized sector needs to be recognized as the result of privatization: it is not a naturally occurring phenomenon; it is something governments create for good and bad reasons. Privatization is everywhere and is always a political process that creates both owners and nonowners. It has most often been used to create winners and losers. Privatization is a tool that should only be used if and when both owners and nonowners benefit from it.

The citizens, through the landholding corporation they call their "government," are the nation's landlord. They own all the associated rights to tax, regulate, and redistribute property titles. To reject the people's right to choose to hold property this way for any reason other than a specific historical claim for rectification is to make a patterned argument against the concentration of wealth—a clear violation of the unpatterned principles that supposedly motivate propertarianism. The citizens of a nation have the same reason to profit from taxation as any landowners have to profit from rent: *because they inherited that right from their ancestors.*

Conclusion

Chapter 16

CONCLUSION

This book has told six histories: the intellectual histories of three widely believed empirical claims, and the political and economic histories that refute those claims. Part One shows how many people throughout history have asserted conflicting explanations for why inequality is natural, inevitable, or a necessary by-product of freedom, when in fact many free, small-scale stateless societies have maintained political, social, and economic equality. Part Two shows that many people claim that the market economy promotes negative freedom better than any other, when in fact the hunter-gatherer band economy promotes negative freedom much better. Part Three shows that propertarians rely on the belief that there is something natural about private property, when in fact the private property system owes its existence to a long history of violent aggression.

One simple conclusion is that advocates of strong, unequal private property rights are not entitled to the terms "libertarian," "liberal," or any term associated with freedom and liberty. They do not promote liberty. They promote property rights for the elite at the expense of liberty and of equality before the law. The term "propertarian" is far more apt. The more important conclusion of this book is that propertarianism relies on false empirical claims about equality, freedom, and the origin and nature of property rights in the past and as a stand-in for some kind of imagined universal human nature. We have said enough about that theory now.

We can move on to the consideration of other lessons we might be able to draw from this history. One lesson is that normative arguments by reference to a single form of "human nature," or other innate or universal dynamics of human social organization, are doomed to failure. Human societies have been endlessly variable in the past and the present; and there is no one way that we humans are destined or obliged to organize ourselves in the future. We can choose the paths that best suit our political and economic goals; or, perhaps more pointedly, the paths that best fulfill our moral duties and ethical obligations in terms of how we treat our fellow humans, and do so without reference to what we happen to think about human nature at any given moment. An important lesson of anthropology is that different rules are possible. There is nothing natural and inevitable in any society's system of rules. Modern states are only beginning to learn how to build true democracy, freedom, and equality.

In contrast, when people have tended to make normative arguments with reference to some natural or inevitable way of doing things, it has almost always taken the form of the justification for how they are already doing something, or some set of things, that benefits them or is otherwise in their interest. This characterization was as true of Plato, Locke, and Nietzsche as it was of Hitler and Pol Pot—because the underlying logic is the same. Propertarian philosophers may take offense at such comparisons, but we have a question to put to them: do you *really* believe that these stories you tell about the past in order to justify your political positions are true? Or do you tell them because you want them to be true so that your conception of moral order remains intact?

We hope that this book and our previous book help people look for ways to use our understanding of human variability to provide an empirical basis for generating and evaluating normative political philosophies. Many philosophers and anthropologists have complained—out loud and in print—about the dangers of anthropological accounts, and especially of ethnographic accounts of modern peoples, as the basis for normative theorizing. For one thing, this complaint has always seemed shallow to us, especially coming from philosophers who were content to accept the centuries-old racist speculation of their intellectual ancestors as hard fact when it comes to things like the "state of nature"—which, by the way, is a form of empirical evidence about human variation; it's just *bad* empirical evidence.

Likewise, anthropologists have warned us against essentializing, primitivizing, romanticizing, "othering," etc., modern indigenous peoples and doing so to their detriment. The complaint is again ironic because *so many* political philosophers and anthropologists have done all of these things without little or no self-reflection. Let's be clear: we don't think modern indigenous people can stand in for our evolutionary past, the state of nature, or any of the many other overlapping concepts meant to contrast with how people in Western industrial societies do things today. Our point is simply that humans have been profoundly variable when both prehistoric and modern indigenous societies are considered and that we now know things about that variability that undermine some of the centuries-old ideas about human nature and/or the state of nature.

The final lesson that we draw here is that, if we choose to prioritize negative freedom as a prime goal of our political-economic systems, then there are concrete things that we can do to enhance negative freedom—by emulating conditions that were prevalent over the bulk of human prehistory and that have persisted among a dwindling number of small-scale societies into the modern world. Above all, we have found, negative freedom flows from "the power to say no" (Widerquist 2013), including all of its economic, social, and political dimensions. Several conditions have ensured this capability for members of small-scale societies, each of which deserves some thought now.

The first and foremost condition is "[a]ccess of all to the 'forces of production,'" (Leacock and Lee 1982: 9). In other words, equal access provided to all individuals to produce the things that they need for survival without dependency on others in any of its many possible forms. The major way in which this tends to be achieved in small-scale societies is through universal access to the commons, which, by providing direct access to the means of economic production, is the central element maintaining each individual's power to refuse cooperation with potential oppressors. All else being equal, the more access people have to a commons, the freer and more equal society tends to be. As Jean-Jacques Rousseau (1984) put it, "[I]t is impossible to make any man a slave, unless he be first reduced to a situation in which he cannot do without the help of others."

Similarly, the political right to confront individuals seeking to dominate others also grows out of security in one's access to the means of production and, thus, frequently in terms of economic access to a commons. For those living in egalitarian band societies, they can be assured that they can shame or ridicule a would-be aggrandizer or refuse the orders of a potential dominator—or employ many of the other leveling mechanisms that egalitarian hunter-gatherers use in maintaining the distinctively human reverse dominance hierarchy (Boehm 2001), since their access to the means of production is not substantively threatened. Under those circumstances, people can leave, move to a new village, form a new village, live by themselves, or whatever else they choose—all without fear of threat to their means of survival.

For virtually everyone alive on Earth today, however, the commons is closed. Disadvantaged people are subject to a host of political rules favoring the advantaged. Most modern people are not fully free to confront the rich and the powerful, to leave bad jobs, or sometimes even to escape from a violent spouse—all because of the fear of economic desolation. They have nowhere to go to avoid these rules. And so, billions of people today are forced to do jobs that they do not want, for people that they don't want to work for, controlled by governments who make rules that disadvantage them and uphold values in which they do not believe. None but the independently wealthy is free to choose noncooperation with potential oppressors. If we really believe in liberty, then we must give all people the economic power to say no to those who would force them to labor for economies they do not wish to participate in, or, for that matter, for governing principles in which they do not believe.

Some will no doubt resort to the superficial complaint that it is impractical or even impossible literally to provide all people with access to a physical commons in which they could forage or plant crops, etc. Indeed, though such commons are not uncommon in the world today, as we have pointed out previously in this book, not everyone can be afforded the direct opportunity to hunt, fish, gather, farm, or herd, and produce their own food in doing so. Some of us might be happy if we could; most would not be; and few would have the knowledge or desire to figure out the details even if enough land and resources were available. This is not what we are suggesting. Instead, if we take the importance of the common right seriously, we have to find a substitute that increases people's power to refuse cooperation with those who try to dominate them. That substitute has to give the least advantaged people genuine power over their own lives.

Propertarians are right to say that private ownership of property helps protect people from the dangers of other people's power in any form. But property only works for people who own it. Everybody else, which is nearly all of us, has only the appearance of being able to refuse cooperation. Without direct, individual access to the resources they need to survive, disadvantaged people in the modern, globalized economy are subjugated in ways that most of our ancestors would have seen as a fundamental violation of their humanity.

In our previous book (Widerquist and McCall 2017), we argued that, in order for social contract formulations of the state to be justified according to the Lockean proviso, all people alive today must be as well- or better-off than the most well-off individual in a stateless society (of the kind so many political philosophers have imagined as the state of nature). Here, we argue that, in order for property rights regimes to be justified, and if liberty is indeed the prime goal, we must find a way to provide all living people with as much negative freedom as they could have expected if they lived in an egalitarian hunter-gatherer society.

To approximate the independence available to people with access to a commons, we need to cede a great deal more power to the disadvantaged than any of the world's governments do now. One of the authors of this book has argued elsewhere on the importance of independence, on the ways contemporary state societies consistently deny this power to disadvantaged individuals, on the benefits of securing it for all, and on an unconditional basic income as one reasonable way to support independence when direct access to a physical commons is impractical.

One of the authors of this book has discussed this issue extensively (Widerquist 1999, 2006b, 2010b, 2011, 2013, 2019). We don't need to reiterate those arguments here. The central idea is that by robustly defending the power of noncooperation for everyone including the most disadvantaged, society creates an important check on both political and economic power, which is otherwise held exclusively by the privileged few or at best the privileged half of the population.

Universal Basic Income would, in a sense, provide all people with direct access to the means of economic production by giving them a slice of the economic product as a whole. Universal Basic Income is not a literal replacement for a commons but it would provide individuals with many of the same structural points of leverage in demanding better wages, working conditions, ethnic and gender relations, and so on.

After hundreds of millennia in which all humans had direct access to the commons, it took only a few centuries for enclosure, colonialism, capitalism, and industrialization to cut off the vast majority of people on Earth from direct access to the means of economic production and therefore to rob them of the power to say no. It took only a few generations to convince most people that this situation was natural and inevitable. That false lesson needs to be unlearned.

REFERENCES

Adams Jr., R. M. (2017), *The Evolution of Urban Society: Early Mesopotamia and Prehispanic Mexico*. New York: Routledge.

Alexander, C. F. (2013), "All Things Bright and Beautiful," in *Hymns for Little Children* (1848). Retrieved October 2, 2020 from https://hymnary.org/text/each_little_flower_that_opens

Altman, J. C. and N. Peterson (1988), "Rights to Game and Rights to Cash among Contemporary Australian Hunter-gatherers," in T. Ingold, D. Riches and J. Woodburn (eds.), *Hunters and Gatherers 2: Property, Power and Ideology*. Oxford: Berg Publishing, 75–94.

Ames, K. M. (2007), "The Archaeology of Rank," in R. A. Bentley, H. D. G. Maschner and C. Chippindale (eds.), *Handbook of Archaeological Theories*. Lanham, MD: Altamira Press.

Anderson, D. G. (1998), "Property as a Way of Knowing on Evenki Lands in Arctic Siberia," in C. M. Hann (ed.), *Property Relations: Renewing the Anthropological Tradition*. Cambridge: Cambridge University Press, 64–84.

Andreasson, S. (2006), "Stand and Deliver: Private Property and the Politics of Global Dispossession," *Political Studies*, 54: 1, 1–21.

Arneson, R. J. (2003), "Equality, Coercion, Culture and Social Norms," *Politics, Philosophy & Economics*, 2: 1, 139–163.

Arnold, J. E. (1996), "The Archaeology of Complex Hunter-Gatherers," *Journal of Archaeological Method and Theory*, 3: 1, 77–126.

Ashcraft, R. (1987), *Locke's Two Treatises of Government*. Hemel Hempstead: Allen & Unwin.

Attas, D. (2005), *Liberty, Property and Markets*. Aldershot: Ashgate.

Ault, W. (2013), *Open-Field Farming in Medieval Europe: A Study of Village By-laws*. London: Routledge.

Bailey, M. J. (1992), "Approximate Optimality of Aboriginal Property Rights," *Journal of Law and Economics*, 35, 183.

Bandy, M. S. (2004), "Fissioning, Scalar Stress, and Social Evolution in Early Village Societies," *American Anthropologist*, 106: 2, 322–333.

Banner, S. (1999), "Two Properties, One Land: Law and Space in Nineteenth-Century New Zealand," *Law and Social Inquiry*, 24: 4, 807–852.

Banner, S. (2000), "Conquest by Contract: Wealth Transfer and Land Market Structure in Colonial New Zealand," *Law and Society Review*, 47, 72–73.

Banner, S. (2002), "Transitions between Property Regimes," *Journal of Legal Studies*, 31: S2, S359–S371.

Bar-Yosef, O. (1986), "The Walls of Jericho: An Alternative Interpretation," *Current Anthropology*, 27: 2, 157–162.

Bard, K. A. (2008), *An Introduction to the Archaeology of Ancient Egypt*. Oxford: Blackwell Publishing.

Barkai, R. and R. Liran (2008), "Midsummer Sunset at Neolithic Jericho," *Time and Mind*, 1: 3, 273–283.

Barnard, A. and J. Woodburn (1988), "Property, Power, and Ideology in Hunter-Gathering Societies: An Introduction," in T. Ingold, D. Riches and J. Woodburn (eds.), *Hunters and Gatherers 2: Property, Power and Ideology*. Oxford: Berg Publishing, 4–31.

Barth, F. (1953), *Principles of Social Organization in Southern Kurdistan*. Oslo: Brødrene Jørgensen.

Bastiat, F. (1996), *Economic Harmonies*. Irvington-on-Hudson, NY: The Foundation for Economic Education.

Beckett, J. V. (1989), *A History of Laxton: England's Last Open-field Village*. Oxford: Basil Blackwell.

Bellwood, P. (1987), *The Polynesians*. London: Thames and Hudson.

Benneh, G. (1973), "Small-scale farming systems in Ghana," *Africa*, 43: 2, 134–146.

Benson, B. L. (1989), "Enforcement of Private Property Rights in Primitive Societies: Law Without Government," *The Journal of Libertarian Studies*, IX: 1, 1–26.

Benson, B. L. (1990), *The Enterprise of Law: Justice without the State*. San Francisco, CA: Pacific Institute for Public Policy Research.

Benson, B. L. (2007), "Legal Evolution in Primitive Societies", in E. P. Stringham (ed.), *Anarchy and the Law: The Political Economy of Choice*. Oakland, CA: The Independent Institute.

Berlin, I. (1969), "Two Concepts of Liberty," in I. Berlin (ed.), *Four Essays on Liberty*. Oxford: Oxford University Press.

Berlin, I. (1978), "Equality", in I. Berlin (ed.), *Concepts and Categories: Philosophical Essays*. London: Hogarth Press, 81–102.

Berns, W. (1987), "John Milton," in L. Strauss and Cropsey (eds.), *History of Political Philosophy*. Chicago: University of Chicago Press, 440–455.

Béteille, A. (2003), *The Idea of Natural Inequality and Other Essays*. Oxford: Oxford University Press.

Binford, L. R. (2001), *Constructing Frames of Reference: An Analytical Method for Archaeological Theory Building using Hunter-gatherer and Environmental Data Sets*. Berkeley: University of California Press.

Binford, L. R. (2006), "Bands May Exist only in the History of Anthropology," in F. Sellet, R. D. Greaves and P.-L. Yu (eds.), *Archaeology and Ethnoarchaeology of Mobility*. Gainesville: University of Florida Press, 3–22.

Binford, S. R. and L. R. Binford (1968), *New Perspectives in Archaeology*. Chicago: Aldine.

Bird-David, N. (1990), "The Giving Environment: Another Perspective on the Economic System of Gatherer-Hunters," *Current Anthropology*, 31: 2, 189–196.

Bird-David, N. (1992), "Beyond the 'Original Affluent Society': A Culturalist Reformulation," *Current Anthropology*, 33: 1, 25–47.

Bird-David, N. (1994), "Sociality and Immediacy: Or, Past and Present Conversations on Bands," *Man*, 29: 3, 583–603.

Black, B. D. and R. P. Thomas (1974), "The Enclosure Movement and the Supply of Labor During the Industrial Revolution," *Journal of European Economic History*, 3: 2, 401–423.

Blackstone, W. (2016 [1753]), *Commentaries on the Laws of England*. Carmel, IN: Online Library of Liberty.

Blurton-Jones, N. G. (1987), "Tolerated Theft, Suggestions about the Ecology and Evolution of Sharing, Hoarding, and Scrounging," *Social Science Information*, 26: 1, 31–54.

Boaz, D. (1997), *Libertarianism: A Primer*. New York: Free Press.

Boehm, C. (1993), "Egalitarian Behavior and Reverse Dominance Hierarchy," *Current Anthropology*, 34: 3, 227–254.

Boehm, C. (2001), *Hierarchy in the Forest: The Evolution of Egalitarian Behavior*. Cambridge, MA: Harvard University Press.

Bogaard, A., D. Filipovic, A. Fairbairn, L. Green, E. A. Stroud et al. (2017), "Agricultural Innovation and Resilience in a Long-Lived Early Farming Community: The 1,500-year Sequence at Neolithic to Early Chalcolithic Çatalhöyük, Central Anatolia," *Anatolian Studies*, 67, 1–28.

Brown, D. (2007), *Bury my Heart at Wounded Knee: An Indian History of the American West*. New York: Macmillan.

Burns, T. (2002), "Sophocles' Antigone and the History of the Concept of Natural Law," *Political Studies*, 50: 3, 545–557.

Burns, T. (2003), "The Tragedy of Slavery: Aristotle's Rhetoric and the History of the Concept of Natural Law," *History of Political Thought*, 24: 1, 16–36.

Burt, W. H. (1943), "Territoriality and Home Range Concepts as Applied to Mammals," *Journal of Mammalogy*, 24: 3, 346–352.

Byccellati, G. (1996), "The Role of Socio-Political Factors in the Emergence of 'Public' and 'Private' Domains in Early Mesopotamia," in M. Hudson and B. A. Levin (eds.), *Privatization in the Ancient Near East and Classical World*. Cambridge, MA: Peabody Museums of Archeology and Ethnology, 129–152.

Calhoun, J. C. (1851), "Disquisition on Government." Retrieved February 18, 2013 from http://www.constitution.org/jcc/disq_gov.htm

Carneiro, R. L. (1970), "A Theory of the Origin of the State," *Science*, 169: 3947, 733–738.

Carson, J. (2007), *The Measure of Merit: Talents, Intelligence, and Inequality in the French and American Republics, 1750–1940*. Princeton, NJ: Princeton University Press.

Carson, K. (2011), *Communal Property: A Libertarian Analysis*. Tulsa, OK: Center for a Stateless Society.

Cashdan, E. (1980), "Egalitarianism among Hunters and Gatherers," *American Anthropologist*, 82: 1, 116–120.

Cashdan, E. (1983), "Territoriality among Human Foragers: Ecological Models and an Application to Four Bushman Groups," *Current Anthropology*, 24: 1, 47–66.

Cashdan, E. (1989). "Hunters and Gatherers: Economic Behavior in Bands," in S. Platter (ed.), *Economic Anthropology*. Stanford, CA: Stanford University Press, 21–48.

Chambers, C. and P. Parvin (2010), "Coercive Redistribution and Public Agreement: Re-evaluating the Libertarian Challenge of Charity," *Critical Review of International Social and Political Philosophy*, 13: 1, 93–114.

Chambers, J. D. (1953), "Enclosure and Labour Supply in the Industrial Revolution," *The Economic History Review*, 5: 3, 319–343.

Childe, V. G. (1950), "The Urban Revolution," *Town Planning Review*, 21: 1, 3.

Childe, V. G. (1957), "Civilization, Cities, and Towns," *Antiquity*, 31: 121, 36–38.

Christmas, B. (2018), "Rescuing the Libertarian Non-Aggression Principle," *Moral Philosophy and Politics*, 5: 2, 305–326.

Christmas, B. (2019), "Ambidextrous Lockeanism," *Economics and Philosophy*, 35: 1, 1–23.

Clutton-Brock, T. H. (1989), "Review Lecture: Mammalian Mating Systems," *Proceedings of the Royal Society of London. B. Biological Sciences*, 236: 1285, 339–372.

Cobo, B. (1979), *History of the Inca Empire*. Austin: University of Texas.

Cohen, G. A. (1988), *History, Labour, and Freedom: Themes from Marx*. Oxford: Clarendon Press.

Cohen, G. A. (1995), *Self-Ownership, Freedom, and Equality*. Cambridge: Cambridge University Press.

Cohen, G. A. (1998), "Once More Into The Breach Of Self-Ownership: Reply To Narveson And Brenkert," *The Journal of Ethics*, 2: 1, 57–96.

Cohen, G. A. (2011). "Freedom and Money", in M. Otsuka (ed.), *On the Currency of Egalitarian Justice, and Other Essays in Political Philosophy*. Princeton, NJ: Princeton University Press, 166–192.

Conklin, H. C. (1961), "The Study of Shifting Cultivation," *Current Anthropology*, 2: 1, 27–61.

Connah, G. (2001), *African Civilizations: An Archaeological Perspective*. Cambridge: Cambridge University Press.

Dahlman, C. J. (2008), *The Open Field System and Beyond*. Cambridge: Cambridge Books.

Dahrendorf, R. (1968), *Essays in the Theory of Society*. London: Routledge and Kegan Paul.

Davies, M. I. (2009), "Wittfogel's Dilemma: Heterarchy and Ethnographic Approaches to Irrigation Management in Eastern Africa and Mesopotamia," *World Archaeology*, 41: 1, 16–35.

Davis, K. and W. E. Moore (1945), "Some Principles of Stratification," *American Sociological Review*, 10: 2, 242–249.

de Tracy, A. L. C. D. (1970 [1817]), *A Treatise On Political Economy To Which Is Prefixed A Supplement To A Preceding Work On The Understanding Or, Elements Of Ideology*. New York: Augustus M. Kelley.

de Waal, F. (2005), *Our Inner Ape: The Best and Worst of Human Nature*. New York: Riverhead Books.

Dennis, T. A. (2002), "The Principality of Sealand: Nation Building by Individuals," *Tulsa Journal of Comparative & International Law*, 10: 1, 261–296.

Dowling, J. H. (1968), "Individual Ownership and the Sharing of Game in Hunting Societies," *American Anthropologist*, 70, 502–507.

Drennan, R. D. and C. E. Peterson (2006), "Patterned Variation in Prehistoric Chiefdoms," *Proceedings of the National Academy of Sciences of the United States of America*, 103: 11, 3960–3967.

Dubreuil, B. (2010), *Human Evolution and the Origins of Hierarchy*. Cambridge: Cambridge University Press.

Dyson-Hudson, R. and E. A. Smith (1978), "Human Territoriality: An Ecological Reassessment," *American Anthropologist*, 80: 1, 21–41.

Earle, T. (ed.) (1991a), *Chiefdoms: Power, Economy, and Ideology*. Cambridge: Cambridge University Press.

Earle, T. (1991b), "The Evolution of Chiefdoms," in T. Earle (ed.), *Chiefdoms: Power, Economy, and Ideology*. Cambridge: Cambridge University Press, 1–15.

Earle, T. (1997), *How Chiefs Come to Power: The Political Economy in Prehistory*. Stanford, CA: Stanford University Press.

Earle, T. (2000), "Archaeology, Property, and Prehistory," *Annual Review of Anthropology*, 29, 39–60.

Earle, T. (2002), *Bronze Age Economics: The First Political Economies*. Boulder, CO: Westview Press.

Edzar, D. O. (1996), "Private Land Ownership and its Relation to 'God' and the 'State' in Sumer and Akkad", in M. Hudson and B. A. Levine (eds.), *Privatization in the Ancient Near East and Classical World*. Cambridge, MA: Peabody Museums of Archeology and Ethnology.

Ellingson, T. (2001), *The Myth of the Noble Savage*. Berkeley, CA: University of California Press.

Endicott, K. (1988), "Property, Power and Conflict Among the Batek of Malaysia," in T. Ingold, D. Riches and J. Woodburn (eds.), *Hunters and Gatherers 2: Property, Power and Ideology*. Oxford: Berg Publishing, 110–127.

Endicott, K. and K. L. Endicott (2008), *The Headman Was a Woman: The Gender Egalitarian Batek of Malasia*. Long Grove, IL: Waveland Press.

Enloe, J. (2003), "Food Sharing Past and Present: Archaeological Evidence for Economic and Social Interactions," *Before Farming*, 2003: 1, 1–23.

Epstein, R. A. (1978–1979), "Possession as the Root of Title," *Georgia Law Review*, 13, 1221–1244.

Epstein, R. A. (1995), *Simple Rules for a Complex World*. Cambridge, MA: Harvard University Press.

Evans-Pritchard, E. E. (1951), *The Nuer*. Oxford: Oxford University Press.

Evola, J. (2002), *Men Among the Ruins: Postwar Reflections of a Radical Traditionalist*. Rochester, VT: Inner Traditions.

Fein, M. L. (2012), *Human Hierarchies: A General Theory*. New Brunswick, NJ: Transaction Publishers.

Feinberg, R. (1982), "Some Observations on a Polynesian Naming System: Personal Names and Naming on Anuta," *The Journal of the Polynesian Society*, 91: 4, 581–588.

Feser, E. (2000), "Taxation, Forced Labor, and Theft," *The Independent Review*, 5: 2, 219–235.

Feser, E. (2005), "There is No Such Thing as an Unjust Initial Acquisition," *Social Philosophy and Policy*, 22: 1, 56–80.

Filmer, S. R. (1949 [1680]), *Patriarcha and Other Political Works*. Oxford: Basil Blackwell.

Finberg, H. P. R. (1949), "The Open Field in Devonshire," *Antiquity*, 23: 92, 180–187.

Fischer, M. H., M. Hout, M. Sánchez Jankowski, S. R. Lucas, A. Swidler et al. (1996), *Inequality by Design: Cracking the Bell Curve Myth*. Princeton, NJ: Princeton University Press.

Flannery, K. V. (1999), "Process and Agency in Early State Formation," *Cambridge Archaeological Journal*, 9: 1, 3–21.

Flannery, K. V. and J. Marcus (2012), *The Creation of Inequality: How Our Prehistoric Ancestors Set the State for Monarchy, Slavery, and Empire*. Cambridge, MA: Harvard University Press.

Forrester, D. B. (1987), "Martin Luther and John Calvin," in L. Strauss and J. Cropsey (eds.), *History of Political Philosophy*. Chicago: University of Chicago Press, 318–355.

Fortin, E. L. (1987a), "St. Augustine," in L. Strauss and J. Cropsey (eds.), *History of Political Philosophy*. Chicago: University of Chicago Press, 176–205.

Fortin, E. L. (1987b), "St. Thomas Aquinas," in L. Strauss and J. Cropsey (eds.), *History of Political Philosophy*. Chicago: University of Chicago Press, 248–275.

Freuchen, P. and D. Freuchen (1965), "Book of the Eskimos." Retrieved November 28, 2014 from http://books.google.com/books?id=HRwtHQAACAAJ

Freyfogle, E. T. (2007), *On Private Property: Finding Common Ground on the Ownership of Land*. Boston, MA: Beacon Press.

Fried, M. H. (1967), *The Evolution of Political Society: An Essay in Political Anthropology*. New York: Random House.

Friedman, J. (1997), "What's Wrong With Libertarianism," *Critical Review*, 2: 3, 407–467.

Gaius (1904), *Institutes of Roman Law*. Oxford: Clarendon Press.

Gardner, P. M. (1991), "Foragers Pursuit of Individual Autonomy," *Current Anthropology*, 32, 543–572.

Geertz, C. (1956), "Capital-Intensive Agriculture in Peasant Society: A Case Study," *Social Research*, 23: 4, 433–449.

Gellner, E. (1995), *Anthropology and Politics*. Oxford: Blackwell.

George, H. (1976), *Progress and Poverty*. New York: Dutton.

Gibbard, A. (2000), "Natural Property Rights," in P. Vallentyne and H. Steiner (eds.), *Left-Libertarianism and its Critics*. Basingstoke: Palgrave Macmillan, 23–30.

Gintis, H., C. van Schaik and C. Boehm (2015), "Zoon Politikon: The Evolutionary Origins of Human Political Systems," *Current Anthropology*, 56: 3, 327–353.

Gison, T. (1988), "Meat Sharing as a Political Ritual: Forms of Transaction Versus Modes of Subsistence," in T. Ingold, D. Riches and J. Woodburn (eds.), *Hunters and Gatherers 2: Property, Power and Ideology*. Oxford: Berg Publishing, 165–179.

Glausser, W. (1990), "Three Approaches to Locke and the Slave Trade," *Journal of the History of Ideas*, 51: 2, 199–216.

Goldschmidt, W. (1951), "Ethics and the Structure of Society: An Ethnological Contribution to the Sociology of Knowledge," *American Anthropologist*, 53: 4, 506–524.

Goodall, J. (1990), *Through a Window: My Thirty Years with the Chimpanzees of Gombe*. Eastbourne: Soko Publications.

Gosepath, S. (2011), "Equality," in E. N. Zalta (ed.), *The Stanford Encyclopedia of Philosophy*. Stanford, CA: Stanford University Press.

Graeber, D. (2011), *Debt: The First 5,000 Years*. Brooklyn, NY: Melville House.

Graeber, D. and D. Wengrow (2018), "How to Change the Course of Human History (at Least, the Part that's Already Happened)," *Eurozine*. Retrieved October 2, 2020 from https://www.eurozine.com/change-course-human-history/

Gray, P. (2009), "Play as a Foundation for Hunter-gatherer Social Existence," *American Journal of Play*, 1: 4, 476–522.

Greaves, R. D. (1997), "Hunting and Multifunctional Use of Bows and Arrows: Ethnoarchaeology of Technological Organization Among Pumé Hunters of Venezuela," in H. Knecht (ed.), *Projectile Technology*. New York: Plenum Press, 287–320.

Gurven, M. (2006), "The Evolution of Contingent Cooperation," *Current Anthropology*, 47: 1.

Hallowell, A. I. (1943), "Nature and Function of Property as a Social Institution," *Journal of Legal and Political Sociology*, I: 1, 115–138.

Hamilton, A. (1982), "Descended from Father, Belonging to Country: Rights to Land in the Australian Western Desert," in E. Leacock and R. B. Lee (eds.), *Politics and History in Band Societies*. Cambridge: Cambridge University Press, 85–108.

Hann, C. (1998a), "Introduction: The Embeddedness of Property," in C. Hann (ed.), *Property Relations: Renewing the Anthropological Tradition*. Cambridge: Cambridge University Press, 1–47.

Hann, C. (ed.) (1998b), *Property Relations: Renewing the Anthropological Tradition*. Cambridge: Cambridge University Press.

Hann, C. (2005), "Property," in J. G. Carrier (ed.), *A Handbook of Economic Anthropology*. Cheltenham: Edward Elgar, 110–124.

Harari, Y. N. (2015), "Sapiens: A Brief History of Humankind." Retrieved June 23, 2016 from http://erenow.com/common/sapiensbriefhistory/54.html

Hardin, G. (1968), "The Tragedy of the Commons," *Science*, 162: 3859, 1243–1248.

Harlan, J. R. (1971), "Agricultural Origins: Centers and Noncenters," *Science*, 174: 4008, 468–474.

Harris, M. (1977), *Cannibals and Kings: The Origins of Culture*. New York: Random House.

Hasian, M. A. (1996), *The Rhetoric of Eugenics in Anglo-American Thought*. Athens: University of Georgia Press.

Hasnas, J. (2003), "Reflections on the Minimal State," *Politics, Philosophy & Economics*, 2: 1, 115–128.

Hasnas, J. (2005), "Toward a Theory of Empirical Natural Rights," *Social Philosophy and Policy*, 22: 1, 111–147.

Hawkes, K. (2001), "Is Meat the Hunter's Property? Big Game, Ownership, and Explanations of Hunting and Sharing," in C. B. Stanford and H. T. Bunn (eds.), *Meat-Eating and Human Evolution*. Oxford: Oxford University Press, 219–236.

Hawkes, K., J. F. O'Connell and N. G. Blurton Jones (2001), "Hunting and Nuclear Families: Some Lessons from the Hadza about Men's Work," *Current Anthropology*, 42: 5, 681–709.

Haworth, A. (1994), *Anti-Libertarianism: Markets, Philosophy and Myth*. New York: Routledge.

Hayden, B., M. Deal, A. Cannon and J. Casey (1986), "Ecological Determinants of Women's Status among Hunter/Gatherers," *Human Evolution*, 1: 5, 449–473.

Hayek, F. A. (1944), *The Road to Serfdom*. London: Routledge.

Hayek, F. A. (1960), *The Constitution of Liberty*. Chicago: University of Chicago Press.

Hayek, F. A. (1973), *Law, Legislation, and Liberty, Vol. 1, Rules and Order*. Chicago: University of Chicago Press.

Headland, T. and L. Reid (1989), "Hunter-gatherers and their Neighbors from Prehistory to the Present," *Current Anthropology*, 30: 1, 43–66.

Hegmon, M. (2003), "Setting Theoretical Egos Aside: Issues and Theory in North American Archaeology," *American Antiquity*, 68: 2, 213–243.

Helbaek, H. (1960), "Ecological Effects of Irrigation in Ancient Mesopotamia," *Iraq*, 22: 1–2, 186–196.

Henrich, J., M. Chudek and R. Boyd (2015), "The Big Man Mechanism: How Prestige Fosters Cooperation and Creates Prosocial Leaders," *Philosophical Transactions: Biological Sciences*, 370: 1683, 1–13.

Herbinger, I., C. Boesch and H. Rothe (2001), "Territory Characteristics Among Three Neighboring Chimpanzee Communities in the Taï National Park, Côte d'Ivoire," *International Journal of Primatology*, 22: 2, 143–167.

Hernstein, R. C. and C. Murray (1994), *The Bell Curve: Intelligence and Class Structure in American Life*. New York: Free Press.

Herodotus (1998), *The Histories*. Oxford: Oxford University Press.

Hershkovitz, I., Y. Garfinkel and B. Arensburg (1986), "Neolithic Skeletal Remains at Yiftahel, Area C (Israël)," *Paléorient*, 12: 1, 73–81.

Hill, K. and A. M. Hurtado (1996), *Ache Life History: The Ecology and Demography of a Foraging People*. New York: Aldine de Gruyter.

Hitchcock, R. K. (2005), "Sharing the Land: Kalahari San Property Rights and Resource Management," in T. Widlok and W. G. Tadesse (eds.), *Property and Equality: Ecapsulation, Commercialization, Discrimination*. London: Berghahn Books, 191–207.

Hobbes, T. (1962 [1651]), *Leviathan: Or the Matter, Forme and Power of a Commonwealth Ecclesiasticall and Civil*. New York: Collier Macmillan.

Hobbes, T. (1996 [1651]), *Leviathan*. Cambridge: Cambridge University Press.

Hobhouse, L. T. (1913), "The Historical Evolution Of Property, In Fact And In Idea," in C. Gore and L. T. Hobhouse (eds.), *Property; Its Duties and Rights: Historically, Philosophically and Religiously Regarded*. London: Macmillan and Co., Limited.

Hoebel, E. A. (1954), *The Law of Primitive Man*. Cambridge, MA: Harvard University Press.

Hogbin, H. I. (1934), *Law and Order in Polynesia: A Study of Primitive Legal Institutions, with an Introduction by B. Malinowski*. London: Christophers.

Holcombe, R. G. (2005), "Common Property In Anarcho-Capitalism," *Journal of Libertarian Studies*, 19: 2, 3–29.

Honoré, T. (1987), *Making Law Bind*. Oxford: Oxford University Press.

Hoppe, H.-H. (1995), "The Political Economy of Monarchy and Democracy, and The Idea of a Natural Order," *Journal of Libertarian Studies*, 11: 2, 94–121.

Hoppe, H.-H. (2001), *Democracy, the God that Failed: The Economics and Politics of Monarchy, Democracy, and Natural Order*. New Brunswick, NJ: Transaction Publishers.

Hoppe, H.-H. (2006), *The Ethics and Economics of Private Property*. Auburn, AL: Ludwig von Mises Institute.

Horne, T. A. (1990), *Property Rights and Poverty: Political Argument in Britain, 1605–1834*. Chapel Hill: University of North Carolina Press.

Hudson, M. (1996a), "The Dynamics of Privatization, from the Bronze Age to the Present," in M. Hudson and B. A. Levine (eds.), *Privatization in the Ancient Near East and Classical World*. Cambridge, MA: Harvard University Press, 33–72.

Hudson, M. (1996b), "Summary Review: Early Privatization and its Consequences," in M. Hudson and B. A. Levine (eds.), *Privatization in the Ancient Near East and Classical World*. Cambridge, MA: Peabody Museums of Archeology and Ethnology, 293–308.

Hudson, M. and B. A. Levine (eds.) (1996), *Privatization in the Ancient Near East and Classical World*. Cambridge, MA: Harvard University Press.

Huxley, T. H. (1998), "On the Natural Inequality of Men," in *Collected Essays*. Retrieved May 1, 2013 from http://aleph0.clarku.edu/huxley/CE1/NatIneq.html

Ingold, T. (1986), *The Appropriation of Nature: Essays on Human Ecology and Social Relations*. Manchester: Manchester University Press.

Ingold, T. (1999), "On the Social Relations of the Hunter-gatherer Band," in R. B. Lee and R. Daly (eds.), *The Cambridge Encyclopedia of Hunters and Gatherers*. Cambridge: Cambridge University Press, 399–410.

Isakson, H. R. and S. Sproles (2008), "A Brief History of Native American Land Ownership," in R. A. Simons, R. M. Malmgren and G. Small (eds.), *Indigenous People and Real Estate Valuation*. New York: Springer, 1–13.

Jefferson, T. (1905), *The Writings of Thomas Jefferson*. Washington, DC: Thomas Jefferson Memorial Association.

Johnson, A. (1989), "Horticulturalists: Economic Behavior in Tribes," in S. Platter (ed.), *Economic Anthropology*. Stanford, CA: Stanford University Press, 49–77.

Johnson, A. and T. Earle (2000), *The Evolution of Human Societies: From Foraging Group to Agrarian State*. Stanford, CA: Stanford University Press.

Johnson, J. W. (1927), *God's Trombones: Seven Negro Sermons in Verse*. New York: The Viking Press.

Jost, J. T. and O. Hunyady (2005), "Antecedents and Consequences of System-Justifying Ideologies," *Current Directions in Psychological Science*, 14: 5, 260–265.

Katz, C. J. (1997), "Private Property versus Markets: Democratic and Communitarian Critiques o Capitalism," *American Political Science Review*, 91: 2, 277–289.

Katz, R., M. Biesele and V. S. Denis (1997), *Healing Makes our Hearts Happy: Spirituality and Cultural Transformation among the Kalahari Ju/'hoansi*. Rochester, VT: Inner Traditions/Bear & Co.

Kelly, R. L. (1995), *The Foraging Spectrum: Diversity in Hunter-Gatherer Lifeways*. Washington, DC: Smithsonian Institution Press.

Kenyon, K. M. (1957), *Digging up Jericho*. New York: Praeger.

Kershnar, S. (2004), "Why Equal Opportunity is not a Valuable Goal," *Journal of Applied Philosophy*, 21: 2, 159–172.

Kevles, D. J. (1985), *In the Name of Eugenics: Genetics and the Uses of Human Heredity*. New York: Knopf.

Kirch, P. V. (1984), *The Evolution of Polynesian Chiefdoms*. Cambridge: Cambridge University Press.

Kirch, P. V. and R. C. Green (2001), *Hawaiki, Ancestral Polynesia: An Essay in Historical Anthropology*. Cambridge: Cambridge University Press.

Kirk, R. (1985), *The Conservative Mind: From Burke to Eliot*. Washington, DC: Regnery Publishing, Inc.

Kirzner, I. M. (1981), "Entrepreneurship, Entitlement, and Economic Justice," in J. Paul (ed.), *Reading Nozick: Essays on Anarchy, State, and Utopia*. Oxford: Basil Blackwell, 380–411.

Kirzner, I. M. (1989), *Discovery, Capitalism, and Distributive Justice*. Oxford: Basil Blackwell.

Knauft, B. M. (1991), "Violence and Sociality in Human Evolution," *Current Anthropology*, 32: 4, 712–713.

Kropotkin, P. A. (2011), *Mutual Aid: A Factor of Evolution*. Salt Lake City, UT: Project Gutenberg.

Kuper, A. (1994), *The Chosen Primate: Human Nature and Cultural Diversity*. Cambridge, MA: Harvard University Press.

Layton, R. H. (2001), "Hunter-gatherers, their Neighbors and the Nation State," in C. Panter-Brick, R. H. Layton and P. Rowley-Conwy (eds.), *Hunter-Gatherers: An Interdisciplinary Perspective*. Cambridge: Cambridge University Press, 292–321.

Leacock, E. (1954), "The Montagnais 'Hunting Territory' and the Fur Trade," *American Anthropologist*, 56: 5, Part 2, Memoir No. 78.

Leacock, E. (1978), "Women's Status in Egalitarian Society: Implications for Social Evolution," *Current Anthropology*, 19: 2, 247–275.

Leacock, E. (1998), "Women's Status in Egalitarian Society: Implications for Social Evolution," in J. Gowdy (ed.), *Limited Wants, Unlimited Means: A Reader on Hunter-gatherer Economics and the Environment*. Washington, DC: Island Press, 139–164.

Leacock, E. and R. B. Lee (1982), "Introduction," in E. Leacock and R. B. Lee (eds.), *Politics and History in Band Societies*. Cambridge: Cambridge University Press, 1–20.

Leage, R. W. (1961), *Roman Private Law*. London: Macmillan.

Lee, R. B. (1979), *The !Kung San: Men Women, and Work in a Foraging Society*. Cambridge: Cambridge University Press.

Lee, R. B. (1982), "Politics, Sexual and Non-sexual, in an Egalitarian Society," in E. Leacock and R. B. Lee (eds.), *Politics and History in Band Societies*. Cambridge: Cambridge University Press, 37–59.

Lee, R. B. (1988), "Reflections on Primitive Communism," in T. Ingold, D. Riches and J. Woodburn (eds.), *Hunters and Gatherers 1: History, Evolution and Social Change*. Oxford: Berg Publishing, 252–268.

Lee, R. B. (1990), "Primitive Communism and the Origin of Social Inequality," in S. Upham (ed.), *The Evolution of Political Systems: Sociopolitics in Small-Scale Sedentary Societies*. Cambridge: Cambridge University Press, 225–246.

Lee, R. B. (1992), "Art, Science, or Politics? The Crisis in Hunter-gatherer Studies," *American Anthropologist*, 94: 1, 31–54.

Lee, R. B. and R. Daly (1999), "Foragers and Others," in R. B. Lee and R. Daly (eds.), *The Cambridge Encyclopedia of Hunters and Gatherers*. Cambridge: Cambridge University Press, 1–19.

Lee, R. B. and I. DeVore (eds.) (1968a), *Man the Hunter*. New York: Aldine.

Lee, R. B. and I. DeVore (1968b), "Problems in the Study of Hunter and Gatherers," in R. B. Lee and I. DeVore (eds.), *Man the Hunter*. New York: Aldine, 3–12.

Leoni, B. (1972), *Freedom and the Law*. Los Angeles, CA: Nash Publishing.

Lerner, M. J. (1980), *The Belief in a Just World: A Fundamental Delusion*. New York: Plenum Press.

Lerner, R. (1987), "Moses Maimonides," in L. Strauss and J. Cropsey (eds.), *History of Political Philosophy*. Chicago: University of Chicago Press, 228–247.

Levine, B. A. (1996), "Farewell to the Ancient Near East," in M. Hudson and B. A. Levine (eds.), *Privatization in the Ancient Near East and Classical World*. Cambridge, MA: Peabody Museums of Archeology and Ethnology, 223–252.

Levmore, S. (2002), "Two Stories about the Evolution of Property Rights," *Journal of Legal Studies*, 31: S2, S421–S451.

Locke, J. (1960 [1689]), *Two Treatises of Government*. Cambridge: Cambridge University Press.

Lomasky, L. (1987), *Persons, Rights, and the Moral Community*. Oxford: Oxford University Press.

Long, R. (1996), "In Defense of Public Space," *Formulations*, 3: 3.

Long, R. (1998), "A Plea for Public Property," *Formulations*, 5: 3.

Lovejoy, A. O. (1960), *The Great Chain of Being: A Study of the History of an Idea*. New York: Harper & Row.

Lucas, J. R. (1965), "Against Equality," *Philosophy & Public Affairs*, 40: 154, 296–307.

McCall, G. J. and P. A. Resick (2003), "A Pilot Study of PTSD Symptoms Among Kalahari Bushmen," *Journal of Traumatic Stress*, 16: 5, 445–450.

McCall, G. J. and J. L. Simmons (1969), *Issues in Participant Observation: A Text and Reader*. Chicago: Addison-Wesley Publishing Company.

McCall, G. S. (2000), "Ju/'hoansi Adaptations to a Cash Economy," *African Sociological Review/Revue Africaine de Sociologie*, 4: 1, 138–155.

McCall, G. S. (2009), "Exploring the Origins of Human Warfare Through Cross-Cultural Research on Modern and Prehistoric Foragers," *International Journal of Contemporary Sociology*, 46: 2, 161–181.

McCall, G. S. and N. Shields (2008), "Examining the Evidence from Small-Scale Societies and Early Prehistory and Implications for Modern Theories of Aggression and Violence," *Aggression and Violent Behavior*, 13: 1, 1–9.

McCall, G. S. and K. Widerquist (2015), "The Evolution of Equality: Rethinking Variability and Egalitarianism Among Modern Forager Societies," *Ethnoarchaeology*, 7: 1, 21–44.

MacCallum, G. C. (1967), "Negative and Positive Freedom," *The Philosophical Review*, 76: 3, 312–334.

McCloskey, D. N. (1991), "Open Field System," in J. Eatwell, M. Milgate and P. Newman (eds.), *The World of Economics*. London: Palgrave Macmillan.

McClosky, H. (1958), "Conservatism and Personality," *The American Political Science Review*, 52: 1, 27–45.

McDaniel, R. A. (1998), "The Nature of Inequality: Uncovering the Modern in Leo Strauss's Idealist Ethics," *Political Theory*, 26: 3, 317–345.

Macfarlane, A. (1998), "The Mystery of Property: Inheritance and Industrialization in England and Japan," in C. M. Hann (ed.), *Property Relations: Renewing the Anthropological Tradition*. Cambridge: Cambridge University Press, 104–123.

Machan, T. R. (1989), *The Moral Case for the Free Market Economy: A Philosophical Argument*. Lewiston, NY: The Edwin Mellen Press.

Machan, T. R. (1990), *Capitalism and Individualism*. Hemel Hempstead: Harvestor Wheatsheaf.

Machan, T. R. (1997), "Does Libertarianism Imply the Welfare State?" *Res Publica*, 3: 2, 131–149.

Machan, T. R. (2006a), *Libertarianism Defended*. Aldershot: Ashgate.

Machan, T. R. (2006b), "Two Philosophers Skeptical of Negative Liberty," in T. Machan (ed.), *Libertarianism Defended*. Aldershot: Ashgate, 269–284.

Mack, E. (1995), "The Self-Ownership Proviso: A New and Improved Lockean Proviso," *Social Philosophy and Policy*, 12, 186–218.

Mack, E. (2002a), "Self-ownership, Marxism, and Egalitarianism: Part I: Challenges to Historical Entitlement," *Politics, Philosophy & Economics*, 1: 1, 75–108.

Mack, E. (2002b), "Self-ownership, Marxism, and Egalitarianism: Part II: Challenges to the Self-ownership Thesis," *Politics, Philosophy & Economics*, 1: 2, 237–276.

Mack, E. (2006), "Non-Absolute Rights and Libertarian Taxation," *Social Philosophy and Policy*, 23: 2, 109–141.

McLynn, F. (2009), *Marcus Aurelius: A Life*. Jackson, TN: De Capo Press.

Mahdi, M. (1987), "Alfarabi," in L. Strauss and J. Cropsey (eds.), *History of Political Philosophy*. Chicago: University of Chicago Press, 206–227.

Maine, H. S. (1861), *Ancient Law: Its Connection with the Early History of Society, and its Relation to Modern Ideas*. London: John Murray.

Maisels, C. K. (1990), *The Emergence of Civilization: From Hunting and Gathering to Agriculture, Cities, and the State in the Near East*. New York: Routledge.

Maistre, J. de (1996), *Against Rousseau: "On the State of Nature"; and "On the Sovereignty of the People."* Montreal: McGill-Queen's University Press.

Malinowski, B. (1921), "The Primitive Economics of The Trobriand Islandees," *The Economic Journal*, 31: 121, 1–16.

Malinowski, B. (1934), "Introduction," in H. I. Hogbin (ed.), *Law and Order in Polynesia: A Study of Primitive Legal Institutions*. London: Christophers, xvii–lxxii.

Malinowski, B. (1947), *Freedom and Civilization*. London: George Allen and Unwin Ltd.

Malinowski, B. (1956), *Coral Gardens and Their Magic, Volume I: Soil-Tilling and Agricultural Rites in the Trobriand Islands*. London: George Allen and Unwin Ltd.

Malinowski, B. (1966), *Crime and Custom in Savage Society*. London: Routledge & Kegan Paul.

Malinowski, B. (1972 [1922]), *Argonauts of the Western Pacific*. London: Routledge & Kegan Paul.

Manning, D. (2013), "Reality: We Accept the Reality of the World with which we are Presented." Retrieved May 27, 2013 from http://www.reellifewisdom.com/reality_we_accept_the_reality_of_the_world_with_which_we_are_presented

Mansfield, H. J. (1987), "Edmund Burke," in L. Strauss and J. Cropsey (eds.), *History of Political Philosophy*. Chicago: University of Chicago Press, 687–709.

Marshall III, J. M. (2002), *The Lakota Way: Stories and Lessons for Living*. New York: Penguin.

Marshall III, J. M. (2005), *The Journey of Crazy Horse: A Lakota History*. New York: Penguin.

Marshall, L. (1960), "!Kung Bushman Bands," *Africa*, 30: 4, 325–355.

Martin, P. S. and R. G. Klein (eds.) (1984), *Quaternary Extinctions: A Prehistoric Revolution*. Tucson: University of Arizona Press.

Marx, K. (1994), *Selected Writings*. Indianapolis, IN: Hackett Publishing Company Inc.

Marx, K. (n.d.), "Critique of the Gotha Programme." Marxists Internet Archive. Retrieved September 2020 from https://www.marxists.org/archive/marx/works/download/Marx_Critque_of_the_Gotha_Programme.pdf (p. 10).

Mayor, T. (2012), "Hunter-Gatherers: The Original Libertarians," *The Independent Review*, 16: 4, 485–500.

Mead, M. (1930), "Social Organization of the Manu'a," *Bulletin*, 76. Honolulu, HI: Bishop Museum Press.

Mill, J. S. (1859), "On Liberty," in J. M. Robson (ed.), *Collected Works of John Stuart Mill*. Toronto: University of Toronto Press.

Mingay, G. E. (2016), *Enclosure and the Small Farmer in the Age of the Industrial Revolution*. New York: Macmillan International Higher Education.

Mitani, J. C. and P. S. Rodman (1979), "Territoriality: The Relation of Ranging Pattern and Home Range Size to Defendability, with an Analysis of Territoriality Among Primate Species," *Behavioral Ecology and Sociobiology*, 5: 3, 241–251.

Montesquieu, B. d., Charles de Secondat (2001), *The Spirit of the Laws*. Kitchener, ON: Batoche Books.

Moore, J. A. (1985), "Forager/Farmer Interactions: Information, Social Organization, and the Frontier," in J. Robinson (ed.), *The Archaeology of Frontiers and Boundaries*. Elsevier, 93–112.

Morgan, L. H. (1877), *Ancient Society; Or, Researches in the Lines of Human Progress From Savagery, Through Barbarism to Civilization*. New York: Henry Holt and Company.

Murray, C. (1997), *What it Means to be a Libertarian*. New York: Broadway Books.

Narveson, J. (1988), *The Libertarian Idea*. Philadelphia, PA: Temple University Press.

Narveson, J. (1998), "Libertarianism vs. Marxism: Reflections on G. A. Cohen's *Self-Ownership, Freedom and Equality*," *The Journal of Ethics*, 2: 1.

Neeson, J. M. (1993), *Commoners: Common Right, Enclosure and Social Change in England, 1700–1820*. Cambridge: Cambridge University Press.

Nine, C. (2008), "A Lockean Theory of Territory," *Political Studies*, 56, 148–165.

Nozick, R. (1974), *Anarchy, State, and Utopia*. New York: Basic Books.

Nye, P. H. and D. J. Greenland (1960), *The Soil under Shifting Cultivation*. Farnham Royal: Commonwealth Agricultural Bureaux.

O'Connell, J. F. (1995), "Ethnoarchaeology Needs a General Theory of Behavior," *Journal of Archaeological Research*, 3: 3, 205–255.

Olivecrona, K. (1974), "Appropriation in the State of Nature: Locke on the Origin of Property," *Journal of the History of Ideas*, 35: 2, 211–230.

Olsen, E. J. (2019), "The Early Modern 'Creation' of Property and its Enduring influence," *European Journal of Political Theory*, Online Early, 1–23.

Otsuka, M. (2003), *Libertarianism Without Inequality*. Oxford: Oxford University Press.

Paine, T. (2012), "Agrarian Justice." Retrieved from http://www.ssa.gov/history/paine4.html

Pateman, C. and C. Mills (2007), *The Contract and Domination*. Cambridge: Polity Press.

Patrick, V. K. (2010), "Peopling of the Pacific: A Holistic Anthropological Perspective," *Annual Review of Anthropology*, 39, 131–148.

Peter, F. (2004), "Choice, Consent, and the Legitimacy of Market Transactions," *Economics and Philosophy*, 20: 1, 1–18.

Peterson, N. (1993), "Demand Sharing: Reciprocity and the Pressure for Generosity among Foragers," *American Anthropologist*, 95: 4, 860–874.

Plato (2013a), "Crito." The Internet Classics Archive. Retrieved April 13, 2013 from http://classics.mit.edu/Plato/crito.html

Plato (2013b), *Republic*. Retrieved April 13, 2013 from http://classics.mit.edu/Plato/republic.html.

Pole, J. R. (1978), *The Pursuit of Equality in American History*. Berkeley: University of California Press.

Pospíšil, L. (1971), *Anthropology of Law: A Comparative Theory*. New York: Harper and Row.

Possehl, G. L. and M. H. Raval, with contributions from Y. M. Chitalwala et al. (1989), *Harappan Civilization and Rojdi*. Boston, MA: Brill Archive.

Protevi, J. (2019), *Edges of the State*. Minneapolis: University of Minnesota Press.

Pryor, F. L. (1985), "The invention of the plow," *Comparative Studies in Society and history*, 27: 4, 727–743.

Pugliese, G. (1965), "On Roman Usufruct," *Tulane Law Review*, 40, 523–526.

Ramsay, M. (1722), *An Essay upon Civil Government*. London: Randal Minshull.

Rappaport, R. A. (1968), *Pigs for the Ancestors: Ritual in the Ecology of a New Guinea People*. New Haven, CT: Yale University Press.

Rashdall, H. (1915), *Proptery, its Duties and Rights*. London: Macmillan.

Rauscher, F. (2012), "Kant's Social and Political Philosophy," in E. N. Zalta (ed.), *The Stanford Encyclopedia of Philosophy*. Stanford, CA: Stanford University Press.

Rawls, J. (1971), *A Theory of Justice*. Oxford: Oxford University Press.

Rawls, J. (2001), *Justice as Fairness: A Restatement*. Cambridge, MA: Harvard University Press.

Redfield, R. (1967), "Primitive Law," in P. Bohanan (ed.), *Law and Warfare*. Garden City, NY: The Natural History Press.

Renfrew, C. (2007), *Prehistory: The Making of The Human Mind*. London: Phoenix.

Renger, J. M. (1995), "Institutional, Communal, and Individual Ownership or Possession of Arable Land in Ancient Mesopotamia from the End of the Fourth to the End of the First Millennium BC," *Chicago-Kent Law Review*, 71, 269.

Rigaud, J. P. and J. F. Simek (1987), "Arms Too Short to Box with God," in O. Soffer (ed.), *The Pleistocene Old World*. New York: Springer, 47–61.

Riker, W. H. and I. Sened (1991), "A Political Theory of the Origin of Property Rights: Airport Slots," *American Journal of Political Science*, 35: 4, 951–969.

Ringmar, E. (2020), "The Anti-Nomadic Bias of Political Theory," in J. Levin (ed.), *Nomad-State Relationships in International Relations: Before and After Borders*. Basingstoke: Palgrave.

Roberts, J. T. (1994), *Athens on Trial: The Antidemocratic Tradition in Western Thought*. Ewing, NJ: Princeton University Press.

Roscoe, P. (2002), "The Hunters and Gatherers of New Guinea," *Current Anthropology*, 43: 1, 153–162.

Rosen, S. (1987), "Benedict Spinoza," in L. Strauss and Cropsey (eds.), *History of Political Philosophy*. Chicago: University of Chicago Press, 456–475.

Rossi, E. and C. Argenton (forthcoming), "Property, Legitimacy, Ideology: A Reality Check," *Journal of Politics*.

Rothbard, M. (1978), *For a New Liberty, The Libertarian Manifesto*. New York: Libertarian Review Foundation.

Rothbard, M. (1982), *The Ethics of Liberty*. Atlantic Highlands, NJ: Humanities Press.

Rothbard, M. (2006), *For a New Liberty: The Libertarian Manifesto*. Auburn, AL: Ludwig von Mises Institute.

Rothbard, M. (2012), "Egalitarianism as a Revolt Against Nature." Retrieved May 26, 2013 from http://www.lewrockwell.com/rothbard/rothbard31.html

Rousseau, J.-J. (1984), *A Discourse on Inequality*. New York: Penguin Classics.

Rousseau, J.-J. (1998), *A Discourse: What is the Origin of Inequality Among Men, and Is It Authorized By Natural Law?* Austin, TX: Constitution Society.

Ryan, C. (2019), *Civilized to Death: The Price of Progress*. New York: Simon & Schuster.

Sahlins, M. (1963), "Poor Man, Rich Man, Big-Man, Chief: Political Types in Melanesia and Polynesia," *Comparative Studies in Society and History*, 5: 3, 285–303.

Sahlins, M. (1974), *Stone Age Economics*. London: Tavistock.

Sahlins, M. D. (1957), "Land Use and the Extended Family in Moala, Fiji," *American Anthropologist*, 59: 3, 449–462.

Scelza, B. A. (2013), "Choosy but not Chaste: Multiple Mating in Human Females," *Evolutionary Anthropology: Issues, News, and Reviews*, 22: 5, 259–269.

Schiffer, M. B. (2016), *Behavioral Archaeology: Principles and Practice*. New York: Routledge.

Schmidtz, D. (1990), "When is Original Appropriation *Required*?" *The Monist*, October, 504–518.

Schmidtz, D. (1994), "The Institution of Property," *Social Philosophy & Policy*, 11, 42–62.

Schrire, C. (1984), "Wild Surmises on Savage Thoughts," in C. Schrire (ed.), *Past and Present in Hunter-Gatherer Studies*. San Diego, CA: Academic Press, 1–26.

Scott, J. C. (1998a), "Freedom and Freehold: Space, People and State Simplification in Southeast Asia," in D. Kelly, A. Reid and J. Ravenhill (eds.), *Asian Freedoms: The Idea of Freedom in East and Southeast Asia*. Cambridge: Cambridge University Press, 37–64.

Scott, J. C. (1998b), "Property Values: Ownership, Legitimacy and Land Markets in Northern Cyprus," in C. M. Hann (ed.), *Property Relations: Renewing the Anthropological Tradition*. Cambridge: Cambridge University Press, 142–159.

Scott, J. C. (2009), *The Art of Not Being Governed: An Anarchist History of Upland Southeast Asia*. New Haven, CT: Yale University Press.

Scott, J. C. (2017), *Against the Grain: A Deep History of the Earliest States*. New Haven, CT: Yale University Press.

Scott, J. C. (2019), "State Simplification," in R. E. Goodin and P. Pettit (eds.), *Contemporary Political Philosophy: An Anthology*. Oxford: Wiley-Blackwell, 77–104.

Service, E. R. (1962), *Primitive Social Organization: An Evolutionary Perspective*. New York: Random House.

Shachar, A. and R. Hirschl (2007), "Citizenship as Inherited Property," *Political Theory*, 35: 3, 253–287.

Shapin, S. and B. Barnes (1976), "Head and Hand: Rhetorical Resources in British Pedagogical Writing, 1770–1850," *Oxford Review of Education*, 2: 3, 231–254.

Shapiro, D. (2002), "Egalitarianism And Welfare-State Redistribution," *Social Philosophy and Policy*, 19: 1, 1–35.

Shepperd, J., W. Malone and K. Sweeny (2008), "Exploring Causes of the Self-serving Bias," *Social and Personality Psychology Compass*, 2: 2, 895–908.

Silberbauer, G. B. (1982), "Political Process in G/wi bands," in E. Leacock and R. B. Lee (eds.), *Politics and History in Band Societies*. Cambridge: Cambridge University Press, 23–36.

Skidmore, T. E. (1829), *The Rights of Man to Property!* New York: Alexander Ming, Jr.

Smith, A. (1976 [1776]), *The Wealth of Nations*. Oxford: Oxford University Press.

Smith, A. (1982), *Lectures on Jurisprudence. Glasgow Edition of the Works and Correspondence of Adam Smith*. Indianapolis, IN: Liberty Fund.

Smith, H. E. (2000), "Semicommon Property Rights and Scattering in the Open Fields," *Journal of Legal Studies*, 29: 1, 131–169.

Smith, M. E. (2004), "The Archaeology of Ancient State Economies," *Annual Review of Anthropology*, 33: 1, 73–102.

Somos, M. (2019), *American States of Nature: The Origins of Independence, 1761–1775*. Oxford: Oxford University Press.

Spencer, J. E. (1966), *Shifting Cultivation in Southeastern Asia*. Berkeley, CA: University of California Press.

Spengler, O. (1934), "Hour of Decision." Retrieved May 1, 2013 from http://archive. org/details/TheHourOfDecision

Stake, J. E. (2004), "The Property 'Instinct.'" *Philosophical Transactions of the Royal Society B: Biological Sciences*, 359: 1451, 1763–1774.

Standing, G. (2019), *Plunder of the Commons*. London: Penguin Books Limited.

Stark, W. (1998), *America: Ideal and Reality: The United States of 1776 in Contemporary European Philosophy*. London: Routledge.

Stebbins, S. (2019), Who Owns the Most Land in America? *USA Today*. Retrieved October 5, 2020 from https://eu.usatoday.com/story/money/2019/11/25/these-people-own-the-most-land-in-america/40649951/

Steenhoven, G. v. d. (1962), *Leadership and Law among the Eskimos of the Keewatin District*. Rijswijk: Excelsior.

Strathern, M. (1988), *The Gender of the Gift: Problems with Women and Problems with Society in Melanesia (No. 6)*. Berkeley, CA: University of California Press.

Strauss, L. (1953), *Natural Right and History*. Chicago: University of Chicago Press.

Strauss, L. and J. Cropsey (1987), *History of Political Philosophy*. Chicago: University of Chicago Press.

Stringham, E. P. (ed.) (2007), *Anarchy and the Law: The Political Economy of Choice*. Oakland, CA: The Independent Institute.

Tacitus, P. C. (1996), "Germania." Retrieved January 18, 2013 from http://www. fordham.edu/halsall/source/tacitus1.html

Tavov, N. and T. Pangle (1987), "Epilogue: Leo Strauss and the History of Political Philosophy," in L. Strauss and J. Cropsey (eds.), *History of Political Philosophy*. Chicago: University of Chicago Press, 907–934.

Thomas, J. (1999), *Understanding the Neolithic*. London: Routledge.

Tomasi, J. (2012), *Free Market Fairness*. Princeton, NJ: Princeton University Press.

Townsend, E. D. (2007), "Minutes of an Interview Between the Colored Ministers and Church Officers at Savannah with the Secretary of War and Major-Gen. Sherman," in S. F. Miller (ed.), *Freedom: A Documentary History of Emancipation, 1861–1867*. College Park, MD: Department of History, University of Maryland. http://www.history.umd.edu/Freedmen/savmtg.htm

Trigger, B. G. (1990a), "Maintaining Economic Equality in Opposition to Complexity: An Iroquoian Case Study," in S. Upham (ed.), *The Evolution of Political Systems: Sociopolitics in Small-Scale Sedentary Societies*. Cambridge: Cambridge University Press, 119–145.

Trigger, B. G. (1990b), "Monumental Architecture: A Thermodynamic Explanation of Symbolic Behaviour," *World Archaeology*, 22: 2, 119–132.

Trigger, B. G. (2003), *Understanding Early Civilizations: A Comparative Study*. Cambridge: Cambridge University Press.

Turnbull, C. M. (1968), "The Importance of Flux in Two Hunting Societies," in R. B. Lee and I. DeVore (eds.), *Man the Hunter*. New York: Adline, 132–137.

Vallentyne, P. and H. Steiner (2000a), *Left-Libertarianism and its Critics: The Contemporary Debate*. New York: Palgrave.

Vallentyne, P. and H. Steiner (2000b), *The Origins of Left-Libertarianism: An Anthology of Historical Writings*. Basingstoke: Palgrave.

Vallentyne, P., H. Steiner and M. Otsuka (2005), "Why Left-Libertarianism is Not Incoherent, Indeterminate, or Irrelevant," *Philosophy and Public Affairs*, 33: 2, 201–215.

Wagoner, P. L. (1998), "An Unsettled Frontier: Property, Blood and US Federal Policy," in C. M. Hann (ed.), *Property Relations: Renewing the Anthropological Tradition*. Cambridge: Cambridge University Press, 124–141.

Waldron, J. (1988), *The Right to Private Property*. Oxford: Clarendon Press.

Waldron, J. (1993a). "Homelessness and the Issue of Freedom," in J. Waldron (ed.), *Liberal Rights*. Cambridge: Cambridge University Press, 309–338.

Waldron, J. (1993b), *Liberal Rights*. Cambridge: Cambridge University Press.

Waldron, J. (2005), "Property and Ownership," in E. N. Zalta (ed.), *Stanford Encyclopedia of Philosophy*. Stanford, CA: Stanford University Press.

Waldron, J. (2012), "Property and Ownership," in E. N. Zalta (ed.), *The Stanford Encyclopedia of Philosophy*. Stanford, CA: Stanford University Press.

Washburn, S. L. and C. S. Lancaster (1968), "The Evolution of Hunting," in R. B. Lee and I. DeVore (eds.), *Man the Hunter*. New York: Aldine, 293–303.

Watner, C. (1983), "Libertarians and Indians: Proprietary Justice and Aboriginal Land Rights," *Journal of Libertarian Studies*, 7: 1, 147–156.

Weber, M. (2004), *The Vocation Lectures*. Indianapolis, IN: Hackett Publishing Company.

Wenar, L. (1998), "Original Acquisition of Private Property," *Mind*, 107: 428, 799–820.

Wengrow, D. and D. Graeber (2015), "Farewell to the 'Childhood of Man': Ritual, Seasonality, and the Origins of Inequality," *Journal of the Royal Anthropological Institute*, 21: 3, 1–23.

Wheeler, S. C. (2000), "Natural Property Rights as Body Rights," in P. Vallentyne and H. Steiner (eds.), *Left-Libertarianism and its Critics: The Contemporary Debate*. New York: Palgrave, 171–193.

Widerquist, K. (1999), "Reciprocity and the Guaranteed Income," *Politics and Society*, 33, 386–401.

Widerquist, K. (2006a), *Property and the Power to Say No: A Freedom-Based Argument for Basic Income*. Oxford: Oxford University, Department of Politics and International Relations.

Widerquist, K. (2006b), "Who Exploits Who?" *Political Studies*, 54: 3, 444–464.

Widerquist, K. (2008), "The Physical Basis of Voluntary Trade," *Human Rights Review*, Online First.

Widerquist, K. (2009a), "A Dilemma for Libertarianism," *Politics, Philosophy, and Economics*, 8: 1, 43–72.

Widerquist, K. (2009b), "Libertarianism," in P. O'Hara (ed.), *The International Encyclopedia of Public Policy: Governance in a Global Age, Volume 3*. Perth: GPERU.

Widerquist, K. (2010a), "Lockean Theories of Property: Justifications for Unilateral Appropriation," *Public Reason*, 2: 3, 3–26.

Widerquist, K. (2010b), "The Physical Basis of Voluntary Trade," *Human Rights Review*, 11: 1, 83–103.

Widerquist, K. (2011), "Why We Demand an Unconditional Basic Income: The ECSO Freedom Case," in A. Gosseries and Y. Vanderborght (eds.), *Arguing about Justice: Essays for Philippe Van Parijs*. Louvain-la-Neuve, Belgium: Presses universitaires de Louvain, 387–394.

Widerquist, K. (2013), *Independence, Propertylessness, and Basic Income: A Theory of Freedom as the Power to Say No*. New York: Palgrave Macmillan.

Widerquist, K. (2016), "A People's Endowment," in A. Gosseries and I. Gonzalez (eds.), *Institutions for Future Generations*. Oxford, UK: Oxford University Press, 312–330.

Widerquist, K. (2019), "The Pursuit of Accord: Toward a Theory of Justice With a Second-Best Approach to the Insider-Outsider Problem," *Raisons Politiques*, 73: 1, 61–82.

Widerquist, K. and G. S. McCall (2017), *Prehistoric Myths in Modern Political Philosophy*. Edinburgh: Edinburgh University Press.

Wiessner, P. W. (2002), "Hunting, Healing, and Hxaro Exchange: A Long-Term Perspective On !Kung (Ju/'hoansi) Large-Game Hunting," *Evolution and Human Behavior*, 23: 6, 407–436.

Wiessner, P. W. (2005), "Norm Enforcement Among the Ju/'hoansi Bushmen," *Human Nature*, 16: 2, 115–145.

Wilmsen, E. N. (1989), *Land Filled with Flies: A Political Economy of the Kalahari*. Chicago: University of Chicago Press.

Wilson, D. S. (1998), "Hunting, Sharing, and Multi-Level Selection," *Current Anthropology*, 39: 1, 73–97.

Wilson, P. J. (1988), *The Domestication of the Human Species*. New Haven, CT: Yale University Press.

Winter, S. (2014), *Transitional Justice in Established Democracies: A Political Theory*. Basingstoke: Palgrave Macmillan.

Winterhalder, B. (2001), "The Behavioral Ecology of Hunter-Gatherers," in C. Panter-Brick, R. H. Layton and P. Rowley-Conwy (eds.), *Hunter-Gatherers: An Interdisciplinary Perspective*. Cambridge: Cambridge University Press, 12–38.

Wister, O. (1902), *The Virginian: A Horseman of the Plains*. Retrieved April 22, 2013 from http://www.fiction.us/wister/virgin/chap13.html

Wittfogel, K. A. (1957), *Oriental Despotism: A Study of Total Power*. New Haven, CT: Yale University Press.

Wood, B. M. and F. W. Marlowe (2013), "Household and Kin Provisioning by Hadza Men," *Human Nature*, 24: 3, 280–317.

Woodburn, J. (1968a), "An Introduction to Hadza Ecology," in R. B. Lee and I. DeVore (eds.), *Man the Hunter*. New York: Aldine, 49–55.

Woodburn, J. (1968b), "Stability and Flexibility in Hadza Residential Groupings," in R. B. Lee and I. DeVore (eds.), *Man the Hunter.* New York: Aldine, 103–110.

Woodburn, J. (1982), "Egalitarian Societies," *Man,* 17: 3, 431–451.

Woodburn, J. (1998), "'Sharing is Not a Form of Exchange': An Analysis of Property-sharing in Immediate-return Hunter-gatherer Societies," in C. M. Hann (ed.), *Property Relations: Renewing the Anthropological Tradition.* Cambridge: Cambridge University Press, 48–63.

Wrangham, R. W. and D. Peterson (1997), *Demonic Males: Apes and the Origins of Human Violence.* New York: Houghton Mifflin Harcourt.

Wright, H. T. (1977), "Recent Research on the Origin of the State," *Annual Review of Anthropology,* 6: 1, 379–397.

Yelling, J. A. (1977), *Common Field and Enclosure in England, 1450–1850.* Hamden, CT: Archon Books.

Yoffee, N. (2004), *Myths of the Archaic State: Evolution of the Earliest Cities, States, and Civilizations.* Cambridge: Cambridge University Press.

Zuk, M. (2013), *Paleofantasy: What Evolution Really Tells us about Sex, Diet, and How we Live.* New York: W. W. Norton & Company.

Zwolinski, M. (2016), "The Libertarian Nonaggression Principle," *Social Philosophy and Policy,* 32: 2, 62–90.

INDEX